PERSPECTIVES ON ECCLESIOLOGY AND ETHNOGRAPHY

STUDIES IN ECCLESIOLOGY AND ETHNOGRAPHY

Series Editors

Pete Ward, Christian Scharen, Paul Fiddes, John Swinton, and James Nieman

The STUDIES IN ECCLESIOLOGY AND ETHNOGRAPHY series is focused on the development of new forms of cross-disciplinary scholarship in the study of the Church. The series has grown out of a convergence around the attempt to rethink the customary divide between empirical and theological analyses of the Church within Religious Studies, Systematic Theology and Practical Theology. The volumes in the series will explore methodological and substantive issues that arise from theological and empirical studies of the practices and social reality of the Church. Ethnography is defined by the series editors "inclusively" as any form of qualitative research. The series will include both multi-author volumes and monographs.

PUBLISHED VOLUMES

Perspectives on Ecclesiology and Ethnography
    Pete Ward, Editor

Perspectives on Ecclesiology and Ethnography

Edited by

Pete Ward

WILLIAM B. EERDMANS PUBLISHING COMPANY

GRAND RAPIDS, MICHIGAN / CAMBRIDGE, U.K.

Published 2012 by
Wm. B. Eerdmans Publishing Co.
2140 Oak Industrial Drive N.E., Grand Rapids, Michigan 49505 /
P.O. Box 163, Cambridge CB3 9PU U.K.

Printed in the United States of America

18 17 16 15 14 13   7 6 5 4 3 2

Library of Congress Cataloging-in-Publication Data

Perspectives on ecclesiology and ethnography / edited by Pete Ward.
         p.   cm.   — (Studies in ecclesiology and ethnography)
    Includes bibliographical references.
    ISBN 978-0-8028-6726-1 (pbk.: alk. paper)
    1. Church. 2. Ethnology — Religious aspects — Christianity.
    3. Theology — Methodology.   I. Ward, Pete, 1959-

    BV600.3.P48   2012
    262.0089 — dc23

                                        2011039559

www.eerdmans.com

Contents

PART TWO: THE CONVERSATION

Contributors

DEBORAH BHATTI, ARCS project field-worker

LUKE BRETHERTON, Reader in Theology and Politics, King's College, London

HELEN CAMERON, ARCS team member, Research Fellow, Ripon College, Cuddesdon

CATHERINE DUCE, ARCS project field-worker

PAUL S. FIDDES, Professor of Systematic Theology, University of Oxford

NICHOLAS M. HEALY, Professor, Theology and Religious Studies, Associate Dean, College of Liberal Arts and Sciences, St. John's University, New York

MARY McCLINTOCK FULKERSON, Professor of Theology, Duke Divinity School

ALISTER E. McGRATH, Professor of Theology, Ministry, and Education, King's College, London

JAMES NIEMAN, Academic Dean and Professor of Practical Theology, Hartford Seminary

RICHARD R. OSMER, Thomas W. Synnott Professor of Christian Education, Princeton Theological Seminary

ELIZABETH PHILLIPS, Tutor in Theology and Ethics, Westcott House, Cambridge

CHRISTIAN SCHAREN, Assistant Professor of Worship and Theology, Luther Seminary, St. Paul

JAMES SWEENEY, Director of the ARCS project, senior lecturer, Heythrop College, London

JOHN SWINTON, Professor in Practical Theology and Pastoral Care, University of Aberdeen

PETE WARD, Senior Lecturer in Youth Ministry and Theological Education, King's College, London

CLARE WATKINS teaches at the Westminster Seminary, Allen Hall, London, and is a member of the research project Action Research — Church and Society

JOHN WEBSTER, Professor of Systematic Theology, University of Aberdeen

Introduction

Pete Ward

It is the 1980s and Robert Orsi is carrying out his fieldwork. He sits close to the back of the Church of Our Lady of Guadalupe in South Chicago watching groups of people arrive for the evening's novena service in honor of Saint Jude Thaddeus, the patron saint of lost causes. As he observes what is happening, Orsi experiences a wave of pride mixed with anger. "I am here among these working-class people in this postindustrial land-scape because I want to hear their stories. I take their voices seriously. This is what research in religion means, I fume, to attend to the experiences and beliefs of people in the midst of their lives, to encounter religion in its place in actual men and women's lived experience, in the places where they live and work. Where are the theologians from the seminaries on the South Side, I want to know, with all their talk of postmodernism and narrativity? When will the study of religion in the United States take an empirical and so more realistic and humane direction?"[1]

It's a good question: Where are the theologians? The irony, as Orsi suggests, is that theologians, from a range of different positions, appear to be more and more interested in practice, culture, and the embodied social nature of doctrine and the church. Yet, whether through inclination, or disciplinary convention or habit or methodological prejudice, theologians have tended to avoid fieldwork. The result has been that empirical research — generally referred to as "ethnography" — has often been discussed by

1. Robert Orsi, *Between Heaven and Hell: The Religious Worlds People Make and the Scholars Who Study Them* (Princeton: Princeton University Press, 2005), p. 147.

1

theologians as a theoretical move or indeed even as a theoretical or theological necessity, but strangely this is very often divorced from any real or sustained engagement with actual churches and communities.

This book, and the series it inaugurates, takes Orsi's challenge seriously. We are saying, "Here we are." Actually, during the last thirty years a number of theologians, Christian ethicists, and of course practical theologians have been actively engaged in fieldwork of different kinds. Now is the time to start to bring this wealth of experience together. We want not only to talk about the theological significance of empirical research, but also to reflect on the experience of doing fieldwork. We want to explore how the practice of engaging in ethnographic and qualitative research shapes the way we do theology and reflect on the church. This project is of vital significance for the future direction of theological study because we believe the turn toward fieldwork and ethnography represents a vital element in the ongoing debates concerning the practice of the church.

The Proposal

At the heart of our project lies a proposal. Put simply, the proposal is that to understand the church, we should view it as being simultaneously theological and social/cultural. Added to this is the insight that this "understanding" is itself ecclesial. So the very practice of understanding is both theological and social/cultural. This means that to do ecclesiology we must embrace methods of research that are simultaneously theological and "ethnographic" and that these methods arise from our situatedness as church. There will thus be a constant interaction between theories and principles generated from the theological tradition, and careful participative observation of the particularities of an ecclesial situation. Theological generalizations or universals will be reshaped by observation, using tools of social and cultural inquiry, but observation is itself already theological. This proposal is variously articulated in this volume, but at its heart lies a common conviction. This could be expressed in christological terms in the poem in Colossians 1. Christ is "the image of the father, the firstborn of creation, in whom all things have their origin and in whom all things have their reconciliation. In him *all things hold together.*" At the same time, this Christ is "the head of his body, *the church.*" We want to speak simultaneously about the theological and the social/cultural reality of the church because of Christ who is at once the one in whom "all things" hold together and "head of the church." We see understanding as an ecclesial act that is both theological and social/cultural, and this is because of Christ.

To explore our proposal a little further we should perhaps make clear what we are not saying. We are not talking about what is usually called correlation. Our christological starting point does not support a distinction between social/cultural description and theology as it is constructed in correlational method. If all things are "in Christ," then this must relate to social and cultural expressions, and this is also true of the means that might be used to research it. But neither are we saying that "theology" has any kind of innate disciplinary superiority over social science. Interdisciplinary conversations are not constructed around a disembodied and sacred "theology" and a profane and misguided social theory, but arise from the possibility of analogy and dialogue from social and cultural realities that are in Christ. So where there may well be differences of view and contested theories and interpretations, these are a conversation, a dialogue that is held together in the one from whom all things have their origin.

The practice of theology is itself cultural and social or situated. So theoretical conversations are not essentially distinct or distinguished. In embracing ethnography we do not see ourselves as moving across strongly demarcated disciplinary boundaries. Rather, just as there are sociologists, educationalists, and anthropologists who make use of ethnographic methods, so there can be theologians who do the same. Yet in making this move we do not see ourselves as privileging the kind of theology that simply emerges out of social and cultural particulars — what might be termed a theology from "below." We accept that this is a possible way of doing theology, but it is not ours; we see our situated understanding as itself arising from a traditioned ecclesial expression. This expression includes a doctrinal and liturgical canon that forms us as we set about trying to understand the church. So ecclesiology arises from a theological situatedness in the church. But it finds not only its origin but also its purpose in the church. This purpose is also christological. If we practice ethnographic research as ecclesial theologians, we do so in order to share in the "holding together" and the "reconciling" that is attributed to Christ. This does not mean that we have to agree or indeed be particularly sanctified as we set about contributing to the contested and contentious field of ecclesiology, but rather that we see what we are doing as somehow, even in its disagreements, being indwelt by and indwelling Christ.

Toward a Plausible Ecclesiology

Ecclesiology and ethnography argue that the ethnographic "voice" demands our attention because it has the potential to make a significant and urgently needed contribution to the contemporary discussion of the church. This conviction arises from a growing sense that there is often a disconnection between what we say doctrinally about the church and the experience of life in a local parish. This disconnection seriously prohibits how theological study can make any kind of credible contribution to the life of the church. One way of expressing this is in terms of plausibility in ecclesiology.

It is a characteristic of ecclesiology that it must make some kind of reference to churches and communities. We avoid the word "real" here because using it valorizes the social over the transcendent, the cultural over the spiritual. What is "real," however, is not what is at stake in the plausibility of how ecclesiology deals with the experience of faith and life in Christian communities. Plausibility addresses a much more basic concern — methodological laziness in ecclesiology. To put this in very simple terms, it has been the custom in theological circles to talk about social realities in ways that lack credibility. It is interesting to contrast the way we theologians customarily talk about the contemporary church with the way we deal with historical sources or philosophical sources. When it comes to history or philosophy, we proceed with considerable caution. We take great care to make sure that we abide by accepted academic convention and we want to demonstrate that we are proceeding with academic rigor. Then when we talk about the contemporary church, completely different rules seem to apply. It becomes acceptable to make assertions where there is no evidence. We assume a common perception of contemporary church life between author and reader. We base whole arguments on anecdote and the selective treatment of experience. We are prone to a sleight of hand that makes social theory appear to be a description of social reality — which of course it is not. The turn to ethnography challenges these conventions by the simple observation that assertions about the lived reality of the church require a kind of discipline and rigor similar to those that pertain in other areas of theological writing. Taking this disciplinary rigor seriously does not mean that theologians become something they are not. Just as theologians do not necessarily compromise what they are and what they are about when they make use of philosophy or history. It simply means that when we seek to talk about the social and cultural reality of the church, we need to take the academic conventions and disciplines that are customary in this practice much more seriously, and this is precisely what the essays in the book are seeking to do.

The correspondence between the theological representation of church and the lived social reality of Christian communities touches in another important way upon plausibility. The credibility of ecclesiology rests not only on the rigor of its assertions but also on its ability to shape and inspire people and the congregations, denominations, and organizations they form. Ethnography does not directly fix this issue — because, as many of the chapters in this book show, ethnographic writing is often as idealized and constructed as more traditional kinds of theological writing. What it does encourage is a way of talking about the church that is closer to or at least more directly concerned with congregational life. This means that ethnographic accounts of the church allow for a kind of analogical correspondence or an imaginative leap between academic work and practice. Fieldwork offers a connection to life that is operative for both the author and the reader. Participation in the life of the church and focused attention on the expression and practices of communities shape the theologian and orientate what the theologian eventually writes. The practice of ethnographic fieldwork has a symbiosis with a theology of person, place, and identification that is rooted in the mission of God. This orientation aligns the writer with the concerns of communities and practitioners in such a way that our ecclesial readers recognize a commonality between our research and their own calling and vocation. It is this recognition that offers the potential of plausibility.

Qualitative research offers plausibility in ecclesiology in a third way. The ethnographic turn allows for a "soft" test of theological assertion. There are certain kinds of ecclesiology that are not amenable to examination through empirical means. A good example might be the idea that the church is the body of Christ. It is hard to see how this kind of theological idea could be tested through social scientific methods. Having said this, ecclesiology is full of assertions about the social and communal nature of the church. So, for instance, if the idea of unity and diversity in the church that arises from the image of the body of Christ could be explored through participant observation and semistructured interviews, it might be possible to explore how people in a local congregation relate. From this a picture of "the body" might be developed that makes reference to the various social connections and disconnections that characterize a particular community's life. It is, of course, a theological move to then decide on the relative significance of the empirical data and the theological or doctrinal notions of unity. Adopting a more disciplined and rigorous approach to social and cultural reality, however, does not of itself prejudge how we settle ourselves in terms of theological priorities. Different theologians will make their moves in different ways. The point we would want to contend in this book is that these kinds of normative judgments, far from being skewed or subverted by the empirical, are simply enhanced and finessed. Ecclesiology needs ethnography.

Ethnography

While its roots lie in nineteenth-century anthropology, what is meant in contemporary research by the word "ethnography" is not always clear. Martyn Hammersley and Paul Atkinson suggest that the boundaries have been blurred between ethnography and terms such as "qualitative inquiry," "fieldwork," "interpretative method," and "case study."[2] This shift in the use of the term "ethnography," while not entirely uncontested — especially by anthropologists mindful of their heritage — has come about as a range of different academic disciplines has started to make use of qualitative methodologies. So in recent research ethnography, or qualitative methods of inquiry, has been adopted in a range of disciplinary contexts. These include education, criminology, geography, business studies, media studies, as well as the social sciences more generally.[3] In this context the interest in "ethnography" in theology forms part of a more general "turn" toward practice and the lives that can be seen across many disciplinary fields.

In this series we use the term "ethnography" inclusively. Ethnography refers to a way of seeing or a way of approaching social research. Julie Scott Jones and Sal Watt describe this more general idea of ethnography as a "sensibility" that while it is diverse in method and defies a single definition, it does have a number of shared values. They describe seven core ethnographic values: participation; immersion; reflection, reflexivity, and representation; thick description; an active participative ethics; empowerment; and understanding.

Participation traditionally relates to the method of participant observation, but Scott Jones and Watt point out that the fully immersed par-

---

2. Martyn Hammersley and Paul Atkinson, *Ethnography: Principles into Practice*, 3rd ed. (London: Routledge, 2007), p. 1.

3. Julie Scott Jones and Sal Watt, eds., *Ethnography in Social Science Practice* (London: Routledge, 2010), p. 6.

ticipant observer is not always a possibility — for instance, in research into prisons. Participation has therefore come to mean an approach or a willingness to participate in social worlds in a range of different ways. These might include physical, social, mental, and emotional (and we might add spiritual and theological) kinds of participation.[4] The core value of immersion in ethnographic research is seen in the willingness of the researcher to enter deeply into social and cultural worlds through fieldwork. It means learning the language of the people one is studying both literally and metaphorically. Robert Park, the Chicago School sociologist, expressed the idea of immersion as the researcher being willing to get the seat of his or her pants dirty.[5] Reflection, reflexivity, and representation cluster a series of approaches to research. Ethnographers are constantly reflecting on their fieldwork and their methods. Qualitative research is not a fixed method that researchers simply apply to situations. It is an evolving and shifting dialogical approach or attitude. This process of revision and conversation is particularly significant in relation to researchers' own sense of themselves in relation to the processes of research. It is therefore a recognized part of qualitative method to be reflexively concerned with the interaction between the site of study and the self as a gendered, positioned, and traditioned subject. Representation takes these reflective and reflexive concerns into a continual critical examination of the way that communities and individuals are represented in and through the research process. In particular, attention to representation reflects the issues and problems that emerge as studies are written up. The core value of thick description refers to the way that ethnographers attempt to describe the situations they study in as much detail as possible. Ethics forms a continual concern in ethnographic work. Going from this ethical commitment, researchers are actively engaged in issues of participation and power in relation to the individuals and the groups they study. The final core value is understanding. Understanding in ethnographic work, Scott Jones and Watt argue, has been influenced by Max Weber's notion of *verstehen* with its aim of "creating interpretative bridges" or frameworks for understanding. Understanding the social world as Clifford Geertz suggested involves creating relationships in the field in such a way that the process is like "grasping a proverb, catching an illusion . . . reading a poem."[6]

4. Scott Jones and Watt, *Ethnography,* p. 7.
5. Scott Jones and Watt, *Ethnography,* p. 7.
6. Scott Jones and Watt, *Ethnography,* pp. 9-10.

Methods

Seen inclusively, ethnography becomes a cluster of values that shape how research is conducted rather than a specific, closely defined methodology. This inclusive approach to the ethnographic does however involve certain clearly defined methods of inquiry. There are four main methods, says David Silverman, that are common to all kinds of qualitative research. The first of these is observation.

Observation is foundational to a range of research traditions starting with the pioneering studies by anthropologists such as Malinowski and Radcliffe-Brown and the sociology of the Chicago School sociologists. From these beginnings, observation, says Silverman, has often been the "chosen method to understand another culture."[7] In congregational studies observation has become one of the main ways to develop a picture of the lived experience of a church community. The second method relates to analyzing texts and documents. This kind of qualitative research focuses on exploring the different categories that are used by participants. Examples of this kind of work might include the analysis of stories that are told, for instance, in preaching, or ways that organizations organize and deal with documents, like the various documents and minutes of church councils or descriptions of congregational life found over the years in church magazines. The third method identified by Silverman is interviewing. In qualitative research, interviews are focused on the attempt to discover an authentic voice rather than a representative or reliable sample. So the aim is to try to find ways to capture the authentic voice of a participant; this is most usually achieved through open-ended questions. For example, a researcher might ask a group of Christian young people to describe what attending a church service means to them. The final method is the use of recordings and transcripts. Qualitative researchers, says Silverman, often make use of different kinds of recordings; for example, audio or digital cameras might be used to make a record of a worship service or a sermon. These provide a reliable point of reference after an event has happened. Recordings are often combined with transcription, which allows for different kinds of data analysis.[8] Recordings and transcriptions could be made, for instance, when researching the var-

---

7. David Silverman, *Interpreting Qualitative Data: Methods for Analysing Talk, Text, and Interaction* (London: Sage, 1993), p. 9.

8. Silverman, *Interpreting Qualitative Data*, pp. 9-11.

ious conversations that take place in a church mums and tots club or in a Bible study meeting.

The turn toward the ethnographic represents a strategic intervention in Christian theology. Methods of research are never neutral. They situate the researcher in relation to the area of study. They structure how we see, what we see, and what we eventually come to write. Qualitative methods constitute a particular kind of perspective or voice within different disciplinary conversations. Whatever the disciplinary field and whatever the particular point at issue, the ethnographic "voice" focuses attention on the lived and the local.

The Conversation and the Proposal

The chapters in this book have been divided into two sections. The first section has chapters written by four of the editors of the Studies in Ecclesiology and Ethnography: Paul Fiddes, John Swinton, Christian Scharen, and Pete Ward. We have called these contributions collectively "The Proposal." Each chapter explores the idea of ecclesiology and ethnography as a theological method from a slightly different perspective. Together they constitute a common view on how the church and its study can be viewed as simultaneously theological and social/cultural. We explore how an embodied understanding of the church and the study of embodied expressions of church contribute to each other. The chapters describe, in slightly different ways, how ethnographic research can be informed and shaped from our ecclesial situatedness and how theological ideas are reformed through this process. Thus through our social/cultural theological traditioning in liturgical life and through the ecclesial practice of academic writing we are shaped as researchers, and this shaping informs and locates how, and why, and to what eventual ends we might engage with the lived expression of the church through ethnographic methods of inquiry.

We have termed our contribution a proposal because, while we see it as a coherent and common view, we do not see it as the last word or a settled position but rather as a starting point for dialogue. In this spirit we have given the second section of the book the title "The Conversation." Many of these chapters have come from the discussions we have had at the ecclesiology and ethnography workshops and conferences we have been holding over the last few years. Others have been invited to join these discussions by simply writing for this volume. As this is a conversation, we see it as essential that interesting and diverse people are gathered around the table. We have not simply invited people who will agree with our proposal. There has been no agreed line or "take" that determines who is included in this volume. Nevertheless, whether this has come about through the process of debate and mutual sharing within the network or perhaps through the self-selection that comes from those who have an interest in ecclesiology and ethnography, the papers as a whole track a very similar path to our central proposal — with of course some important correctives and emphases.

PART ONE

The Proposal

CHAPTER 1

Ecclesiology and Ethnography: Two Disciplines, Two Worlds?

Paul S. Fiddes

E Is For . . .

What has ecclesiology to do with ethnography? Apart, of course, from a pleasing alliteration of initial letters and a similar plurality of syllables? These two disciplines may seem to be worlds apart, the first being, it seems, quite deductive in method, and the second fundamentally inductive. Ecclesiology, as employed by theologians, is deeply rooted in a doctrine of the triune God, and so seems to take its sources "deductively" from the Holy Scriptures, the tradition of the church, and its liturgy. Ethnography, as employed by social scientists, is rooted in observing the life and practices of a specified group of human people and drawing conclusions "inductively" from them. In the deductive method of inference, conclusions are drawn quite tightly and inevitably from accepted premises, in this case the beliefs held by the Christian community. In the inductive method of inference we move from particularities to more general suppositions, so that the situations and experiences we face in the world make certain conclusions at least plausible. The difference might also be put in terms of "the one and the many": theology is sure that it has the sense of a whole, a metanarrative that will make sense of everything, while social science is concerned with the multiple, contingent details of everyday life and only aims to construct theory after observation. Further, one might reflect with the poet Chaucer on "the life so short, the craft so long to learn," and conclude regretfully that there is just not enough time to become skilled in two disciplines to the extent that it would be productive to integrate them.

Despite all this, the present volume is the first in a series bridging ecclesiology and ethnography, and it is my contention that it is actually essential for *theology* to attempt to bring the two disciplines together. Since I am a theologian and not a social scientist, I am bound to look at the issue from this angle, and I must leave it to colleagues in the social sciences to propose the necessity of *ecclesiology* for their own discipline if they wish. I can only state that, while remaining in the craft of a theologian, I do not think it is possible to do theology properly without taking at least an amateur interest in the methods and results of "ethnographers." In this chapter I want to explore the distinctively theological reasons for this claim, and in particular to suggest that it presupposes a certain vision of God, or a certain view of the relation between God and the world. There are not two worlds but one — and the question is how to conceive of the relation of this one created world to uncreated and final reality.

However, in making this proposal I should make clear from the outset that I am taking a wide interpretation of the term "ethnography," and I believe this is in line with the present series of books. In its classical form, ethnography is the study of a particular group of people who supposedly share a single culture, an investigation mainly using one method — living for a considerable length of time with the group, becoming as far as possible "one of them," thoroughly getting to know their beliefs and practices through careful observation over a long period, and then writing up an interpretation by employing established categories.[1] The "outsider" tries to become the "insider," and to feel the "otherness" or strangeness of the group within his or her own self. The interpretation arrived at belongs essentially to the external observer, though it may be shared with those inside.

Under the catchword "ethnography" I want to include other methods of investigation, such as shorter-term observation, interviews, analysis of speech patterns appearing in the discourse of the group, study of journals kept by members of the group, use of surveys (supplementing other means), and introduction into the group of texts to be read and reflected upon. These methods are largely qualitative, though some — such as the survey — have a quantitative element to them. Recently the term "action research" has appeared.[2] According to this kind of approach, the investiga-

---

1. For a classic description of "participant observation," see H. Russell Bernard, *Research Methods in Anthropology: Qualitative and Quantitative Approaches* (London: Sage, 1994), pp. 136-54.

2. See the chapter later in this volume by Clare Watkins; for an example of the

tors (usually a team) may not strictly be outsiders at all but may share the same culture and convictions; since the point of bringing ethnography and ecclesiology together is to study the life of the Christian church, the investigators are likely to be members of the church, although not necessarily of the same Christian communion being studied. The interpretation that is the goal of the study may then emerge between the investigators and a team from the group, and the result is expected to be transformative and not just descriptive. This approach is a variation of what has come to be called the "pastoral cycle" in practical theology, where reflection on practice leads to new actions, which then become the stuff of further reflection.[3] In short, the *e* for ethnography has a significant alliteration with *e* for "empirical." I am interested here in *many* ways of bringing empirical investigation of a Christian community into interaction with the Christian doctrine of the church, or ecclesiology. The term "ethnography" nevertheless remains useful as pointing to the need for all these empirical methods to include, or be accompanied by, at least some element of participative observation.

This more flexible approach to ethnography may actually make more sense from the standpoint of contemporary social theory. Although the magisterial *Oxford English Dictionary* still defines "ethnography" as a "scientific description of nations or races of men, with their customs, habits, and points of difference," a great deal of late-modern suspicion has arisen around studying groups of people as if they were homogeneous units within a tight cultural boundary. There is critique of the notion of a culture as a self-contained unit — a unified and consistent whole of beliefs and values, discontinuous with other cultures around it. A late-modern approach to culture sees diverse cultures as *sharing* cultural elements, with open boundaries between them.[4] In the earlier modern anthropological

---

method in operation, see the report *Living Church in the Global City: Theology in Practice* (London: Heythrop College; Cuddesdon: Ripon College Cuddesdon, 2008).

3. This was first popularized by Laurie Green in *Let's Do Theology: A Pastoral Cycle Resource Book* (London: Mowbray, 1990; Continuum, 2004), and has been widely drawn upon. For another variation, see Elaine Graham, Heather Walton, and Frances Ward, *Theological Reflection: Methods* (London: SCM, 2005), pp. 170-99.

4. See, e.g., Daniel Cottom, *Text and Culture* (Minneapolis: University of Minnesota Press, 1988), pp. 18ff. For a critique of cultural "wholism," see Clifford Geertz, *The Interpretation of Cultures* (New York: Basic Books, 1973), p. 408. For an application of the postmodern sense of "place" to congregational study, see Mary McClintock Fulkerson, *Places of Redemption* (Oxford: Oxford University Press, 2007), pp. 24-54.

analysis of culture, a cultural identity (a "way of life")[5] was thought to be bounded at the same points as a distinct social group and localized in a defined geographical space. But all cultures or ways of life show creativity in consuming other cultures (as Michael de Certeau proposes),[6] and those that are marginalized or powerless like the Christian church often show the most originality and ingenuity. As Kathryn Tanner points out, it is difficult to sustain the notion of the church as an alternative social world;[7] the interesting question is *how* the church absorbs influences from other cultures and how it employs them, not whether it does so or not. There are good social science reasons, then, for abandoning the classical notion of a dispassionate, outside observer setting out to identify with a "strange people"; this has overtones of the patronizing, indeed the imperialistic, to it.[8] There should be no bar to the investigator sharing the Christian culture of the group under study, though he or she will probably have a different "style" in blending elements of the Christian tradition with other contemporary cultures.

But my interest here is less in social theory than in theology, beginning from the concept of the church as not merely a social grouping but as a community that is engaged in the communion of the triune God. *E* here is for engagement. Recent "*koinonia* ecclesiology," to be found in all Christian churches,[9] emphasizes that the *koinonia*, or "fellowship," of the church reflects — and indeed participates in — the *koinonia* of Father, Son, and Holy Spirit in God.[10] If we think of the relational movement in God that is

5. See, e.g., Alfred L. Kroeber and Klyde Kluckhohn, *Culture: A Critical Review of Concepts and Definitions* (Cambridge: Harvard University Press, 1952), pp. 50ff.; Raymond Williams, *The Long Revolution* (Harmondsworth, U.K.: Penguin, 1965), p. 57.

6. Michael de Certeau, *The Practice of Everyday Life* (Berkeley: University of California Press, 1984), pp. 21, 43.

7. Kathryn Tanner, *Theories of Culture: A New Agenda for Theology* (Minneapolis: Fortress, 1997), pp. 97-102.

8. See James Clifford and George E. Marcus, *Writing Culture: The Poetics and Politics of Ethnography* (Berkeley: University of California Press, 1986).

9. See William C. Ingle-Gillis, *The Trinity and Ecumenical Church Thought* (Aldershot: Ashgate, 2007), pp. 9-11, 36-38.

10. E.g., Miroslav Volf, *After Our Likeness: The Church as the Image of the Trinity* (Grand Rapids: Eerdmans, 1998), pp. 191-220; Catherine Mowry LaCugna, *God for Us: The Trinity and Christian Life* (San Francisco: HarperCollins, 1991), pp. 278-305; John D. Zizioulas, *Being as Communion: Studies in Personhood and the Church* (London: Darton, Longman and Todd, 1985), pp. 49-66; Leonardo Boff, *Trinity and Society* (Maryknoll, N.Y.: Orbis, 1988), pp. 11-24, 106-7, 153-54, 209-10.

like a Father sending out a Son, expressed from without beginning in an "eternal generation," and subsequently sent on mission into the created world, then this shapes all the movements of mission in the church as it gives itself generously for the life of society around; the key thought will be "as the Father has sent me, so I send you" (John 20:21). If we think of the relational movement in God that is like a Son responding to the Father and glorifying him through his obedient acceptance of the task laid upon him, then this shapes all movements of discipleship and worship in the church. If we think of the relational movement in God that is like a Spirit of love and hope, opening up the divine relations to new depths in themselves and to a real future, then this shapes all movements of openness in the church, to others and to a future unconstrained by the conditions of the present. Since these movements in God are self-giving and suffering love, then we can also think of them with different genders in appropriate circumstances, so that we can imagine relations that are like those between a mother and a daughter (or a mother and a son, or a father and a daughter) and that similarly impress themselves on the life of the church.

Further, if we think of the interweaving *(perichoresis)* of the three distinct modes of divine relation, different in role but equal in divine reality, then we shall strive for an equality of all members in the church, each freed from oppression by the other and necessary to the other. Later I shall return to the idea of "relational movements" in God, but for the moment I want to affirm that ecclesiology is grounded in God, and its story is nothing less than an engagement in the metanarrative of the Trinity. This is a narrative given through the self-disclosure of God at key moments in human history, and through human reflection on this encounter, prompted by its impact on the human mind. But I want to assert that a Trinitarian ecclesiology cannot *only* be deduction from the Scripture and tradition that witness to this self-unveiling of God, and to make this assertion for good theological (in fact, Trinitarian) reasons.

Inadequacy of Deduction or "Application"

The alternative to taking induction from empirical investigation seriously would be simply to *apply* a preexisting doctrine of ecclesiology to a particular situation. The presupposition here would be that Christian theology is a set of unchanging truths that only need to be *translated* into different cultural contexts, like translating a text from ancient Hebrew into modern

English. We might then take the New Testament concept of the church as the body of Christ, elaborated in the church fathers as the theology of a eucharistic community, and then ask how any local church matches up to this vision. Or we might begin with a theory of God as "communion," and then examine the way that a church reflects or fails to reflect such a model. This is often called the "deductive" method, working from large principles to application in particular situations. I do want to affirm that the deductive movement of thought, working from established principles or from canonical texts to particular situations, certainly has a place in the project of ecclesiology. But there are problems if this becomes the predominant approach. There are many reasons why we must take the contextualization of theology more seriously than this.[11]

In the first place, there are reasons *external* to the work of Christian theology that make us question this "application" model, just as we have found reasons to question a unitary view of ethnography. We might think of the way that Western thought forms, in which much traditional theology has been done, do not make sense within the unique cultural patterns of other parts of the world. This problem has become more acute as regional churches have become aware of their national identity and self-worth and become resistant to colonization. We may admit further that traditional theology has tended to oppress or at least overlook certain social groups in every society, such as the poor, the powerless, and women. Finally, it is now clear that human culture is not a universal and permanent phenomenon, but a set of *changing* meanings and values that shape a way of life. To take culture seriously means to listen carefully to the stories that people tell about themselves in a particular historical and geographical situation.

But it is not just external factors that raise questions about an "application" model of ecclesiology. There are reasons *internal* to Christian theology, which are part of its own momentum. There are the central, linked ideas of incarnation, sacrament, and revelation. In the first place, there is incarnation. Christian faith affirms that God has become flesh not in a general, universal way but particularly as a Jewish male in first-century Palestine. This focus of the divine presence happens in the context of God's continuous involvement with a particular people, engaging in a costly way in all the (often messy) particularities of their history. If we are to share in this mission of God, we must also share in the process of incar-

---

11. See further Stephen B. Bevans, *Models of Contextual Theology* (Maryknoll, N.Y.: Orbis, 1992).

nation, communicating Christian truth in a way that is truly grounded in a culture that is European, Asian, African, poor, or sophisticated. So, taking *incarnation* seriously means more than applying existing principles. This leads to a kind of "sacramental" understanding of reality in which God is encountered in an embodied way, through concrete realities, and not merely through ideas. The ordinary things of life can become transparent to God's presence; culture itself can be sacramental, in the sense of providing places of transforming encounter with the triune God. *Sacrament* means taking bodies seriously.[12] This then further involves a view of *revelation* as the self-unveiling or the self-offer of God rather than a direct communication of propositional truths.[13] God communicates God's own self through actions, relationships, and symbols in daily life, though this self-offering is fully expressed only in the person of Jesus. So we cannot simply impose a set of revealed truths on a situation.

In other words, for theological reasons an element of *induction* is necessary, working from the details of the actual situation to theological principles. Perhaps the outstanding recent exemplar of this method is Elaine Graham, and especially in her book *Transforming Practice*. She begins from the actual practices of faith communities as they can be observed here and now, and envisages the task of practical theology as interpreting and helping communities in their pastoral practice; such theology should enable them to understand better the relation between their beliefs and their actions, to achieve consistency between what they say and what they do, and to articulate this in the public arena.[14] A purely inductive approach has, however, the dangers of relativism and a floating free from the Christian tradition.

Faith is not a mere matter of words but is *embodied;* it takes bodily form in the life of a community as people live together, and communities cannot operate without some kinds of institutions and structures. Ecclesiology should seek to express the *theological* dimension within these embodied forms. "Theology" means talk about God, and so we are asking what the triune God is doing in and through these bodily shapes of life, finding what we can say about the activity of God in creation and redemption. As Schleiermacher understood it, practical theology was the method

12. So Sallie McFague, *The Body of God* (London: SCM, 1993), pp. 180-87.

13. "Revelation is the Person of God speaking": Karl Barth, *Church Dogmatics* I/1 (Edinburgh: T. & T. Clark, 1975), p. 304.

14. Elaine L. Graham, *Transforming Practice: Pastoral Theology in an Age of Uncertainty* (London: Mowbray, 1996), pp. 112-41.

of "maintaining and perfecting the church," and so was essentially a study of the tasks involved in "church leadership."[15] We might say that such a study took the church as a whole body seriously, and allowed theological principles to interact with its corporate life — with its worship, provision of education, and government. Roughly speaking, it included structures as well as individuals.

In recent years, "pastoral theology" has tended to be regarded as restricted to the church, and "practical theology" as being theological reflection on the whole life of the world. Practical theology — its advocates assert — tries to understand what God is doing to renew life in economic and political structures, in *secular* bodies as well as in the Christian community. But this is a rather artificial distinction. One pastoral theologian, Don Browning, certainly regards pastoral theology as being concerned with the life cycle of individuals in community, but understands the community to be that of *society* as a whole.[16] Pastoral theology seeks to find Christian ethical norms, he argues, which govern the life cycle of *all* human beings. It will be basic to my own exploration of ecclesiology to find deep connections between a "theological" vision of the church community and communities outside the walls of the church. We cannot, however, confine this continuity to ethical values: we must find connections also in the aesthetic dimensions of human life, not only in the human sense of living in the face of moral values and demands, but also in the experience of beauty and creativity. In developing an ecclesiology, we are thus concerned with the interplay between beliefs and practices, whether inside or outside the Christian community.[17] This does not mean there is no difference between "church" and "world," but it is to resist separation.

Since faith *is* embodied in worldly and secular forms, it is appropriate that ecclesiology should use some secular tools to analyze these forms. In our age these are predominantly the tools of the human sciences, but since this is *theology*, these are not to be used as if they were autonomous disciplines; they are to be used in the service of theological reflection, to assist us to find the theological dimension in the worldly forms of life.

---

15. Friedrich Schleiermacher, *Brief Outline of the Study of Theology*, trans. Terence N. Tice (Richmond, Va.: John Knox, 1966), pp. 91-94.

16. D. S. Browning, *The Moral Context of Pastoral Care* (Philadelphia: Westminster, 1976).

17. So James Woodward and Stephen Pattison, eds., *The Blackwell Reader in Pastoral and Practical Theology* (Oxford: Blackwell, 2000), pp. 6-7.

Method in the Sciences and Human Sciences

However, if all this be accepted, the question arises: *How* do the secular tools of analysis relate to the theological tools of inquiry? How do induction and deduction come together? Here we are bound to begin with thinking about method in the physical sciences. This is itself a rather scandalous way into our subject, since it is a widespread view today that the Enlightenment project of gaining knowledge is deeply flawed. It is right to protest that the scientific method has become an idol to which everything else has had to conform — whether it is history, sociology, or indeed theology. However, it is still illuminating to begin with the "classic" form of method in science. Here the first task is largely *descriptive* and involves collection of data; the second is *inductive*, moving inferentially from particular instances to a general theory, or the making of concepts. This movement is also predictive, in formulating a theory that will account not only for present observation but also for any further data collected in the future. Finally, the theory is tested by repeatable experiments, and this third movement of testing involves an element of *deduction* from the theory or concepts that have been established. Theory is correct if the results can be repeated.

There is a good deal of truth in this account, but as Ian Barbour has shown in his Gifford Lectures, *Religion in an Age of Science,* the situation is more complicated than this.[18] One of the complications, in comparison with our initial account, is that scientists do not move directly from observation and description of data to the *theory* stage by inference or induction alone; they have to make what Barbour calls "acts of creative imagination for which no rules can be given";[19] these acts or imaginative leaps involve the use of analogies and models. For instance, gas particles might be pictured as billiard balls colliding and bouncing off each other, and from this model a kinetic theory of gases can be developed — the way gases move. The third movement from theory to experiment is also more complex. Any process of testing is bound to be influenced by the network of theories and concepts that make up the store of scientific knowledge and tradition, that have been built up in the community. Moreover, "community" here means both the narrower scientific community and the wider society that

18. Ian Barbour, *Religion in an Age of Science,* Gifford Lectures, 1989-1991, vol. 1 (London: SCM, 1990), pp. 31-33.
19. Barbour, *Religion,* p. 32.

has been influenced by scientific discovery. In fact, the very first process of observation and collection of data has been influenced in the same way already. The element of "deduction" is thus far wider than the testing of a theory; it is a drawing upon stored traditions.

This more complicated account has already taken onboard *some* criticisms of the Enlightenment project. On the way to theories, imagination and metaphor play a part. On the way to observation of the world, we need to recognize the nature of society as a linguistic community. The way we see the world is shaped by the language games we play. Our experience is deeply influenced by language, which might be called the "grammar" of life itself. In so-called postmodern reactions against the confidence of the Enlightenment period, language may even become God, the creator of all. Without going so far, even scientists should recognize that they are creatures of words, inheritors of traditions and stories.

This is even more clearly the case when we consider method in the *human* sciences, concerned with observing human behavior, which have built on method in the physical sciences. Observation and collection of data in this process will involve kinds of "measurement" that would not be proper for the physical sciences. For example, if you wanted to measure how religious someone was, you could ask the person a number of questions such as "How often do you attend church?" and "How important is the reading of the Bible to you?" and "Do you pray regularly?" and so on. A useful tool for this kind of measurement is the survey.[20] Another useful tool, more obviously qualitative, is taking a verbatim account of a conversation, to be reflected upon in the light of various questions.

A social scientist or psychologist of religion will then be interested in predicting when and where things will be most likely to happen, to say, "If someone feels or acts in *this* way, that person will be more likely also to feel or act in *that* way." We might, for instance, predict that people who take the parable of the Good Samaritan seriously will be more likely to give to charity; or that someone who believes in life after death will be more likely to approach death in a peaceful way than someone who does not. This has some similarity with the predictions of scientific method, which belong to the second, inductive movement from description to theory.

Like the process in the physical sciences, we cannot get to the stage of

---

20. See Catherine Marsh, *The Survey Method: The Contribution of Surveys to Sociological Explanation* (London: Allen and Unwin, 1982); Claus A. Moser, *Survey Methods: A Social Investigation* (London: Heinemann, 1967).

prediction, however, without passing through the *making of models*. In the human sciences, this usually takes the form of "correlation," in which two variables are measured to see how they relate to each other. This helps us to understand our observations better, showing that one kind of behavior is usually related to another. For example, the high rate of unemployment among young people might be correlated with the high level of crime among young people. The theory or prediction arrived at is that young people who have no jobs are more likely to commit crimes. To take another example, the low self-esteem of people who are depressed may be correlated with statistics for suicide, leading to the prediction that those who have a low sense of self-worth are more likely to take their own lives.

These correlations lead as yet only to a prediction, not to an *explanation*. We have to go one step further to arrive at an explanation, such as that the desperation induced by unemployment *causes* crime. The method of correlation itself cannot tell us why the two variables are related. If we return to one of the predictions already discussed, that those who have a belief in an afterlife approach death more peacefully, this might be because such a belief causes peace; but it might also be because those who approach death in a peaceful way are also more disposed to believe in an afterlife. Or there may be a third variable we have not considered, such as the influence of people around them. But, despite these difficulties, social scientists are more interested than physical scientists in pressing on beyond the question *how* to the question *why*. Theories in the social sciences move toward an explanation of why things happen, where in the physical sciences they tend to remain explanations of how they happen, predicting that they will happen consistently if conditions are similar.

To *test* an explanation (the third movement), the human scientist will introduce an "experiment." That is, one variable will be changed to see how it affects the situation. Usually it is changed in one group of people and left unchanged in another (a control group). But to conduct a good experiment, the researcher must have a theory suggesting that one thing will cause a change in another. Like the physical sciences, the experiment sets out to test the usefulness of the theory of how things happen; but it also tries to test *why*. The result will hopefully be understanding. Experiments with human beings are of course much more difficult to achieve (and raise ethical issues), and I will return to this aspect from a theological standpoint in a moment.

We noticed that in the "revised" account of science, there was a deductive element in the part played by the life of the community in shaping both observation in the first place, and the process of testing a theory. This is even more obvious in the human sciences, not least because of the number of conflicting explanations brought forward! The influence of traditions of interpretation held within the community makes a considerable impact.

Methods in Theology: An Experiment in Thought

The more complex account of the scientific and human scientific methods explored above brings them quite close to the methods of theology. In his own account Ian Barbour offers a flowchart at this point,[21] and with a great deal of hesitation I offer a version of my own that has some similarities with (but also considerable differences from) his.

Barbour finds a very close similarity between method in science and religion. Scientific "theories" are replaced by beliefs, and "data" comes in the form of religious experiences, rituals, and the great stories of the faith. The kinds of experiences relevant here are wonder (sense of the holy), unity with the infinite (mysticism), reorientation of life (conversion), courage (in the face of suffering and death), obligation (a sense of moral demands), and the experience of the world as both ordered and creative. In the inductive movement from collecting data to making theory, Barbour points out that, like science, theology too uses "models" — examples in theology would be images of God — to present meaning and to evoke understanding. In both cases, too, the "data" is being observed and interpreted by a community in which there is a whole network of belief and understanding built up over the years, so that there is an element of deduction from received "doctrine," practiced in rituals. The movement of "experimentation" is more problematic in the areas of religious belief and experience than in science, and so Barbour shows it by a broken arrow, as I do in the chart below. He does, however, think there are some criteria in experience for judging the adequacy of beliefs.

My own version of the flowchart appears on page 25. My view is that there are indeed similarities between method in the physical and human sciences on the one hand, and in theology on the other, but there are also profound differences. My own flowchart tries to represent these, and I want to draw attention to three differences in particular.

---

21. Barbour, *Religion*, p. 36.

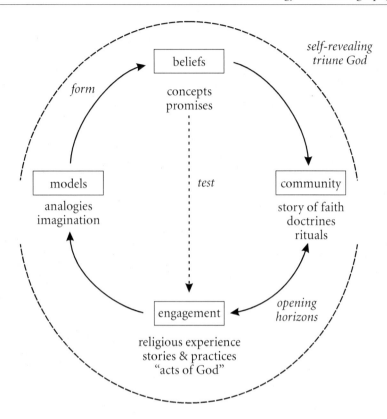

The first huge difference is a belief in *revelation,* which is represented in the diagram by the all-embracing sphere. God is not an object like other objects in the world and so cannot be observed, but this does not mean that all we have to go on is the data of human religious experience. Theology, I suggest, presumes that we live in the presence of a self-revealing God. Indeed, we live in the environment of the triune God, who is always opening and manifesting God's self to us. I began with some reflections on a Trinitarian or *koinonia* ecclesiology; this makes most sense if we think of what are traditionally called "persons" in God as nothing more or less than movements of relationship. Taking a clue from Augustine and Aquinas, who, in different cultural contexts, proposed that "the [divine] names refer to the relations"[22] or "person signifies relation,"[23] I maintain that what the

22. Augustine, *De Trinitate* 5.6.
23. Aquinas, *Summa Theologiae* 1a.29.4.

church fathers called *hypostases* are not *subjects* who *have* relations, but the very relations themselves. The relations are *hypostases,* a term best translated as "distinct reality," insofar as they are distinct ("other") from each other and more real than any subjects can be. Taking a further clue from Karl Barth's insistence that "with regard to the being of God, the word 'event' or 'act' is final,"[24] we may speak of God as an "event of relationships," or perhaps "three movements of relationship subsisting in one event."

Of course, it is not possible to visualize, paint, or etch in stone or glass three interweaving relationships, or three movements of being characterized by their relations, without subjects exercising them. But then this ought to be a positive advantage in thinking about God, who cannot be objectified like other objects in the world. The triune God cannot be conceptualized as either subject or object, and so cannot be known by observation but only by participation.[25] We "know" God when we engage in relations of love, compassion, and justice that rely on relations that are deeper, richer, and more life-enhancing than our own, and by which we can think of God. The language of relations must remain analogical, since literal talk about God is impossible, but the analogy is with the *relations* in which we engage as human beings, not with those beings themselves. Talk about God is thus apophatic and kataphatic at the same time, eluding all human conception and yet open to analogies that are given by revelation, creation, and incarnation.

This is why I have put the word "engagement" in the flowchart where "observation" might be expected in other disciplines. While of course we observe objects in the world, "engagement" is common ground between the data of human experience and religious talk about "acts of God." We cannot observe God, but we can engage in the life of God, participating in the relationships we may call Father, Son, and Spirit. This is the greatest challenge to the assumption of the Enlightenment that human beings are the great subjects in the world, and that the remainder of nature is an object to be mastered and controlled. We need to get beyond subject-object thinking to a kind of thinking characterized by engagement and participation. Such participation applies to all created reality, since everything created participates in the relations of the triune God, or exists in the space opened up by

24. Barth, *Church Dogmatics* II/1 (Edinburgh: T. & T. Clark, 1957), p. 263.
25. I have worked this out in detail in my *Participating in God: A Pastoral Doctrine of the Trinity* (London: Darton, Longman and Todd, 2000), pp. 34-50, 81-86.

the interweaving relations of God. God makes room in God's self for us to dwell. Relations do not exist in space, as in a Newtonian receptacle of space-time, but space exists in relations. As Leibniz put it, space is not a container in which bodies are put, but a compendium of relations.[26]

This does not mean that all created things participate in God *in the same way*, or that there is no difference between the *koinonia* of church and the world. Theologian Hans Urs von Balthasar offers a crucial insight: since "there is nothing outside God," there is only one place where even the human "no" of rejection of God can be spoken, and that is — ironically — within the glad response of the Son to the Father. Just as our "yes" to God leans upon the movement of thanksgiving and obedience that is already there in God, like the relation of a Son to a Father, so we speak our pain-giving "no" in the same space. Our "no" is a kind of "twisted knot" within the current of love of the Son's response.[27] The drama of human life can only take place within the greater drama of the divine life. Our dance of relationships can only happen within the patterns of the larger dance. As Balthasar puts it, "The creature's No resounds at the 'place' of distinction within the Godhead."[28]

Now, if all created reality exists in the space made by Uncreated Reality, then it also receives the self-disclosure of God, whatever kind of response it makes, whether "yes," "no," or a blend of the two.[29] This Trinitarian account of the relation between God and the world makes empirical investigation *essential* for ecclesiology. It brings together the theological search for the "One" or the grand metanarrative (nothing less than the story of the Trinity itself) with a respect for the many details of the world that are held in God. The place of revelation also highlights a difference from the method of the natural and human sciences, and this first great difference leads in turn to others.

It means, second, that the "data" to be observed and measured will not only be the repeatable phenomena of everyday experience, both individual and social. Describing present practice and experience will perhaps be the most straightforward part of any project on ecclesiology and ethnography,

---

26. Leibniz, *Die Philosophischen Schriften*, ed. G. J. Gerhardt, vol. 7 (Hildesheim: G. Olms, 1890), pp. 389-420.

27. Hans Urs von Balthasar, *Theo-Drama: Theological Dramatic Theory*, vol. 4, *The Action*, trans. G. Harrison (San Francisco: Ignatius, 1994), p. 330.

28. Balthasar, *Theo-Drama*, 4:333-34.

29. So Karl Rahner, *Foundations of Christian Faith*, trans. W. Dych (London: Darton, Longman and Todd), pp. 100-102.

and the tools of social and psychological science may certainly be drawn upon to *measure* this. We must listen to the stories that people tell *here and now* about themselves. But the "data" will also include the particular events in the past to which the community of faith bears witness as being especially disclosive of the nature and acts of God (on the flowchart, noted as "story of faith"). The fact that these events are told in a way that has been shaped by the faith of the community will not rule them out as "data," since all observation is influenced and shaped by the worldviews of the community in which the observer stands. Nor will the fact that certain events witnessed to are nonrepeatable (especially the resurrection of Jesus) rule them out. After all, the positivist view that history is totally uniform in events ("we do not see resurrections now so they do not happen") is only a particular interpretative framework, a copying of the strictly scientific method.[30]

The story of Jesus, in the backward context of Israel and the forward context of church tradition, will be brought into interaction with the story of contemporary life. There will be a hermeneutics of an "opening of horizons" between the past story and the present, a dialogical approach in which contemporary culture is both allowed to shape our understanding of the past story and to be challenged by it. This is represented on the flowchart by a two-way arrow. There is inevitably an element of deduction in this process; we are bound, for instance, to ask how the story of a Jesus who invited the outcasts, the marginal, and the oppressed of society to sit at his table illuminates the situations in which we find ourselves today. In the relation between induction (on the left-hand side) and deduction (on the right) lie some of the most contested areas. What we should avoid, however, is any kind of rigid, mechanical extraction of application from the stories and witnesses of the past. We must be open to imagination at this stage as well as in the making of models; there can be a creative interplay between the past story and the present one, room for the making of lateral leaps and imaginative jumps, as they are placed alongside each other. This two-way movement has, I suggest, some similarity to the "extended case method" developed by the sociologist Michael Burawoy, who proposes to expose preexisting theory or principles to the particularities of a situation, especially where they are anomalous to generalizations already held, in order to *reconstruct* theory and achieve new generalizations or universals. This he contrasts with the simple inductive strategy that moves

---

30. So Wolfhart Pannenberg, *Basic Questions in Theology,* trans. H. Kehm, 3 vols. (London: SCM, 1970), 1:66-80.

from particulars in time and space toward universals, as held by forms of "grounded theory."[31]

Third, this opening of horizons makes a difference to the making of models, compared with other disciplines. On the way to theological concepts (see the flow on the left-hand side of the diagram), we create models to talk about God and God's action in the world. Such models or metaphors cannot exactly describe God, who cannot be objectified. Yet (as Janet Martin Soskice argues),[32] metaphors can indicate a reality without exactly describing it. These models we create will not only arise out of contemporary experience and action, as tends to be the case with the natural and human sciences. *Decisive* paradigms have emerged from events in the past, which belong to the identity of the Christian community and which cannot be lost in whatever "paradigm shifts" may rightly happen. The very concept of Trinity, for instance, as a model for community, emerged from the first disciples' experience of the life of Jesus, his obedient Sonship, and his empowering by the Spirit; it was shaped in the life of the early church by their experience of worship in a particular cultural context. The resurrection is also an indispensable sign of hope for the Christian community, by which cruciform experiences of desolation and despair are to be interpreted. Another persistent metaphor is that of the church as the body of Christ, and I want to return to this image in particular when we consider the interplay of models between disciplines.

An Integrated Method in Ecclesiology

Everything said so far on method in theology is obviously relevant to ecclesiology, but is not restricted to it. Having surveyed methods in natural science, human science, and theology in general, we can now see how they interact in ecclesiology in particular. I have already suggested that since faith is embodied in worldly forms, and these forms exist within the relational life of God, the theologian exploring them must draw on the insights of the various sciences that set out to analyze the world. The concern

31. Michael Burawoy et al., *Ethnography Unbound: Power and Resistance in the Modern Metropolis* (Berkeley: University of California Press, 1991), p. 280. I am indebted to Luke Bretherton for alerting me to the thought of Burawoy: compare his own use of "the extended case method" in his chapter below.

32. Janet Martin Soskice, *Metaphor and Religious Language* (Oxford: Clarendon, 1987), pp. 118-41.

of the theologian working in ecclesiology is to find the theological dimension within the worldly forms of community, to be able to reflect on the presence, nature, purpose, and activity of the triune God that can be perceived within and through the form. This leads, I suggest, to at least three aspects of method.

First, the theologian should attempt to develop a *sharing of models* by means of which the community and events within it are interpreted. The making of models in all areas of knowledge must be taken seriously if we adopt a vision of the created world as held "in God," and so the kind of correlation done by the social and psychological sciences has to be taken into account. So must models for the nature of the physical world that have emerged from particular cultures, including the modern scientific culture. But these must also interact with the models held in Christian story and belief. Out of a genuine dialogue and not a simple synthesis, both prediction and theory can emerge.

Various types of practical theology have tended to center upon one model or another, and this can be an area of contention when the claims of one model are advanced against others. With regard to community, the model of *liberation* has been much explored in recent years. The work of Stephen Pattison has focused upon it, especially in his book *Pastoral Care and Liberation Theology.* His approach is not to write another liberation theology in itself, but to make an "exercise in critical pastoral theology designed to bring about a reorientation of focus and practice of pastoral care." He urges that the release of people from oppression is relevant to a wide range of pastoral issues, including the way people with mental health problems are treated not only in church, but also in hospital and society more widely. Models developed in the social sciences, relating to the analysis of oppression and liberation, are here brought into interaction with Christian images of freedom.[33] Peter Sedgewick makes the interesting attempt to bring together the model of contract in social and political sciences with the biblical model of covenant, in the service of a liberation theology that is relevant to community.[34] There is, however, a huge amount left to do in this attempt to share models, and a key example concerns the image of the "body of Christ."

---

33. Stephen Pattison, *Pastoral Care and Liberation Theology* (London: SPCK, 1997), pp. 48-49.

34. Peter Sedgewick, "Liberation Theology and Political Theory," in *The Blackwell Reader in Pastoral and Practical Theology,* pp. 165-71.

If God makes room in the divine life for all created things, then ecclesiology will need to reflect on living in the tension between several expressions of the body of Christ.[35] In the New Testament the phrase "body of Christ" has a threefold reference — to the glorious resurrection body of Christ (who is to be identified with the earthly Jesus of Nazareth), to the church, and to the eucharistic bread in which the community shares.[36] But developing the witness of Scripture, in line with our Trinitarian vision, we will want to speak of the embodiment of Christ in the world beyond the walls of the church. In the words of Dietrich Bonhoeffer, Christ "takes form" in the world;[37] we may discern the form and presence of Christ, for example, in a group that is working for racial equality, or providing refuge for women who have suffered violence from their husbands, or offering medical care in refugee camps. Different spatial dimensions of the body of Christ — incarnate, eucharistic, ecclesial, and secular — are thus related but not simply identical. We may say that the human Jesus, in his body, offered an obedient response to God his Father that was exactly the same as the movement of responsive love within God's life that we call the eternal Son. Thus the relation between a Son and a Father in the life of Jesus can be exactly mapped over the movement in the triune life that is like that of a Father sacrificially sending forth a Son and a Son saying yes to the Father in a Spirit of hope and openness to the future.

So the church can occupy this space in God, shaped like a child's relation to a parent, because the space is Christ-shaped. Mapped onto the life in God, it is not just *like* a body — it *is* the body of Christ. Likewise, the actions of breaking bread and pouring wine can fit into the movement of self-breaking and self-outpouring within God, becoming the place where we encounter in an ever deeper way the self-giving of Christ. But wherever in the world people give themselves to others or sacrifice themselves for others, these actions will also match the movement in God that is like a Son going forth on mission in response to the purpose of a Father; their acts share in the patterns of love in God, and so in them we can discern the body of Christ. Wherever there is the movement of a measure of music, or of a stroke of a brush, or of a blow of a chisel, or of a sequence of thought

35. For greater detail, see Paul S. Fiddes, *Tracks and Traces: Baptist Identity in Church and Theology* (Milton Keynes, U.K.: Paternoster, 2003), pp. 167-92.

36. E.g., resurrection body: Rom. 7:4; Phil. 3:21; John 2:21; church: 1 Cor. 6:15; 12:4-31; Rom. 12:3-8; Eph. 4:1-16; Col. 1:18; eucharistic bread: 1 Cor. 10:17; 11:24, 27, 29.

37. Dietrich Bonhoeffer, *Ethics,* ed. Eberhard Bethge, trans. N. Horton Smith (London: SCM, 1971), pp. 66-68; cf. p. 170.

in the arts or sciences, which reflects God's truth and beauty, this too shares in the dynamic flow of the life of God.

Different bodies in the world — the individual bodily form of Jesus Christ; the sacraments of bread, wine, and water; the eucharistic community; groups in society; and all the variety of matter in nature — are then all related to a common space. The space they occupy in God is not a kind of container, but a reality characterized by relationships, and in this way Christ can be embodied in all of them; his form can be recognized in them, and in all of them he can take flesh. The body of the world is thus shaped and formed by being held in relational movements in God. Living and moving in God (Acts 17:28), the world takes on the form of a text, a pattern of signs that points toward its creator. The church as the body of Christ, however, will not be simply the same as bodies in the world; it will be shaped in a distinctive way and will signify in its own way by its deliberate living in the relations of God, in its telling of the story of Christ, and by its sharing in the body of Christ in baptism and Eucharist.

This understanding of the different forms of the body of Christ means that there is scope for interaction between the ecclesial model of the body of Christ and models of body developed in the social sciences, which are likely to be drawn on in empirical studies. For instance, there is the model of body as *habitus,* as in the social philosophy of Pierre Bourdieu. The self is understood as an "embodied history" where the body is a site in which social structures are internalized over a length of time. Social customs and conventions are "written" on the body, and this *habitus* determines our response to the situation in which we are placed. What is learned by the body, Bourdieu comments, is not something that one has but something that one *is.*[38] The *habitus* is thus an embodied "system of structured, structuring dispositions, which is constituted in practice and is always orientated towards practical functions."[39] Bourdieu aims to overcome the dualism between subject and object, and there is obvious overlap here with the Christian model of the body of Christ, which is — as we have seen — a highly participative idea.

Social theorists also point out that in our present culture there is a reaction against the definition of self by means of established social spaces,

38. Pierre Bourdieu, *The Logic of Practice,* trans. Richard Nice (Cambridge: Cambridge University Press, 1995), p. 73.

39. Bourdieu, *The Logic of Practice,* p. 52; cf. Bourdieu, *Outline of a Theory of Practice,* trans. Richard Nice (Cambridge: Cambridge University Press, 1997), pp. 78-79.

characterized by narrow practices taking place within them and directed by a particular, dominant force. We experience our bodies today in the setting of new configurations of space. We live in a world where space is less the confined space of established social groups, and more the open arenas of global networks of information and communication. This globalization can be seen in the music, fashion, film, and travel industries, and most strikingly in the phenomenon of cyberspace.[40] All this makes us aware that the individual body is shaped not in a dualistic way by the powerful spirit of an individual or a particular group, but by living in interactive networks. This fits in with the earlier phenomenological perception that body is about participating in the widest possible space, and engaging in self-giving relations with others rather than protecting our own boundaries. As Maurice Merleau-Ponty puts it, bodiliness is about touching and being touched, about being "enfolded" in a kind of embrace that has no horizons, and where the divisions between our body and that of others collapse.[41] The overlap of these models of body with the Christian concept of body as engaging in the "wide space" of the Trinity is obvious.

A second point about method in ecclesiology is that, in comparison with a merely scientific or sociological perspective on community, it will look for something *unexpected* in the area of "theory" — that is, proposing how and why events happen as they do. On the basis of a sharing of theological models with secular models, it is bound to be alert to the elements of the grace of God and the action of God. This is why I have changed the term "prediction," which belongs to the second movement of method in the natural and social sciences, to "promise" in the theological flowchart; the researcher in ecclesiology is looking for the ways in which God will fulfill the divine promises, and this has room within it for the unexpected, for an openness that mere prediction does not have. The biblical notion of God's promise is not a tight, enclosed sequence of prediction and outcome, but has scope for divine and human freedom in bringing about something genuinely new in fulfillment, something surprising.

This also means that the researcher who is using empirical methods in the service of ecclesiology needs a theological conviction about the way God acts in the world; ecclesiology cannot be done without sorting this

---

40. See Scott Lash and Jim Urry, *Economies of Signs and Space* (London: Sage, 1994), pp. 13-28, 54-59.

41. Maurice Merleau-Ponty, *Visible and Invisible*, trans. Alphonso Lingis (Evanston: Northwestern University Press, 1969), pp. 248-49.

out. Is God's activity in the world coercive, unilateral, and interventionist? Or is it always persuasive, cooperative, and immanent? The latter belongs more obviously to the vision of a world held within the movements of a relational God.[42] However, it is not just the theological question of the *way* that God acts that might be in contention, but the bringing of the very attempt to discern God's action at all into the bounds of an academic discipline. In an important essay, Alastair Campbell asks, "Do practical theologians have the temerity to suggest that they can discern where God is at work, say in international politics, or in the works of writers and artists, or in the dilemmas of modern technological society?" He answers himself: "Perhaps one must answer that such boldness is indeed required."[43] Because ecclesiology is being done in the context of a university faculty, there will be a tendency to assimilate it entirely to the norms and methods of other branches of knowledge, and so to be comfortable in discussing objectively the phenomenon of how a community *believes* that God is at work redemptively in individuals and structures. But the interaction of beliefs and actions in this discipline has its own integrity; at the stage of theory, we must talk about the way God acts, remembering that this will have an unexpectedness about it that is not under our control. Unlike other theologians,[44] however, I do not think this emphasis on the integrity of theology rules out collaboration with other disciplines, for the theological reasons I have given.[45]

What, thirdly (following the movement of the natural and human sciences), can we say about the stage of "test" or experiment marked on the diagram above? This will be directed by the theory of how and why things happen, which — as we have seen — must have a theological dimension to it. This rules out even more clearly the conducting of the kinds of experiments that manipulate people; even if this were possible, let alone desirable, God is not amenable to experiment in this way. However, there *are* two kinds of testing in which the applied theologian is involved, one having to do with reflection, and the other in the mode of action.

42. See Paul S. Fiddes, *Participating in God: A Pastoral Doctrine of the Trinity* (Louisville: Westminster John Knox, 2001), pp. 115-48.

43. Alastair Campbell, "The Nature of Practical Theology," in *The Blackwell Reader in Pastoral and Practical Theology*, p. 86.

44. See, e.g., John Webster, *Theological Theology: An Inaugural Lecture Delivered before the University of Oxford on 27 October 1997* (Oxford: Clarendon, 1998), p. 3; also Webster, *Holiness* (Grand Rapids: Eerdmans, 2003), p. 2.

45. See pp. 18-20 above.

In the first place, although we cannot in ecclesiology deliberately *change* social variables to see what happens, we can observe the way that people act and react in different contexts, seeing the way that "theory" is worked out in different cultures. This means a cross-cultural approach, with investigation of the shape of church in different contexts. In the second place, there can be a testing out of theory in action that is not academic and experimental, but simply pastoral practice. One of the outcomes of an empirical-ecclesiological study should be *transformed practice*. Sharing interpretation of data between investigators and investigated should make a difference to people and situations in the contemporary world. Insights gained through the use of models and from the making of theory are put back again into action — whether this is dealing with third-world debt or the mission of the local church. This is more than a theological reflection on the church by detached observers; investigators and observed community develop a shared *habitus* (in the sense described above) and so develop a "bodily" wisdom beyond the merely conceptual.

Finally, then, let us sum up reasons why the integration of the empirical and the ecclesiological might be contentious. Different emphases may be put on induction and deduction, and on the balance between the vision of the "one" and the observation of the "many" in theological method. There may be a difference of opinion about the models to be selected as a focus for bringing together the tools of theology and the human sciences. There may be different theological understandings of the way God relates to the world. And there may be higher or lower degrees of nervousness about bringing talk about discerning the renewing action of God into an academic environment. Despite all this, there is a discipline here in its own right, contested though it is. In its very tensions and conflicts there lie the interest and the adventure of the subject. It is much more than the rather cynical dismissal of practical ecclesiology, by Don Cupitt, as "the gentle art of running a church that makes a healthy profit."[46]

---

46. Don Cupitt, *After All* (London: SCM, 1994), p. 20.

Attention and Conversation

Pete Ward

On a hot and sunny Pentecost Sunday in 2009, Paul Fiddes and I set out on a collaborative journey as participant observers. We had agreed that as part of the Ecclesiology and Ethnography project we would work together, and this resolve led us to join the crowds of students and young people attending a service of adult baptism at St. Aldate's Church in Oxford. As observers, we had spent a short while reflecting on our task and we had formulated preliminary research questions. In our discussions we had agreed that our interest lay in the relationship between theology and its expression in worship. With this basic orientation Paul and I shared in the worship as attentive researchers.

A much more formal account of our research will be published in an accompanying volume to this one.[1] But in broad terms through our observation of the service, and then as we reviewed it on the videos and in the transcripts we had made, our attention became focused on two areas. Paul was drawn to consider the theological implications of the particular practices of baptism that we observed at the service. I was taken up with the interplay and mix of different evangelical and charismatic cultural expressions in the service. Looking back on this, I suppose I might say there's not much of a surprise here. Our attention was drawn to the kinds of things we like to think about and write about. Paul is a Baptist and writes about systematic theology, and I am an Anglican with charismatic roots and I write about culture and theology. I am not trying to say that our "bias" or "inter-

---

1. Christian Scharen, ed., *Explorations* (Grand Rapids: Eerdmans, forthcoming).

est" distorted our research or that these elements were not observable or verifiable — we have the data recorded in a variety of forms and we have been careful to make a case to support our findings. The point is that what we saw, and indeed what we eventually chose to say about what we saw, emerged from and was shaped by our interests. We were attentive observers, but attentive in certain ways.

It is conceivable that different observers might have seen and chosen to write about different things. I could imagine, for instance, that another researcher's attention might have been drawn to the various references to the British general election and to the looming economic crisis. This might have led to a paper about evangelicalism and politics. Someone else might have been taken up with the social mix in this Oxford church and written about the interplay of social privilege and theology. The service might also have been ripe for analysis in terms of gender roles and the interplay with the presentation of the self in charismatic Christianity. Then again, given the number of overseas students present, it might have been interesting to explore the relationship between this very English church and issues of globalization, postcolonialism, and identity formation. As it was, Paul and I followed our research question and eventually wrote about the representation of theological themes within the performance of worship.

Qualitative Research and Conversations

Following a research question forms part of the accepted methodology in qualitative research. Martyn Hammersley and Paul Atkinson talk about research questions as being a kind of "foreshadowing."[2] This refers to the way that theoretical debates and concerns influence and shape how research is conducted. Research is "foreshadowed" by conversations because they direct attention and interest. As the research takes place these conversations continue, and as a consequence research questions are refined and changed.[3] The reformulation of research questions takes place before and during data collection and into the process of data analysis and writing.

Foreshadowing research questions arise from and contribute to wider conversations. Facts do not "speak for themselves," says David

2. Martyn Hammersley and Paul Atkinson, *Ethnography: Principles into Practice,* 3rd ed. (London: Routledge, 2007), p. 24.
3. Hammersley and Atkinson, *Ethnography,* p. 24.

Silverman; rather, qualitative research is "theory driven."[4] Research questions are situated in theoretical conversations. They arise from within, and contribute to, theoretical debates and discourses. Attention to the particular research setting grows out of and feeds into these more general conversations. As a result, qualitative inquiry is always "partisan" and "opinioned." James Clifford speaks of ethnographic truths as being "inherently partial — committed and incomplete."[5] What we see and what we eventually write are always conditioned not simply by the social and cultural reality we are researching, but also by our own contingent location within conversations. So the researcher is situated within these discipline-related theoretical conversations. Conversations therefore serve to shape the subjectivity of the researcher. The researcher's sense of self comes from a formation within and a continued interest in particular kinds of disciplinary conversations.

This chapter explores the idea of disciplinary conversations through six qualitative or ethnographic studies of the church. The studies are the following: Susan Friend Harding, *The Book of Jerry Falwell;* R. Stephen Warner, *New Wine in Old Wineskins;* Paul Heelas and Linda Woodhead, *The Spiritual Revolution;* David Mellott, *I Was and I Am Dust;* Nancy Ammerman, *Congregation and Community;* and Mary McClintock Fulkerson, *Places of Redemption.*[6] These books are very different from one another; they deal for instance with individual congregations, with a number of churches and religious groups in a small town, with the spiritual experience of an individual, with a representative spread of different churches experiencing change in urban life, and with the theological communication in the complex of ministries in a megachurch. Yet while they

---

4. David Silverman, *Interpreting Qualitative Data: Methods for Analysing Talk, Text, and Interaction* (London: Sage, 1993), pp. 36-37.

5. James Clifford, "Introduction: Partial Truths," in James Clifford and George E. Marcus, *Writing Culture: The Poetics of Ethnography* (Berkeley: University of California Press, 1986), p. 7.

6. Susan Friend Harding, *The Book of Jerry Falwell: Fundamentalist Language and Politics* (Princeton: Princeton University Press, 2000); R. Stephen Warner, *New Wine in Old Wineskins: Evangelicals and Liberals in a Small-Town Church* (Berkeley: University of California Press, 1988); Paul Heelas and Linda Woodhead, *The Spiritual Revolution: Why Religion Is Giving Way to Spirituality* (Oxford: Blackwell, 2005); David M. Mellott, *I Was and I Am Dust: Penitente Practices as a Way of Knowing* (Collegeville, Minn.: Liturgical Press, a Pueblo Book, 2009); Nancy Tatom Ammerman, *Congregation and Community* (New Brunswick, N.J.: Rutgers University Press, 1997); and Mary McClintock Fulkerson, *Places of Redemption: Theology for a Worldly Church* (Oxford: Oxford University Press, 2007).

may be substantively different, they exemplify, albeit with slightly different methodological emphases, the kind of attentive engagement with the social and cultural reality of church that characterizes qualitative and ethnographic research. Yet methodological commonality is at the same time variously articulated through different kinds of conversation. The writers are attentive in different kinds of ways. They are shaped by particular research questions, and these questions in turn locate each of these studies within conversations. A common feature in all the works is that the writers are conscious of their own disciplinary subjectivity. In most cases they self-identify as a theologian, or as a sociologist, or as an anthropologist. So, while each may be looking at the church, each looks in a very different way driven by different kinds of research questions that situate each's writing within different conversations.

A Political Conversation

Susan Friend Harding's study of Jerry Falwell focuses on the political significance of theological communication within fundamentalism. Falwell rose to prominence as the leader of what became known as the Moral Majority, but he was also the pastor of a megachurch in Lynchburg, Virginia. In the 1980s Falwell's church and the associated Liberty College and other media-based ministries employed around a thousand people. Harding calls this Falwell's fundamentalist empire. "Falwell's empire was in effect a hive of workshops, of sites of cultural production, that smelted, shaped, packaged, and distributed myriad fundamentalist rhetorics and narratives."[7]

Harding's work features a series of in-depth analyses of the different kinds of communication that characterize the cultural production within Falwell's organization. These include witnessing, testimony, biography, and preaching. Through a close and extended reading of these different forms of theological communication, she paints a vivid and complex picture of shifting theological sensibilities within American fundamentalism. As she puts it, Falwell and his followers were engaged in a process of tearing up the tacit contract that had held sway in public and political discourse in the United States since the Scopes trial in 1925. This contract proscribed any attempt to mix politics with "premodern" forms of religious faith. The effect of this was that fundamentalist Christians had been effec-

---

7. Harding, *Book of Jerry Falwell*, p. 15.

tively quarantined both culturally and politically. As a result, fundamentalists had for more than fifty years retreated into their own churches and institutions, leaving the public and political arena as a sphere that accepted only "modern" forms of "rational" discourse.[8]

By the early 1980s Falwell, and others, had been able to challenge the existing consensus and had begun to reassert a fundamentalist Christian voice in the public sphere. This was achieved through what were primarily "theological" forms of communication, in particular biblical exegesis and preaching. Central to this enterprise, Harding argues, was the ability to form alliances between fundamentalists, Pentecostals, charismatics, and noncharismatics. These previously antagonistic groups began to rally around a shift in theological language as to what constituted a Christian. The shorthand for this was the term "born again." Born-again Christianity rested on a simplified version of the gospel that was learned in the first instance from evangelists such as Billy Graham. Born-again Christians were people who realized they were sinners, asked Jesus to forgive them, and asked Jesus into their hearts.[9] This abbreviated form of evangelical theology forged the collective identity that allowed Falwell to claim that he represented a "moral" majority in the United States.

Most of the content in *The Book of Jerry Falwell* is theological, but it is not situated in a theological conversation. Susan Harding is very clear that she is an anthropologist who went to Lynchburg to study the political activism of fundamentalist groups. What she found, however, surprised her and forced her to reevaluate what constituted politics. At the start of her fieldwork she expected to find forms of political action such as protests and political meetings. What she actually found was a church and Christian organizations that spent their time talking about the Bible, preaching, teaching, and witnessing. "Eventually I realized that while I saw little in the way of routine protest in Falwell's Lynchburg community, it was rife with another kind of politics, with what might be called cultural politics."[10] These cultural forms of political expression, Harding sees as being carried in and transmitted through theological rhetoric. Moreover, this theological form of communication was not so much aimed at the political sphere as at fundamentalist Christians themselves. Harding sees Falwell's agenda as being primarily concerned with the conversion of fundamentalists who

8. Harding, *Book of Jerry Falwell*, p. 21.
9. Harding, *Book of Jerry Falwell*, p. 19.
10. Harding, *Book of Jerry Falwell*, p. 10.

saw their only role as evangelism into conservative evangelicals who sought "worldly power and influence in the name of Christian values."[11] So, although Harding discusses theology, her work is shaped by research questions that find their point of origin in a discussion about the changing nature of religion in American civil life.

Nancy Ammerman's book *Congregation and Communities* is different from Harding's in that she studies multiple congregations. Yet her focus is also on ecclesial change and, like Harding, she locates this interest in a conversation about the "political" significance of church. The study looks at the changing fortunes of congregations as they adapt to changes in urban life. Harding makes a great deal of her position as a lone researcher. Ammerman's project reproduces this in a multiple form with a number of different researchers engaged on what was a large-scale project. Each of these researchers was located in a particular community for six months studying multiple congregations. The research was designed to explore different kinds of challenges represented by changes in communities. The changes in urban life affecting these congregations were grouped into three main categories: cultural change, such as the need to adapt to a growing gay and lesbian community or large-scale immigration; economic change, such as the stresses associated with stratification in the African American community; and social changes linked to suburbanization.[12] Nine communal locations were selected to give the research a spread of different kinds of urban changes as well as different kinds of congregations. Across these community settings eighteen "focus" congregations and a number of other related congregations were studied.[13]

The research describes four main responses to the changes that take place in communities. Some congregations faced with significant challenges simply decline. They may manage to continue for some time as they are weakened, but all their attempts to adapt do not work. Other congregations reorientate themselves either by relocating to another environment or by transitioning into a translocal congregation attracting members from a much wider area. The third type of congregation finds ways to adapt to the new situation by seeking out a new constituency. Some have to change their style in response to these newcomers, but others manage to stay the same. The final group of congregations experienced a process of rebirthing and

---

11. Harding, *Book of Jerry Falwell*, p. 10.
12. Ammerman, *Congregation and Community*, p. 6.
13. Ammerman, *Congregation and Community*, p. 42.

transformation that takes them through the crisis of communal change. As Ammerman puts it, "births, deaths, adaptions, and reorientations to locale are, then, the broad categories in which congregational response to change occurs. In communities whose social infrastructure was being reconstructed, one of the most active institutional sectors we discovered was the changing religious ecology."[14]

Ammerman is interested in churches and how they change, but she situates this within a political conversation. She is interested in the contribution that congregations make to local communities. Her argument is that in communities that are undergoing significant processes of change, churches and congregations represent a source for vitality, social connection, and social capital. As such they serve as a kind of glue or connecting web within these communal settings. When in many ways social connections are stretched and at a low ebb, congregations are still to be found in localities praying, worshiping, eating together, and distributing aid. And it is for this reason that they form such an important part of the communal infrastructure in the United States.[15] Ammerman's work offers a powerful advocacy for Christian communities, but this advocacy comes through the articulation of church to a conversation about the politics of civic life.

A Conversation about the Changing Nature of Religion

The Spiritual Revolution has many similarities with Ammerman's work. Both studies investigate multiple congregations. Paul Heelas and Linda Woodhead's project, however, is based in one town in the English Lake District. And rather than a political conversation, *The Spiritual Revolution* is set within the continuing debate within the sociology of religion concerning the changing nature of religion. In particular, the research was designed to test the theory that a crucial shift was taking place in the religious life of the United Kingdom. This shift is described as a move from religion to spirituality. Heelas and Woodhead link this shift to what they call the "subjectivization thesis," or the turn to the subject.[16] "The turn is shorthand for a major cultural shift of which we all have some experience. It is a turn away from life lived in terms of external or 'objective' roles, duties and

---

14. Ammerman, *Congregation and Community*, p. 45.
15. Ammerman, *Congregation and Community*, pp. 361-70.
16. Heelas and Woodhead, *The Spiritual Revolution*, p. 2.

obligations and a turn towards life lived by reference to one's own subjective experiences (relational as well as individualistic)."[17]

The study deals with what they term the "congregational domain" of churches and chapels, but also the "holistic domain" of alternative New Age spirituality. Central to the research is a categorical distinction between religion as a system, which expects the subjugation of the self to external higher authority, and spirituality, which is orientated around the subjective life. The first they call "life-as" religion, and the second, "subjective-life" spirituality. In the congregational domain the study discusses the variety of ways in which different Christian churches situate the individual in cultural/theological narratives of relative subjection. They divide the congregations into different types according to how they situate the self. "Congregations of Humanity" expect followers to be wholly subject to the service of God and fellow human beings. "Congregations of Difference" teach that God is external to human beings and can only be approached through obedience, while "Congregations of Experiential Difference and Experiential Humanity" are most willing to see God as not simply external to humanity but as also dwelling within the individual.[18] In the holistic domain the study found a range of different practices, but these all shared an approach that situated the spiritual within subjective life. Heelas and Woodhead locate their study in a wider conversation about church decline and the rise of spirituality. "We are interested in the idea that the great historical bond between western cultures and a Christianity whose characteristic mode is to make appeal to transcendent authority is rapidly dissolving and that in its place we are seeing a growth of a less regulated situation in which the sacred is experienced in intimate relationship with subjective lives."

Stephen Warner's study, like that of Heelas and Woodhead, centers on the changing nature of religion. His book *New Wine in Old Wineskins* is a detailed study of a church in Mendocino, California. He traces the way this church has adapted to a different social and political climate. The changes that happened locally are seen as kind of a mirror that reflects the wider changes in the church. In the 1950s the Presbyterian church in Mendocino functioned as a kind of social club. Then in the early 1960s it appointed a young Chinese American pastor. It was the first Presbyterian church to appoint a person of color to the pulpit. Suddenly the emphasis

17. Heelas and Woodhead, *The Spiritual Revolution*, p. 2.
18. Heelas and Woodhead, *The Spiritual Revolution*, p. 17.

in the church shifted toward issues of racial and social justice, and the community was taken up in political issues, struggles, and protests. During this period it experienced a decline in numbers. In the early seventies the congregation appointed a conservative evangelical pastor, and for the next ten years the church began to grow. In fact, it became for a period the fastest-growing Presbyterian church in the United States. Warner's research tells this story of ecclesial adaptation through a rich and detailed narrative. At the heart of the book lie the shifting fortunes of religious movements of the left and of the right. We are introduced to the political activism and social engagement of the "prophetic clergy," the hippies and beatniks that were attracted to the town, and the resurgent evangelism of itinerants who sought to convert the hippies and renew the church.[19]

Through a close study of the Mendocino church Warner develops a typology of faith. First there is what he calls institutional liberalism. This form, typical of the 1950s, is orientated toward a kind of civic religion. Its content is framed primarily around ethics. The second type is nascent liberalism. Nascent liberalism refers to a faith that seeks to make an impact on the social and political environment. In the 1960s, says Warner, the walls of the sanctuary seemed to collapse and religion became a presence that marched in the streets.[20] As well as nascent liberalism there is also a nascent form of evangelicalism. Nascent evangelicalism, the third type, also seeks to make an impact on the world. Finally there is an institutional form of evangelicalism that is focused on the worship of the church and its own internal discourses.[21]

New Wine in Old Wineskins is a deeply sympathetic account of the rise of movements of the "right" in a local church. Warner situates this narrative in a conversation, which prefigures Susan Friend Harding's work, concerning the resurgence and political significance of evangelicalism in the United States. Underlying this conversation is a kind of liberal academic puzzlement about the reasons why people who are likable, intelligent, and, as Warner tells us, so hospitable turn to conservative religion. His attention is drawn to explore why these forms of conservative religion are growing and seem to be so vibrant. Evangelicals, he notes, are focused on the locality, and they seem to be on the "periphery" of the flow of liberal centers of discourse such as universities or major cities, but, as

19. Warner, *New Wine,* pp. xi-xii.
20. Warner, *New Wine,* p. 285.
21. Warner, *New Wine,* pp. 286-87.

Warner says, "the periphery is anything but isolated, it extends throughout the country."

A Conversation about Theology and Embodiment

Mary McClintock Fulkerson's *Places of Redemption* and David Mellott's *I Was and I Am Dust* have little in common on the face of it. Mellott's research focuses on Roman Catholic *Penitente* groups in northern New Mexico, while Fulkerson's deals with a United Methodist congregation in a small city in the American South. What they share is an account of how, through ethnographic methods, theologians can explore difference and the "other" in ecclesiology and the theological challenges and themes that emerge from this encounter. Mellott situates his study in his own experience of theological education and the "traditioning" that comes with being a seminary-trained Roman Catholic priest. He tells a story from early in his ministry of the practice of lighting votive candles in his local parish. This practice was discouraged following the Vatican II reforms, but local people seemed to persist in this kind of devotion. The priests in the community wanted to discourage what they had been instructed to regard as superstitious and primitive forms of petition. They had been educated and "enlightened" into the right forms of Catholic worship, and they saw their role as correcting the mistakes of the local people. He and his fellow priests never thought to ask the people what lighting candles meant to them; "we assumed we knew more about their practices than they did."[22] *I Was and I Am Dust* is an account of the author's journey away from this kind of clerical superiority toward valuing the experience and the voice of lay Catholics.

The book centers on extended interviews with Larry T. Torres, who was a Roman Catholic *Penitente*. *Penitentes* means "the penitent ones." The full name of the group in Spanish is *La Fraternidad Piadorsa de Nuestro Padre Jesus Nazereno* (The Pious Fraternity of Our Father Jesus of Nazareth).[23] Through his research Mellott is taken into the spiritual experience of Torres to places of intense and dark enlightenment. In one of these exchanges Torres describes the rituals and practices that take place in the brotherhood's *morada* on Good Friday for the ceremony of Tienieblas.[24]

---

22. Mellott, *I Was,* p. x.
23. Mellott, *I Was,* p. 3.
24. The three quotations that follow come from Mellott, *I Was,* pp. 78-79.

As the lights are being doused one at a time and we pray for the souls of widows and orphans and people who are jailed or imprisoned . . . there's a sense of forgiveness that comes over you, that brings such peace. . . . The last candle is extinguished and you hear the mourning of the dead as they try to break in. You hear the clanking of the chains, the rattling of the chains, there watching you . . . in the dark and the eyes of the saints are glowing on the altar.

There's a way of feeling it at the very gut level. To be lain on a . . . packed earth floor, on your belly with no shirt on, feeling the damp-ness of the earth, smelling it right next to your nostrils, and realising that . . . part of what you are is that very dirt. That you are that dirt. And maybe whipped a couple of times trying not to react or not feel the sting of it.

[Y]ou are just bone and dirt, you're bones and dust. It is a living death . . . from which there is resurrection of course, fifteen minutes later when the light of Christ comes back and they throw open the doors and all the dead are no longer there.

These accounts of extreme and embodied spirituality challenge Mellott. He finds that he is no longer the teacher but instead has become the one being taught. The strange authenticity of the *Penitentes* forces him to see encounter with God in new ways.

Mary McClintock Fulkerson's research takes her on a very similar journey. Her study takes her into an encounter with a racially diverse con-gregation that also included a significant number of worshipers with a range of disabilities. Fulkerson explores her own subjectivity in relation to difference and othering as a route toward a liberative theology. Her own response to the community she was studying came as a surprise to her. She describes herself as a "feminist, race-conscious, progressive wannabee" who set out to zealously investigate "a community that might have liberatory lessons for the secular society."[25] Yet she found "the theo-logical" in her ethnographic research to be a scarce commodity. People didn't seem to talk in terms that might be recognized by academics as "theology."[26] But in a search for the "theological" her attention was drawn to practices and historic patterns of behavior. She began to examine what

25. Fulkerson, *Places of Redemption*, p. 3.
26. Fulkerson, *Places of Redemption*, p. 10.

she calls the "hidden inheritances" and the "habituated bodies" that constitute a situation.[27]

The starting point for theological reflection emerges from the experience of the research process. Fulkerson explores her own reaction to being in the church for the first time as a sudden coming to terms with her own whiteness and her own able-bodiedness. "My feeling of strangeness in response to the unaccustomed 'blackness' of the place and the presence of people with disabilities at that first visit suggests that my conscious commitments to inclusiveness were not completely correlated to my habituated sense of the normal."[28] What she experienced was a disruption of her sense of self that she realized was situated within a dominant framework. Through her fieldwork encounters she became aware that there may be a disconnection between what she espoused and what she actually felt and experienced. She describes this disjuncture as a "wound" that arises from "interpersonal forms of obliviousness and aversiveness" that are supported by larger sociopolitical systems. This insight serves as a touchstone for Fulkerson to drive a liberatory agenda into the *habitus* of the embodied and affective self. Through her study of the congregation at the Good Samaritan Methodist Church, the author starts to see a place where obliviousness and aversion are to some extent overcome. It is a place where people previously experienced as "other" seem to "appear" and to become part of community.[29] The church is seen as a place of redemption.

Many and Various Conversations

This brief survey of ethnographic work demonstrates the range of conversations that shape the research process. In each of these studies the church formed the substantive field of study and yet the research is variously articulated within different kinds of conversations. These conversations have their roots in much wider disciplinary fields. They foreshadow the research process in various ways. They form the researchers' sense of self and their disciplinary identity; they shape the way research questions are formed; they influence how field research is conducted, how data is analyzed, and eventually how the research is written. One might also add that they serve to shape the reader.

27. Fulkerson, *Places of Redemption*, p. 11.
28. Fulkerson, *Places of Redemption*, p. 15.
29. Fulkerson, *Places of Redemption*, p. 229.

The notion of conversations in ethnographic research is highly significant for ecclesiology. It suggests that a theological perspective can have a place within qualitative method. I originally wrote that last sentence to read "I want to suggest that 'theology' can have a place in qualitative method." The disembodied transcendent use of "theology," however, is precisely not what I am suggesting. Rather, what we see for instance in Mary Fulkerson's and David Mellott's work is that theological attention is variously shaped by interests and conversations. It is hard to imagine Mary writing about the *Penitentes* in the way that David does, or indeed David writing about Good Samaritan church in similar ways to Mary. There is no implied judgment here, simply the observation that a theological conversation is not monolithic or uni-perspectival. "Theology" exists as a contested discursive field. It is operative as an embodied way of experiencing and reasoning in relation to the ethnographic. So in many ways the "theological" in qualitative research is just as "interested" and indeed "partial" as might be the sociological or the anthropological. There is no superior theological place of immunity, but rather there are variously "traditioned" curious observers who see things in different ways. There's nothing very strange or odd here. We are very happy to work with steadily evolving ways of reading history or philosophical writers or indeed the Scriptures. The same is true of social and cultural reality.

This does not mean that all perspectives are equal or indeed that any and all accounts of the social and cultural expression of church are to be taken at face value. Ecclesiology and ethnography is and should be a contested field. It is a conversation that is shaped by and seeks to shape "interest." This conversation needs to take account not simply of the representation of ecclesial communities in research but also of the ways that research questions and conversations foreshadow research. What is at stake here is not simply the possibility of misrepresentation and the "overshadowing" of contexts by theory, although this may well be a possibility; rather, what is in play are the kinds of questions that systematic and practical theologians and Christian ethicists are all too familiar with. What is the social and political importance of the church? How are Christian identities shaped and formed? What is the connection between theological expression and the social formation of the church? What forms of spiritual experience can inform and influence theological understanding? How do we understand redemption in relation to human fragmentation? These kinds of concerns, however, are not the sole preserve of the theologian. They are also of interest to sociologists, anthropologists, geographers, educationalists, and many others. The idea of conversation seeks not only to identify how disciplinary location shapes research but also to offer ways for interdisciplinary dialogue. There are interconnected conversations taking place around the church and much to be learned from listening in, but this does not mean that those who self-identify as "theologians" are in some way inferior or amateur or indeed methodologically trespassing on other people's territory. All qualitative research is conditioned by conversation and therefore interested. Theological interest is not only one among many interests for those who self-identify as theologians; it is their sense of self and it is through that identity and conversation that they will inevitably seek to engage with others. Different kinds of theologians of course will do this in different ways — but maybe that would require a whole other chapter.

CHAPTER 3

Ecclesiology "From the Body":
Ethnographic Notes toward a Carnal Theology

Christian Scharen

In his book *The Origins of Christian Morality,* Wayne Meeks attempts an odd but evocative task: ethnographic investigation of early Christian communities.[1] While he cannot, obviously, enact the traditional fieldwork such a methodology requires, he does argue that the texts allow a sort of observation of local practices. Through attending to the social context of these practices he can offer something approximating a snapshot of the formation of Christian community more than a millennium ago. I begin with this groundbreaking study in part because it raises the question of how traditional theological disciplines — Bible, theology, history — that have been oriented to interpreting texts rather than the living practices of communities and contexts can and perhaps ought to consider methodologies such as ethnography offering just such attentiveness to the level of lived religious practice. I consider this a practical theological question in that it pushes to the foreground not only the issue of the faithfulness of Christian communities but also their living for the sake of abundant life for all.[2]

In pursuing the fruitfulness of this turn to ethnographic work in theology, I wish to start not only with Meeks's methodological starting place

---

1. Wayne Meeks, *The Origins of Christian Morality: The First Two Centuries* (New Haven: Yale University Press, 1995), p. 10.

2. My coauthors and I make the argument for practical theology as fundamentally oriented to the telos of abundant life for all in Dorothy Bass and Craig Dykstra, eds., *For Life Abundant: Practical Theology, Theological Education, and Christian Ministry* (Grand Rapids: Eerdmans, 2008), pp. 13-14.

in mind, but also with the substance of his findings. In particular, I want to focus on Meeks's argument that the ritual of the Lord's Supper (Holy Communion, the Eucharist) worked as a fundamental social practice shaping, reinforcing, and giving meaning to the moral lives of early Christians. The logic of the meal, he argues, played off patterns of inequity in Greco-Roman society where meals reinforced a social hierarchy through a hierarchy of tables, each with matching quality of food and drink. Such social hierarchy strengthened the social honor of the well-placed in and through their proximity to those who had much less, thereby reconstituting the difference between them. Such was Saint Paul's complaint in 1 Corinthians 11 where he reminds the Corinthian church that "when you come together, it is not really to eat the Lord's Supper. For when the time comes to eat, each of you goes ahead with your own supper, and one goes hungry and another becomes drunk." The Lord's Supper depended on and reversed this status hierarchy, following the logic of the Lord whose meal it was, who took the form of a servant, and died for all, even the least. Rather than reinforcing a ritual of self-serving social hierarchy, the Lord's Supper as a social practice depends on one becoming servant to others and becoming one with the body.[3]

This brief description of the early church shows, on the one hand, the social power of Jesus' institution of the meal of his body and blood, a meal centered in one body, as Saint Paul describes it in 1 Corinthians 10: "Because there is one loaf, we, who are many, are one body, for we all share in the one loaf." Yet, on the other hand, I have shown the ways particular bodies complicate the capacity for the rite to "have its way" with us, as some contemporary theologians like Meeks or his Yale colleague George Lindbeck might argue it does.[4] Working at the intersection of congregation, communion, and conflict, I ask the simple question of how people come to understand and experience worship, communal identity, and moral responsibility in different ways. This question matters for those in practical theology who desire to understand in greater clarity the actual theological contours of communal identity, worship, and witness, as well as for pastoral leaders seeking to foster greater faithfulness for the sake of the life of the world. Finding a means, then, to get to the fine detail of actual communal life before God requires at least three main moves. First, in

3. Meeks, *Origins of Christian Morality,* pp. 96-97.

4. George Lindbeck, *The Nature of Doctrine: Religion and Theology in a Post-Liberal Age* (Louisville: Westminster John Knox, 1984), p. 36.

seeking to describe a way of understanding worship as lived, that is, to do justice to practice, I describe David Ford's attempts to do this in theology. Second, moving beyond his proposal for "theologically informed ethnography," I engage three brief case studies portraying different examples of communal worship centered on the ritual of communion. Then third I will work through key approaches to the role of the body in worship — distinguishing between attending to theology of the body as an analysis of the shape of a worshiping community and theology from the body, drawing on its habituation as a primary research tool. Each points toward the possibility of ethnography as sacramental theology and ecclesiology, yet I argue that for the purposes of a practical theology that seeks to foster the church's faithfulness, a theology of worship "from the body" that I call here "carnal theology" is both less appreciated and practiced and more promising.

The Wisdom Embodied in Practice

In a recent book, I described my search for means to understanding rather than explaining the church's public life, seeking immersion in "primary" or "lived" theology observed, heard, seen close at hand, and portrayed by articulation of its practical logic — the wisdom embedded or embodied in practice.[5] Briefly, first, I'll describe how I use the term "practice"; then I'll turn to David Ford's approach to understanding how people actually practice Eucharist within particular worshiping communities. Practice is a term or, better, a concept that has played a central role in numerous threads of important academic and now also popular books.[6] While the terms "practice" and "practices" have given these works a kind of surface family resemblance, they have not always shared the same conceptual underpinning and sometimes have claimed too broad a territory to really be

---

5. See Christian Scharen and Aana Marie Vigen, *Ethnography as Christian Theology and Ethics* (New York: Continuum, 2011), pp. 27-28.

6. Philosophy: Alasdair MacIntyre, *After Virtue: A Study in Moral Philosophy* (Notre Dame, Ind.: University of Notre Dame Press, 1981); social science: Pierre Bourdieu, *Outline of a Theory of Practice*, trans. Richard Nice (New York: Cambridge University Press, 1977); theology: Stanley Hauerwas, *A Community of Character: Towards a Constructive Christian Social Ethics* (Notre Dame, Ind.: University of Notre Dame Press, 1981); Miroslav Volf and Dorothy Bass, *Practicing Theology: Beliefs and Practices in the Christian Life* (Grand Rapids: Eerdmans, 2001).

coherent as distinct practices.[7] I myself have drawn upon multiple frames in various works I have published, from the subtle notion Pierre Bourdieu develops in connection with the idea of *habitus* as a "regulated improvisation," to the more distinct action Alasdair MacIntyre refers to by his definition of practices as a "coherent and complex form of socially established cooperative human activity."[8] While implicit rules for using salad forks and patterns of conversation over dinner point toward Bourdieu's notion of durable, transposable, patterned habits of action, the action of a shared meal as a whole fits more MacIntyre's vision of social practices done for the goods internal to the activity itself. Ted Smith, a theologian at Vanderbilt Divinity School, has articulated the sense in which these two understandings of practice speak "in different registers." MacIntyre's version of practices helps make sense of the telos and goods internal to eating meals together as a whole. Bourdieu's version of practices focuses on a smaller scale, helping to elicit the way most meals "are congeries of practices."[9] This distinction will help us in the concluding section to discern the kinds of embodiments of eucharistic practice shown in the cases I discuss below.

David Ford's excellent book *Self and Salvation* sets up the case studies to follow by posing a basic question about the formation of the self through the practice of Christian meal-sharing often called simply Eucharist. He asks, "What happens to the self shaped through that worship?"[10] Typical works on the Eucharist in sacramental theology tend, Ford writes, to take up questions of "real presence" or to elucidate aspects of "sacrifice" as part of the eucharistic prayer and so on. These important discussions tend to happen in the abstract, however, without particular communities of practice in mind. Ford rather aims to invite a renewed inquiry into actual practice. The difficulties are legion, however, as eucharistic practice

---

7. Nicholas Healy raises this question with vigor in his article, "Practices and the New Ecclesiology: Misplaced Concreteness?" *International Journal of Systematic Theology* 5, no. 3 (November 2003): 287-308.

8. For Bourdieu, see his *Outline*, p. 79, and for my use of this see, among other places, "Baptismal Practices and the Formation of Christians: A Critical Liturgical Ethics," *Worship* 76, no. 1 (January 2002): 62-66; for MacIntyre, see his *After Virtue*, p. 187, and for my use of this see *Faith as a Way of Life: A Vision for Pastoral Leadership* (Grand Rapids: Eerdmans, 2008), pp. 53-54.

9. David D. Daniels III and Ted A. Smith, "History, Practice and Theological Education," in *For Life Abundant*, pp. 214-40.

10. David F. Ford, *Self and Salvation: Being Transformed* (New York: Cambridge University Press, 1999), p. 138.

has been diverse all the way back to the life of the earliest Christian communities.[11] Drawing on Timothy Jenkins's creative deployment of Bourdieu for ethnographic study of local congregations and communities, Ford outlined four aspects of such inquiry into actual practice.[12] These four aspects set up the ways I wish to draw from the case studies to elucidate eucharistic modes of practical knowing, that is, social, religious, and cultural competency through which God inhabits local congregational worship.

Such practical modes of knowing, Ford suggests, are revealed first through acknowledging that what one is seeking are "nonverbal and habitual" ways of knowing. He points to the absolutely basic fact that Christian identity is constituted in and through worship, through a practice, and not through many other things, from law and ethics to an alternative worldview or set of doctrines. Here he introduces Bourdieu's concept of *habitus*, briefly summarizing it as "the durably installed generative principle of regulated improvisations."[13] The ritual of the Eucharist, Ford suggests, is in its many variations "a condensation of the Christian *habitus*." Yet it is not the words nor the confessed theological understandings but rather the "patterns" of "how and why these particular people gather in these ways" alongside "practical meanings" that are not obvious because they are "rooted in distant or recent history" and so on.[14]

Second, and implicit in the first, Ford argues, such embodied knowledge comes by "the apprenticeship undergone by all actors."[15] Noting the "synoptic illusion" that allows supposing a map to be what people follow in traversing the paths of their daily lives, Ford describes the parallel for the Eucharist that requires apprenticeships in practical mastery rather than overviews based on ritual texts or doctrine. Rather, the Eucharist incorporates participants, and distinctively, particularly, in ways not easily articulated in scholastic terms favored by the theologian.

Third, the nature of apprenticeships is intensified by the multiple ap-

---

11. Paul Bradshaw, *The Search for the Origins of Christian Worship: Sources and Methods for the Study of Early Liturgy,* 2nd ed. (New York: Oxford University Press), pp. 118-43.

12. Timothy Jenkins, "Fieldwork and the Perception of Everyday Life," *Man,* n.s., 29, no. 2 (1994): 433-55; Timothy Jenkins, *Religion in English Everyday Life: An Ethnographic Approach,* Methodology and History in Anthropology, vol. 5 (Oxford: Berghahn Books, 1999).

13. Bourdieu, *Outline,* p. 78.

14. Ford, *Self and Salvation,* pp. 140-41.

15. Ford, *Self and Salvation,* p. 141; Jenkins, "Fieldwork," p. 444.

prenticeships within each life that overlay each other creating complexities of many sorts, all coexisting within what Bourdieu calls the "socially informed body" with all its senses.[16] A final anthropological point follows in that this complex, embodied mastery is not easily given representation in language, and in doing so its best path for offering a similarly rich conception of human and divine action comes through being itself diverse. Eucharistic language, Ford argues, includes many genres: "praise, lament, confession, exclamation, narrative, proclamation, petition" as well as "the oral and the written," but both are performed and "resist discursive overview in a somewhat similar way to good drama."[17]

Finally, moving into a more explicitly theological mode, Ford highlights the way the logic of Trinitarian "creativity and abundance" giving way in Christ to a radical singularity in the incarnation offers a way to understand Christian faith as true to itself only in "becoming freshly embodied in different contexts."[18] Life in Christ, Ford argues, is a matter of what Bourdieu calls "necessary improvisation" showing "the distinctive and different realizations of the eventfulness of God."[19] Yet despite the diversity of these fresh embodiments, one can see family resemblances because, as Ford suggests, the habituation of a eucharistic self is not primarily about forming a self for its own sake but to be "responsive to Jesus Christ and other people, and coping with their responses in turn."[20]

His turn in the chapter disappointingly is to biblical interpretation rather than what his finely tuned argument about particularity would suggest: attending closely to formation in particular communities and communion rituals. Not that his deep and fruitful engagement with Scripture is disappointing; Ford rarely disappoints when — and it is happily a regular feature of his theology — he is engaged with Scripture. Yet as he ends the chapter, the all-too-common demurral emerges regarding the claims made without any fieldwork to show them, as it were, in practice. "What will help most in acquiring the *habitus*? At the practical level," Ford writes, "the answer is obvious: practice." Despite his own choice to avoid the difficult process of submitting himself to the field in order to have exemplary portrayals of actual apprenticeships, he "longs to find a full anthropological study of Eucharistic practice along the lines suggested by Jenkins and

16. Bourdieu, *Outline,* p. 124.
17. Ford, *Self and Salvation,* p. 144.
18. Ford, *Self and Salvation,* p. 144.
19. Ford, *Self and Salvation,* p. 144; Bourdieu, *Outline,* p. 8.
20. Ford, *Self and Salvation,* p. 165.

Bourdieu above. That, if it were theologically informed, could be a most helpful accompaniment." As Ford turns, as Meeks does, to biblical portrayals of worship and community in an effort to describe grounded Eucharist, I instead turn to contemporary ethnographic portrayals of religious practice.

Eucharistic Embodiments

In a way, this chapter (and this volume as a whole) seeks to answer Ford's call for theologically informed ethnography. Yet my hope is to move beyond this framing. Yes, I am after ethnography that is theologically informed, but even to suggest that ethnography is theologically informed opens the possibility that it is theologically "charged" from the first. Then the careful work of theological description might itself be a mode of theology, of, in this case, ecclesiology.[21] So what I am after here is to actually pay down on Ford's claim, while also pressing against his too-simple dichotomy of anthropology (ethnography) and sacramental theology (ecclesiology), a point I can return to after showing in three brief case studies how the Eucharist is "true to itself only by becoming freshly embodied in different contexts," as Ford puts it. To open this kind of embodied singularity of the "Eucharist self," I'll highlight Sarah McFarland Taylor's description of green sisters and their culinary Eucharist, Siobhán Garrigan's work on Irish Catholic communion practice, and my own research on the love feast in an African Methodist Episcopal church in Georgia, USA.

Green Sisters

Sarah McFarland Taylor's study of "environmentally activist Roman Catholic vowed religious women," or green sisters, as she puts it, seeks to portray emerging forms of religious culture.[22] In one sense it is not a theologi-

---

21. So Nicolas Adams and Charles Elliott, "Ethnography Is Dogmatics: Making Description Central to Systematic Theology," *Scottish Journal of Theology*, Autumn 2000, pp. 339-64; Don Browning made the case for a "descriptive theological moment" within what he called *A Fundamental Practical Theology: Descriptive and Strategic Proposals* (Minneapolis: Fortress, 1995).

22. Sarah McFarland Taylor, *Green Sisters: A Spiritual Ecology* (Cambridge: Harvard University Press, 2007), p. ix. Page references to this work have been placed in the text.

cal study, in that Taylor does not portray her own work as primarily theological. Yet in her study she literally joins in with these sisters in embodying a new religious movement, finding herself drawn into a life-changing experience with the women. She states that her study is historical ethnography, but without being uncharitable it seems equally that Taylor engages in advocacy — not only for the importance of the ecological issues in general but also for these "green sisters" specifically as important visionaries for another way into our common future on planet Earth. She admits as much, claiming her place as an "intimate outsider" who, while not a vowed member of a Catholic religious order, nonetheless claimed a kind of sisterhood as a Christian laywoman coworker (p. x).

Through over a decade of participation in their religious communities, organic farms, and seminars on faith and ecological sustainability, Taylor felt herself begin to belong, finding herself committed to continued engagement with these sisters, and describing her work as "reciprocal ethnography" in which researcher and subjects interacted regarding data and interpretation (p. xix). This could only happen, she remarks, because on the one hand her own identity as a well-educated Christian woman made her a peer to these very intellectual sisters, swapping books and comparing notes about the meaning of their prayers and practices (p. xvii). But on the other hand, such reciprocity in fieldwork literally depended on working together in the fields, on hands and knees, planting, weeding, harvesting, and cooking local organic food as part of the holistic spirituality of these communities (p. xi).

A key focus for Taylor's work is the Green Mountain Monastery in Greensboro, Vermont. Cofounded by a priest, Thomas Berry, known for his writings on ecology, cosmology, and theology, and nuns Gail Worcelo and Bernedette Bostwick, the monastery seeks to balance engagement in the brokenness of the world while also creating a retreat where alternative ways of life can be practiced. They share deeply rooted connection to the Benedictine patterns of monastic life committed to stability in one place, living a daily pattern of work and prayer. In this respect the community is rather traditional, with daily prayer, Eucharist, and various kinds of daily work. Yet this daily pattern so common to monastic life also embodies the obvious impact of its ecological values. As part of a "Liturgy of the Cosmos" led by Worcelo, the community combines the old practice of *lectio divina,* or sacred reading, with the new awareness of our oneness with the universe. They do this according to a "Feast of the Elements," reading and meditating on the periodic table of elements as a means to a "sacred reading of our origins" (p. 131). This celebration of creation through the basic structure of the cosmos leads into "an Agape, a love feast in remembrance of the birth of Christ," which they claim as the moment the universe "realized its complete oneness with itself and its Source" (p. 132). This liturgy both depends upon and intentionally revisions the traditional liturgy of the Catholic Church, making use of its deep theological and liturgical claims for a new engagement with the ecological frame of the Green Monastery's pattern of life together.

Taylor goes into great detail regarding the particular ways green sisters improvise on Eucharist theology and liturgical practice. They do this primarily through intentional practices of food production, preparation, and meal sharing. As one sister put it, "the concept of food itself is key to the transformation of our ecological crisis" (p. 161). Reading against a problematic history of personal devotion through fasting and renunciation of pleasures of the body — including eating and drinking — as well as the dependence on male priests for celebration of the Holy Eucharist, Taylor finds it nothing short of miraculous how these women religious have revisioned "ecospiritual foodways" in eucharistic terms. The term "foodways" refers to "the eating habits and culinary practices of a particular community, culture, people, region, or historical period." Because of the cosmic Christology embraced by the green sisters, a continuum exists between Christ as the fullness of all things — from the earth body to the human body to the cosmic body. As such, the sisters recast the tending and keeping of organic gardens as well as preparing wholesome food as "priestly practice" and the cooking for the community as "a daily Eucharist" in which they share a sacred communion between these interconnected bodies. Intrinsic to this revisioning of eucharistic practice is the claim that all is holy, an understanding derived partially from sacramental theology of "all things coming into being 'through Christ'" (pp. 161-62).

Such a "culinary Eucharist" is part and parcel of their effort to participate in God's healing work, but they also are intimately aware that this healing work is in response to terrible brokenness, violence, and injustice. In part because of this recognition of brokenness and their commitment to witness to the healing and wholeness God intends for all creation, they revision Christ's suffering on the cross as the earth's suffering. Green Mountain Monastery cofounder Gail Worcelo describes their community's adoption of a traditional Catholic fast from sundown Thursday to sundown Friday as a witness to Christ's "present passion" in the "severe degradation of the earth" (p. 164). Such fasting attentive to the suffering of the planet brings all the more clarity to the sacramental character of ordinary whole food, prepared with dignity and care. Reflecting on the mystical experience of eating a bowl of organic vegetarian chili, one sister noted that "this bowl really held rock and soil, minerals and water, and the energy and heat of the stars . . . it was *gospel* and *eucharist* in a sacrament so simple, so holy, my heart brimmed with gratitude" (p. 174, emphasis in original).

Irish Catholic Communion

In Siobhán Garrigan's study of worship in Ireland, she asks whether embodied worship practices contributed to sectarianism and violence. She thinks so, arguing that "sectarianism, like racism and sexism, works 'behind our backs' keeping us from the deeper changes of hearts and minds that would lead to 'real peace'" (as her title has it).[23] Changes of hearts and minds require careful attention first to what we are doing, second to its effects in sabotaging our peaceful goals, and finally to changes in practices that embody those aims we most hope for our future. A few preliminary points about her argument are in order before turning to her case study of Irish Catholic eucharistic practice, which she considers at length in relation to the problem of sectarianism. Sectarianism may be defined as mere differences in denominational beliefs, but these beliefs are embodied over generations in an attitudinal matrix that extends through politics, economics, and in fact the whole of life. Therefore, the Good Friday Agreement achieved civic and political peace, but the deep and pervasive structure of sectarianism's embodiments — especially seen in terms of segregation — remain.

Garrigan focuses on worship as a way both to understand these embodiments of sectarianism and to imagine means to overcome them. She is not arguing that patterns of Christian worship are the primary cause of sectarianism. Rather, noting that "what human beings do with their bodies sometimes betrays what they do with their thoughts," she argues that how we ritualize together as Christians embodies aspects of our basic beliefs about the world in general and therefore worship can embody and enact sectarianism.[24] Drawing from the work of Nicholas Healy and others, she

23. Siobhán Garrigan, *The Real Peace Process: Worship, Politics, and the End of Sectarianism* (London: Equinox, 2010), p. xv.
24. Garrigan, *The Real Peace Process*, p. 25.

attempts a critical theological ethnography of Irish worship practices aimed at developing a practical-prophetic ecclesiology capable of resisting destructive political realities.[25] In carrying out this ethnographic work in twenty-eight diverse congregations, she notes that her "most important research tool was my own body in the spaces being studied."[26] Aiming at uncovering practices that "work below the level of human consciousness," she took as a starting place that "one can only research ritualizations from within a body that is acted upon and configured in its subjectivity."[27]

Garrigan focuses a significant part of her study on Eucharist as a case study in worship and sectarianism. She does this because, she says, "the fact that no congregant in any of the Roman Catholic churches studied received the cup demands considerable attention." She describes the typical pattern of parishioners processing up to the altar area where a priest or eucharistic minister waits to place a host, "a small, thin, round wafer which has been consecrated," into the open mouth or cupped hands. Thus receiving, the parishioners return to their seats. While nonreception of the cup during communion has a long history in Western Christianity, a history Garrigan sketches, the cup's post–Vatican II reintroduction has resulted in nearly universal return to communion "under both kinds," as the catechism puts it.[28] Yet despite specific encouragement of the Catholic hierarchy and an Irish bishops' report on the matter that encouraged catechesis and renewed practice, across Ireland the practice of reception of the host alone has endured. Garrigan came to understand this practice as an example of the "elision of 'Catholic' with 'Irish'" in that deep-seated folk perceptions stretching back hundreds of years hold "that 'The Protestants, they receive the wine. We do not.' And in some quarters, even: 'If we received the wine, we'd be just like the Protestants.'"[29]

Not content to simply account for this nonreception of the cup as a simple case of sectarian differentiation, Garrigan dug deeper to discover that people's perception of communion was almost entirely mystical. "Communion is adored precisely because it is not quotidian, because it is of God's own world." It turns out that much of the post–Vatican II teaching regarding the renewal of communion treats the sacrament as a meal, an

---

25. Garrigan, *The Real Peace Process*, p. 33; Nicholas Healy, *Church, World, and the Christian Life* (Cambridge: Cambridge University Press, 2000), p. 185.

26. Garrigan, *The Real Peace Process*, p. 32.

27. Garrigan, *The Real Peace Process*, pp. 32-35.

28. *Catechism of the Catholic Church* (1997), paragraph 1390.

29. Garrigan, *The Real Peace Process*, p. 122.

emphasis that exists at some distance from Irish Catholic understandings. To account for the deep-seated cultural aversion to seeing communion as a meal, as an issue related to eating and drinking, Garrigan considers some cultural history. The long legacy of British oppression, including the Great Famine that decimated up to a quarter of the population during the nineteenth century, but also the legacy of British portrayal of the Irish as drunks, less intelligent, and so on, contributes a grim political layer to issues of eating and drinking. Add to this the history of resistance via hunger strikes that have included iconic deaths as part of the Republican protest against British hegemony in Ireland. In such a context, the symbolic resonance of the host as symbolic of Christ's sacrifice for us can catch up and give meaning to the hunger strike as a cruciform sacrifice for the people.[30]

All this leads Garrigan to wonder, drawing on William Cavanaugh's study of the church in Chile, if ecclesiology determines if "the Body of Christ is just one more body created by the state in its own image for its own purposes." That is, she reads the continued nonreception of the cup as complex, and mostly unconscious continuation of a practice that nonetheless works as a perpetuation of the very sectarianism the meal counters in its declaration of a new peace in the one body of Christ.[31] To reform this practice of Eucharist among Irish Catholics, something like her critical theological ethnography is needed. Without "varied, non-streamlined, context-dependant theologies of the Eucharist," it seems unlikely that reform could happen such that, as she tenderly puts it, Irish people could "drink from the cup, safely."[32]

An African Methodist Episcopal Love Feast

In my own research project published as *Public Worship and Public Work,* I offer a cross-comparison between three case congregations — the Shrine, Central Presbyterian, and Big Bethel African Methodist Episcopal (AME) — each of them old, vibrant, downtown Atlanta churches.[33] In that research I asked, taking up theologian Stanley Hauerwas's claims about worship forming Christian community, how do congregational identity, wor-

---

30. Garrigan, *The Real Peace Process,* p. 141.
31. Garrigan, *The Real Peace Process,* p. 146.
32. Garrigan, *The Real Peace Process,* p. 147.
33. Christian Scharen, *Public Worship and Public Work: Character and Commitment in Local Congregational Life* (Collegeville, Minn.: Liturgical Press, 2004).

ship, and social ethics interrelate? In seeking to answer this question through ethnographic congregational study, I especially attended to the ways polity, race, and socioeconomic status, and the community's participation in other formative institutions and cultural traditions, in turn shaped the distinctive ways each church articulated Christian ideals and struggled to embody them in its life. Here I'd like to highlight the practice of Big Bethel's love feast in relation to their typical practice of monthly Holy Communion.

To pursue this research I spent a "season" with Big Bethel, moving through the fall and through Christmas. During that time, encouraged by the pastoral staff (especially an associate pastor I had taught in my courses at Emory's Candler School of Theology), I sought to be as faithful a participant as possible. I threw myself into worship, prayer, and song with the congregation, seeking to learn and share in their patterns of worship. I also attended various other gatherings, both regular Bible studies and staff meetings and the occasional concert or special event. Here, I want to describe their monthly love feast, an adopted tradition made their own as a Saturday morning preparatory service once a month before the Sunday when Holy Communion is offered.

The congregation on a Sunday morning is predominately African American and of all ages. While the congregation is weighted slightly toward middle age to elderly, there are a significant group of younger adults (thirties and forties) and many children. Typical of the more traditional AME churches, dress is very formal with men in suits and women in dresses. A few women had large flowing and pastel-colored hats. While the church has long been home to a fair share of educated professionals, its older members still remember days of working as domestics and in other low-end service jobs. Each younger generation, however, grows in the diversity of its work affiliation; the largely public-sector and self-employed work of the civil rights generation (baby boomers) has given way to much more private-sector employment in the post–civil rights generation (Generation X, or the "busters"). Rev. James Davis has especially tried to draw this youngest group into leadership, "planting the seeds now for Big Bethel's future." One evening he told his Steward Board that "when we have young professionals working at major corporations and IBM trusts them, when Broadcast companies trust them, then the Church has to trust them."[34]

---

34. Scharen, *Public Worship*, pp. 122-23.

The best introduction to the practice is to describe one love feast in particular. Here I quote a description of the first love feast I attended in early fall:

> I took the subway downtown and walked the few blocks to Big Bethel through the early morning chill. As I hurried down Butler Street, I could see the looming steeple of the church bearing the famous neon blue Jesus Saves sign. I was headed to a "love feast," a traditional Methodist ritual that John Wesley learned from Moravians on his boat trip across the Atlantic some two centuries before. Big Bethel holds the Love Feast Prayer Service at 7:30 A.M. on the first Saturday before the first Sunday of the month, the Sunday when they celebrate Holy Communion. I walked through the side doors of the imposing granite building and down into the fellowship hall, where chairs were set up in two rows of five with a middle aisle, six rows deep, for a total of sixty chairs. I found a chair near the rear and waited, noting that in front a table was set up, draped in white linen cloth that covered trays.
>
> People steadily streamed in, and when the prayer service began there were nearly forty people, giving the space a cozy, well-filled feel. For the most part people wore sweat suits, casual clothing such as jeans and sweaters, and only a few people wore dress clothes. The service was coordinated by the Married Couples' Ministry and consisted of an opening hymn ("Blessed Assurance"), invocation prayer ("Dear heavenly Father, we just thank you that you allowed us to gather in your house once again . . ."), a Scripture reading, and then alternating prayers and hymns. Jacques, the energetic minister of music, was there to play the old upright piano in the corner. Each section of prayers had three parts, each prayed by a member in his or her own style, from the heart, and regarding a given topic. For instance, the various sections focused prayer on spiritual maturity and Christian discipleship, on national and local government, on schools and school officials and teachers, and on the hungry and homeless everywhere. While some prayers were quiet meditations guiding us in our "supplication before the Lord," others built a crescendo plea, boldly approaching "the throne of grace."
>
> As this pattern of prayer and hymn singing (we always sang two verses of hymns, never more) continued, more people streamed in and, before long, the place was packed with nearly one hundred people, including at least ten children of varying ages. As the prayers con-

cluded, Rev. Davis moved to the front of the room and offered some words of greeting and asked how many had not been to a love feast before, and I joined about ten people who raised their hands. To this, he and other regulars said, "Praise God!" He noted that it is important for members to keeping reaching out, to keep getting to know others. As if to make his point, he asked, "All right, somebody raise their hand if they know every person in the room." No one did. Then he asked, "Somebody raise their hand if you see three people you don't know." Nearly the whole room raised their hands. He took a moment to have each person find three people they didn't know and introduce themselves — it was an upbeat and friendly break of about five minutes with people milling around, talking, and hugging.

We moved into a large circle, and Rev. Davis asked Rev. Streator to explain what would happen next. While Rev. Davis and Rev. Wood-Powe stepped around the circle with silver communion trays, handing each person a clear plastic communion cup filled with water, Rev. Streator described the "symbolism of the water." Because of the water's transparency and purity, one is encouraged to let go of grudges that prohibit interpersonal transparency. And if one bears a grudge, before going to the altar for communion the next day during Sunday morning service, you should go to that person and make amends. He stated that "the purity of the water symbolized that 'transparency of love' that should mark the community." As if drinking the promise of purity, the others and I tipped back our glasses in unison. Then, each person was given a piece of white bread, about a third of a slice cut lengthwise. I thought we would then eat it in unison as we had drunk the water. Actually, however, no one eats the bread. Each person gets a piece of everyone else's bread. This happens in the following way, and it is, according to Rev. Streator, "intended to build fellowship, to be a symbol of oneness."

Starting with Rev. Davis, the process began; he gave a piece of bread to the person to his left, and that person took a piece of his bread, and they hugged and exchanged God's blessing by saying, "God loves you and so do I." Each subsequent person peeled off and followed Davis, forming a second inner circle moving around the outer circle until everyone had exchanged bread and greetings in a similar way with every other person in the room. I noticed in the process that people stuffed the tidbits of bread they received from others into their little communion cups, and I followed suit. The greetings were sometimes strong hugs and others offered tentative pats on the shoulder, but always faces met, eyes glancing into one another, and smiles. At the end, as if in a collective *eucharista* for the communion we had just shared, all the cups of bread were placed upon the altar table and we sang a stirring rendition of the old gospel hymn "Amazing Grace." Before closing, Rev. Davis introduced Mother Theodora, who stood hunched over her cane near the altar. He reported that she was one of the oldest members and, he said, "she has adopted love feast and comes every time, even today when she doesn't feel well." People applauded and Rev. Davis commented that this might have been the most successful love feast yet.

Woven in and through the process of the bread and greetings, I chatted with Ms. Green, a member since 1948, and a stewardess, that is, a member of the ministry group that hosts the love feast. She noted that this ritual was new for Big Bethel, even though it had deep roots in Methodism generally. In a later interview, she credited this to Rev. Davis being "a deeply spiritual man, and a visionary."[35] Indeed, the love feast and Rev. Davis's enthusiasm for it go to the root of this old church, and account in large part for its current revival. Such a circle ritual has deep roots in the slave "ring shouts" related to me by another old member, Mrs. King. And out of the solace of such song, prayer, and common spirit, gatherings in this fellowship hall have given birth to schools, financial institutions, local civil rights actions, and many programs of social uplift for members and beyond.[36]

Ecclesiology *of* and *from* the Body

Each of the cases offers insight into what I call, following Ford's proposal, eucharistic practice "freshly embodied in different contexts." The cases offer much else besides, as all good ethnographic research does, partly because the complexity of local contexts is multilayered. Yet they each offer grounds from which to now return to Ford's arguments about a theologically informed ethnography of Eucharist, extending his work both methodologically and substantively, connecting sacramental theology and ecclesiology. When one pursues "what happens to the self shaped through worship," as Ford puts it, the body rushes to the fore. Yet as such Ford does

35. Scharen, *Public Worship*, p. 113.
36. Scharen, *Public Worship*, p. 113.

not distinguish the aim of attending to worship *of* the body and *from* the body. As I shall show, his explication of the carnal theological approach rooted in Bourdieu does argue for a preference implicitly, but it remains for me to make it explicit and to say more about its consequences.

Attending to worship of the body from the start separates the observed from the observer, the participant from the researcher. The assumption behind much "participation observation" is that while worshipers are "letting themselves go" in worship and praise, the observer "maintains an analytical frame of mind" seeking to interpret the forms of "letting go" observed all around.[37] One can through this modality come to some understanding of, as one author puts it, "the symbolic function of ecclesial bodiliness in Eucharistic celebration."[38] Yet the presumption here contains its own limits, in that such a perspective takes as axiomatic the observers' outsider perspective. Meaning-making in relationship to worship of the body, then, is "liable to an intellectualist reading, as in the hermeneutic tradition, trapped in the scriptural metaphor of social action as text."[39]

Nicholas Healy has critiqued the ways such intellectualist interpretations of the church merely idealize — and therefore in some important respects miss the reality of — the body. He neatly outlines five key methodological elements characteristic of modern ideal ecclesiologies. Beginning with a single word or phrase (e.g., mystical body of Christ), they declare it the essential characteristic of the church, describing the church as twofold in structure, leaning away from its human toward its normative form. To do this the church must be abstracted from its concrete human form, and thus the result is idealized accounts of the church.[40] Healy offers a summary picture of the result of this procedure in his term "blueprint ecclesiologies." In doing so, he highlights his conviction that they seem to imply we must "get our thinking about the church right first, after which we can go on to put our theory into practice."[41] In fact, then, our capacity

37. James H. S. Stevens, *Worship in the Spirit: Charismatic Worship in the Church of England,* Studies in Evangelical History and Thought (Carlisle and Waynesboro: Paternoster, 2002), p. 42.

38. Bernard J. Cooke, "Body and Mystical Body: The Church and *Communio,*" in *Bodies of Worship: Explorations in Theory and Practice,* ed. Bruce T. Morrill, S.J. (Collegeville, Minn.: Liturgical Press, 1999), pp. 48-49.

39. Loïc Wacquant, "Carnal Connections: On Embodiment, Apprenticeship, and Membership," *Qualitative Sociology* 28, no. 4 (Winter 2005): 466.

40. Healy, *Church,* p. 26.

41. Healy, *Church,* p. 36.

to even see the church *in via* is occluded. For example, Healy offers, the French Catholic ecclesiologist Jean-Marie Roger Tillard argued for the view "that the Eucharist is the most perfect expression of 'communion.'"[42] Such a *communio* ecclesiology — much in fashion over the last fifty years — ironically creates a theology "of the body" in such a way that it lacks the force needed to take account of *actual* bodies. While it may well be true, Healy writes, that Eucharist is on some level the most perfect expression of communion, "Eucharists are concretely and frequently divided by race, class, gender and political ideology, to say nothing of denominational divisions."[43] As such, blueprint ecclesiologies provide little by way of tools for understanding the concrete identity of the church in the complex and ever-shifting contexts from which it is given and within which it has its life. To accomplish this, Healy argues we ought to open up traditional ecclesiologies so that "they include explicit analysis of the ecclesiological context as an integral part of properly theological reflection upon the church."[44]

I have particularly chosen the cases offered in this chapter as studies that could serve as conversation partners about what we might mean by thinking, with Healy, of ecclesiology "more as a practical-prophetic discipline than a speculative and systematic one."[45] Ford's work cited above positions us in relation to Bourdieu's focus on worship's formation of a bodily *habitus*. Added to this is the expectation of multiple apprenticeships that give shape to the particular character of bodies in worship in relation to their contexts. Yet to make the transition beyond the hermeneutical frame that seeks to "read" the symbols that make for some more generalized frame of meaning, we can be helped by seeing in Bourdieu's background Marcel Mauss and his discussion of the social investment of the body through techniques. He, too, used the term *habitus* as Bourdieu occasionally pointed out, but Bourdieu's theoretical development of the term for his overall system covers over the rawness of Mauss's use of the term to get at what he calls "techniques and work of collective and individual practical reason."[46]

---

42. Jean-Marie Tillard, O.P., *Church of Churches: The Ecclesiology of Communion*, trans. R. C. De Peaux (Collegeville, Minn.: Glazier/Liturgical Press, 1992), p. 40.

43. Healy, *Church*, p. 37.

44. Healy, *Church*, p. 39.

45. Healy, *Church*, p. 21.

46. Marcel Mauss, "Techniques of the Body" (1935), in *Sociology and Psychology: Essays*, trans. B. Brewster (London: Routledge and Kegan Paul, 1979), p. 101; see also Talal Asad,

Each of the cases — Taylor's, Garrigan's, and mine — viewed Eucharist or communion as a "particular case of the possible" in relation to the world, a variety of distinct lives, a living tradition, etc., all of which gives way to a complexity of multiple formations.[47] We were able to gain proximity to these congregational worlds and the worshiping selves they produce through a kind of ethnographic apprenticeship, through placing ourselves in the "vortex of action in order to acquire, through practice, in real time, the dispositions of the [worshiper] with the aim of elucidating the magnetism proper to the [doxological] cosmos."[48] Our embodied participation went beyond typical "participant observation," as I have come to understand through the ethnographic writing of Loïc Wacquant on the world of boxing.[49] It was less "observation" and more a throwing oneself into the life of the congregation as far as was possible, seeking as full a "participant" role as possible.

Positing that Bourdieu is right that "we learn by body," we pursued our case studies to an important degree by positioning the worshiper and, in a broader sense, the congregation as a whole not merely as object to be understood, as perhaps a part of the burgeoning sociology or theology *of* the body, but also *from* the body, requiring submitting ourselves to the sometimes difficult and painful apprenticeship in context that allows forging the corporal and mental dispositions that make up the competent worshiper within the crucible of congregational life. A bodily submission, then, to the rigors of apprenticeship *in situ* becomes both the object and means of inquiry, opening, as Merleau-Ponty described, access to sensory-motor, mental, and social aptitudes — a corporal intelligence that tacitly guides "natives" to a particular "familiar universe."[50] It is, as Wacquant argues, a "mutual molding and immediate 'inhabiting' of being and world, carnal entanglement with a mesh of forces pregnant with silent summons

---

"Remarks on the Anthropology of the Body," in *Religion and the Body*, ed. Sarah Coakley (New York: Cambridge University Press, 1997), pp. 46-49.

47. Gaston Bachelard, *Le Nouvel Esprit Scientifque* (Paris: PUF, 1949), p. 58; see also Pierre Bourdieu and Loïc J. D. Wacquant, *An Invitation to Reflexive Sociology* (Chicago: University of Chicago Press, 1992), p. 75.

48. Loïc Wacquant, "Habitus as Topic and Tool: Reflections on Becoming a Prizefighter," in *Ethnographies Revisited: Constructing Theory in the Field*, ed. William Shaffir, Antony Puddephatt, and Steven Kleinknecht (New York: Routledge, 2009).

49. Loïc Wacquant, *Body and Soul: Notebooks of an Apprentice Boxer* (New York: Oxford University Press, 2004), p. 11.

50. M. Merleau-Ponty, *Phenomenology of Perception* (New York: Routledge, 1947/1962).

and invisible interdictions that elude the scholastic distinction between subject and object as they work simultaneously from within, through the socialization of cognition and affect, and from without by closing and opening viable paths for action."[51] Such a "carnal sociology" transfigured into a "carnal theology" illumines dynamics at the heart of Christian faith one might gesture toward in a preliminary way through categories such as God's "in-dwelling," or perhaps better, "in-carnation."

Presumably, the green sisters' "culinary Eucharist," the Irish communion in "one kind," and the "love feast" at Big Bethel AME are the "fresh embodiment" of the body of Christ, the church. Such theologically informed ethnography both portrays the subtlety and fullness of that local practice and opens a view to aspects that are necessary in understanding its particular power for good or ill. The reason why this matters is the practical-prophetic task, as Healy describes it. A "carnal theology" helps get at a level of community, of the church lived, that is not easily observable or interpretable short of the knowing that comes "from the body" through apprenticeship *in situ*. When theologians speak of studying "religion on the ground," they rarely follow Sarah Taylor's submission in which she "dug potatoes, shucked garlic, cut brush, mulched, weeded, harvested and double-dug vegetable beds for intensive planting."[52] When liturgical ecclesiology is written, it is rare that the writer admits, as Siobhán Garrigan does, that "my most important research tool was my own body in the spaces being studied."[53]

Such carnal theology allows for understanding the ways church and communion take form in Catholic communities — in one setting in response to sectarian divides and in another, to ecological divides. Understanding the embodiments of church in context need not be all theologians do, but without such careful submission to and formation in congregational patterns of communion and community, we have little capacity for seeing actual faults and possibilities for reform. We risk missing what David Ford calls "the distinctive and different realizations of the eventfulness of God."[54] If we took only the formal rite out of context, disembodied, the practices of the communities presented here would not make sense. This is on the one hand important for the kind of "confes-

---

51. Wacquant, "Carnal Connections," p. 466.
52. Taylor, *Green Sisters*, p. ix.
53. Garrigan, *The Real Peace Process*, p. 32.
54. Ford, *Self and Salvation*, p. 144.

sional purpose" Healy describes by evoking a practical-prophetic ecclesiology.[55] The subtle apprenticeship, theo-critically engaged, offers a way to see the church's particular participation in broken relationships, and to imagine modes of renewed faithfulness to its Lord. The examples play the confessional dynamic out forcefully, if implicitly. All is not right on the earth (e.g., Taylor's engagement with the green sisters) nor with our human communities (e.g., Garrigan's Irish sectarianism and my work with racism and the reconstitution of community). We need a way to see how our gatherings inhabit brokenness and yet hold within them promised potential for renewal.

It was, to conclude, a theologically necessary apprenticeship amongst the African Methodists at Big Bethel that allowed me to understand that the ritual of the love feast enacted the day prior to communion responded to the disintegrating social power of racism in all its history and current cultural complexity while also deepening their practice of Holy Communion in response by virtue of that communion enacted through the love feast in the laborious process of sharing oneself with another, one by one, as thread stitches cloth, offering and receiving greetings, prayer, confession, reconciliation, singing, cups of water, broken bread, and thanksgiving. To get at the levels of ritualization and communal formation present in this experience, all the typical modes of research were helpful, to be sure, but they emerged from a more basic commitment to understand something of what it is to be *this* gathering, this embodiment of Christ's body sharing communion, for which only a carnal theology, only an ecclesiology "from the body," could have helped.

---

55. Healy, *Church*, p. 185.

CHAPTER 4

"Where Is Your Church?"
Moving toward a Hospitable
and Sanctified Ethnography

John Swinton

> *Christianity, like peace, is not an idea; rather, it is a bodily faith that must be seen to be believed.*[1]

At the conference of the American Academy of Religion in Philadelphia in 2005, I had the pleasure of chairing a panel session on Stanley Hauerwas's theology of disability. The panel was made up of a group of theologians and ethicists with an interest in disability, the intention being to celebrate and discuss a new publication that brought together Hauerwas's essays on disability.[2] During question time a woman from the audience asked Hauerwas: "Where is this community you talk about? Where is your church?" The woman told us she had mental health issues and had suffered significant abuse and rejection from her church community. Her experiences of the empirical church seemed to bear no resemblance to the descriptions of church that Hauerwas was putting forward, and she wanted to know why that was so. Hauerwas's answer made me think: "You are presupposing that the church is a place." The questioner shook her head and

1. Stanley Hauerwas, "Seeing Peace: L'Arche as a Peace Movement" (unpublished paper from the proceedings of the Templeton Foundation Humble Approach Conference, "Living with the Disabled," Trosly, France, 2007). Published in revised form in Hans Reinders, ed., *The Paradox of Disability: Responses to Jean Vanier and L'Arche Communities from Theology and the Sciences* (Grand Rapids: Eerdmans, 2010), pp. 113-27.

2. John Swinton, *Critical Reflections of Stanley Hauerwas' Theology of Disability: Disabling Society, Enabling Theology* (New York: Haworth Press, 2005).

sat down, clearly deeply unsatisfied with the response but presumably re-signed to the fact that that might be as good as it gets. The panel of high-powered "theological experts" shuffled their papers and moved on to the next point. The chairman smiled awkwardly and moved on to the next issue. The question and the response have stuck with me over the years. The encounter embodied for me the difficult tension between what the church should be and what it should look like, and the nature and shape of the church as it actually is. As a practical theologian, this tension matters. Hauerwas's model of church presents a rich critique of modernity and a beautiful vision of what a peaceable kingdom might look like.[3] The woman's experience presents us with something of the reality of what it means to live with a disability in a real church in the here and now. Both descriptions contain truth, but both descriptions are at the same time lacking if they are not brought into conversation.

Is the Church a Place?

It is difficult to know what Hauerwas meant by the assertion that the church was not a place. Clearly he didn't mean that the empirical church doesn't exist or that it should be subsumed within some kind of theological ideal. Elsewhere Hauerwas has shown himself to be convinced that the church, that is, the visible church, is necessary for the proclamation of the gospel and the verification of its truth. The task of the church is to "bear witness" to the truth of the gospel. The fact that the Christian community exists counts as evidence that the gospel is true. "Christianity is unintelligible without witnesses, that is, without people whose practices exhibit their committed assent to a particular way of structuring the whole."[4] That being so, the practices of the empirical church are not inconsequential to the proclamation of the gospel, and as such, should not be substituted for a dissociated, ideal ecclesiology. The Christian's task, in the power of the Holy Spirit, is to *bear witness*.[5] The job of the church is to show to the world what it would look like if Christianity was in fact true.[6] This being

3. Stanley Hauerwas, *The Peaceable Kingdom: A Primer in Christian Ethics* (Notre Dame, Ind.: University of Notre Dame Press, 1983).

4. Stanley Hauerwas, *With the Grain of the Universe: The Church's Witness and Natural Theology* (Grand Rapids: Brazos, 2001), p. 214.

5. Hauerwas, *With the Grain*, p. 210.

6. Hauerwas, *With the Grain*, p. 214.

so, academic theology cannot be separated from Christian community. The empirical church is clearly a place in Hauerwas's ecclesiology. But what kind of a "place" does it have? To answer such a question means we have to look at it, which, as will become clear, is easier said than done!

Perhaps Hauerwas's response related to a more subtle theological point similar to John Milbank's statement that the place where he finds the church in its clearest form is not a "place" or an identity that emerges as the church develops and grows within the dialectics of human history. Rather the church is a gift "given, superabundantly, in the breaking of the bread by the risen Lord, which assembles the harmony of the peoples then and at every subsequent eucharist."[7] In this case, Hauerwas's intention might have been to indicate that the woman's disappointment with the church does not invalidate the fact that it is a gift that remains worthy of reception. It is true that her experience seems to negate something of the authenticity of that gift, but she need not use that experience to reject the possibility that the gift is real and can be seen.[8] Had such a position been expressed to the woman, her disappointment might have been lessened.

Fair enough, but the fact remains that it is a gift that is given in and through a community that is deeply blessed and profoundly fallen but, above all, thoroughly embodied. The gift is not comprehensible apart from the material markers that reflect and respond to its gracious Giver. If these material markers act unfaithfully, as in this woman's experience, then the gift will be occluded and the kingdom cannot be seen; hence her question: "Where is your church?" God's grace is certainly given superabundantly,[9] but that superabundance only becomes comprehensible as it engages with and is revealed through the life and practices of that community that claims to be its recipient: *the church.*

The Eucharist is indeed a powerful mystery. But the practice of the Eucharist is much less mysterious. Someone had to bake the bread and fer-

---

7. John Milbank, "Enclaves, or Where Is the Church?" *New Blackfriars* 73 (June 1992): 341-52.

8. Hence Hauerwas's ongoing reflection on Jean Vanier and L'Arche communities. He sees this form of community as a manifestation of the kingdom of God and a proof that the gospel can be lived. The fact that L'Arche communities exist indicates the possibility that the gospel is true and can be lived. Cf. "Seeing Peace: L'Arche as a Peace Movement," in *The Paradox of Disability.*

9. Eph. 3:20-21. "Now to him who, by the power that is at work within us, is able to do superabundantly, far over and above all that we ask or think. To him be glory in the church and in Christ Jesus throughout all generations forever and ever. Amen."

ment the wine. Someone had to place the elements in their right order. Some real community had to decide on the meaning of this practice and its weighting within the ministries of that particular community. The diversity and fragmentation within the church around the Eucharist would indicate that this gift is received in sometimes radically different ways. The question of why there is no harmony within the churches on the issues that surround this gift is indicative of a need to explore the complexities of why, despite the presence of the risen Lord in the Eucharist (variously defined), there is no universal harmony around the nature and function of the gift. God's superabundance may be a gift revealed in the Eucharist, but the interpretation of the meaning and purpose of that gift is wide and diverse. What is true for the Eucharist is true for many Christian practices.

The paradox is that it may be correct to suggest that the church should not be defined as "a place"; but, at the same time, it *is* very much a place! This is no small point. If the church's task is to bear witness in the ways Hauerwas suggests, then the need to explore the empirical church is of great importance, not for sociological purposes but for theological reasons. Such a suggestion is important for the ways in which we conceptualize and practice ethnography. If ethnographic study of ecclesial communities is perceived as primarily a theological task, then presumably the primary methodological assumptions within any given study will be theological.

We may never know precisely what Hauerwas's response meant. Nevertheless, reflection on his encounter with the mentally disturbed woman in Philadelphia opens up some interesting tensions and possibilities for the conversation between ecclesiology and ethnography. In the remainder of this chapter I will begin to explore why Christians might claim ethnography as a specifically theological enterprise. Social science may be helpful, but the act of looking at the church has theological significance that requires theological approaches and methodologies. My focus here will be on one particular aspect of the social sciences that has become popular with theologians: ethnography. However, my reflections will certainly have implications for the ongoing conversation between theology and the social sciences in all their different forms.

Interpreting the relationship between theology and ethnography in the way I do in this chapter will not be uncontroversial. It will call Christian researchers to explore the implicit and explicit politics of their research and to reflect on the significance of their allegiances to both theology and the social sciences. It may be that the accepted normal aims of publishing in prestigious journals are not the most faithful goals. It may be that offering a specifically Christian approach to ethnography will mean that it sits uneasily with the general tendency toward genericization of methods, approaches, and worldviews. It will certainly be the case that not all readers of this chapter will agree with me. Nevertheless, I offer the following as a contribution to the ongoing conversation around the role of theology within ethnographic research in the hope that together we can move toward ways and modes of researching that are effective and faithful.

The Problem with "Looking"

The suggestion that ethnography should be perceived primarily as a theological enterprise may seem, for some, rather counterintuitive. Is it not the task of ethnography to stand apart from theology and look at what is *actually* going on, thus clearing the way for effective theological reflection? The task of the theologian, usually but not exclusively a practical theologian, is to gather information on church communities using ethnographic methods. Once this picture is composed, varying degrees of theological reflection take place around the ethnographic results. Theology is thus presumed to be a second-order activity that takes place after the rigorous work of ethnography has been carried out. In this way we are enabled to look carefully at the empirical church, reflect on it in the light of Scripture and tradition, and allow that looking to challenge and inspire our ecclesial practices. Thus far, all seems well, until we ask the question: What does it actually mean to *look* at the church?

Ethnography as a Way of Looking

Observation is central to the ethnographic enterprise. One way we might seek to understand ethnography is by viewing it as a particular way of looking at situations and things. This seems quite straightforward until we ask precisely what it means to look at something. At one level the answer seems obvious: to look at an object is to turn one's eyes toward it in order to see what it is. However simple such an action may appear, deeper reflection reveals it to be a much more complex practice. To claim to *see* an object by turning one's eyes toward it requires faith that what you see is what is actually there. This requires an adherence to a particular philosophical perspective that necessarily contains within it a specific worldview: empiricism. Empiricism assumes that only that which falls upon the retina of the eye can be considered factual in terms of truth that is public and verifiable, as opposed to opinion or experiences, which are personal and not publicly verifiable. Such a philosophical position immediately raises a tension with the claims of theology and ecclesial communities. God is spirit, and those who are called to worship God are to do so in spirit and in truth.[10] Such things are beyond the purview of the ethnographic look. That being so, that which drives, motivates, controls, and acts on people's ecclesial lives cannot be seen; it can only be grasped by faith. Ethnography must reduce this spiritual dynamic to "beliefs" and "behaviors" before it can "see what is going on." There may be scope for asserting that such beliefs and behaviors mean a lot to the community and that they are influential in shaping thoughts and behaviors in particular ways, but there is little methodological space to reflect on the fact that they may be real and that a committed theology might be a relevant analytical category alongside psychology and sociology (as opposed to one drawn in after particular modes of observation and analysis have taken place). And yet, theological facts form the foundation of church communities, and the presumed reality of the invisible God is the very reason the church exists. It could of course be argued that ethnography is not in fact empirical in this sense. It is interpretative. This may be true, but to raise the point is simply to shift the methodological discussion into another philosophical frame. The ethnographic look is deeply value laden.

The Problem of Method

This of course raises the problem of method: the methods one chooses to use in one's attempt to look at something will determine what one can see and what one cannot see. Ethnographic looking is not a neutral, value-free endeavor. We tend to choose our methods according to what we assume we will see. In their endeavors to look at particular situations, ethnographers employ various methods designed to enable them to observe and record the environments they are looking at. It is at this point, the issue of method, that we begin to realize just how complex and value-laden the practice of looking actually is.

10. John 4:24. "God is spirit, and his worshipers must worship in spirit and in truth."

What Is Ethnography?

In teasing out the issues surrounding method, it will be helpful to begin by reflecting on what I mean when I use the term "ethnography" in this essay. John Brewer distinguishes between two modes of ethnography: *big* and *little* ethnography. Big ethnography refers to any approach that employs qualitative methods and avoids surveys, statistics, etc. This understanding would be in line with the types of definitions offered by Ward and Fiddes in this volume. Little ethnography has to do with particular fieldwork projects. Here ethnography becomes one specific way of doing qualitative research. The basic argument of this chapter applies to both modes. Formally, Brewer defines ethnography as "the study of people in naturally occurring settings or 'fields' by means of methods which capture their social meanings and ordinary activities, involving the researcher participating directly in the setting, if not also the activities, in order to collect data in a systematic manner but without meaning being imposed on them externally."[11] This definition is quite telling. It informs us that ethnography comprises a series of methods used to collect and collate data from particular contexts that are naturally occurring (as opposed to unnatural or experimental situations). The ethnographer enters into the situation, "sits down," and looks around. To look and record effectively, she draws on particular methods. Brewer describes methods as technical rules, which lay down the procedures for how reliable and objective knowledge can be obtained. As procedural rules they tell people what to do and what not to do if they want the knowledge to be reliable and objective.[12]

Methods help the ethnographer to look closely at, interpret, and understand what is going on. However, these methods are not value-neutral. Methods cannot be separated from the particular methodological framework that provides their legitimation. Methods contain methodologies. The term "methodology" relates to the study of methods. More broadly, it has to do with an overall approach to a particular field. It implies a family of methods that have in common philosophical and epistemological assumptions. Methods are carried out within a particular set of methodological assumptions.[13] Methods thus require and contain certain assump-

---

11. John Brewer, *Ethnography* (Buckingham: Open University Press, 2000), p. 10.

12. Brewer, *Ethnography*, p. 2.

13. John Swinton and Harriet Mowat, *Practical Theology and Qualitative Research* (London: SCM, 2006), p. 75.

tions about the way the world is and how people should function within it. Brewer notes that there are certain necessary judgments within ethnographic methods. Judgments are made regarding

> the object of the research, which is to study people in naturally occurring settings; the researcher's role in that setting, which is to understand and explain what people are doing in that setting by means of participating directly in it; and the data to be collected, which must be naturally occurring and captured in such a way that meaning is not imposed on them from the outside. These issues of technique derive from a set of procedural and philosophical premises — a methodology — so that ethnography-understood-as-fieldwork still describes more than just a set of procedural rules for collecting data (that is, ethnography is more than a method of data collection).[14]

Naturalism, hermeneutics, phenomenology are just three methodological perspectives that emerge from this brief statement. The decision to choose particular methods reflects the way in which the researcher understands the world to be.[15] This being so, the apparently simple act of choosing to use certain methods over and against others already implies a philosophical and epistemological positioning and, as I will suggest later, an implicit or explicit theological position. Such inherent methodological presuppositions will inevitably impact the way the research is constructed, how data is analyzed and interpreted, and the way it is presented. They will also impact the particular audience to whom the findings will be attractive.

So, for example, in phenomenologically oriented methods the researcher might seek to bracket off her own opinions in order to get at the lived experience of participants.[16] In this way she seeks to avoid imposing

---

14. Brewer, *Ethnography*, p. 18.

15. If this is so, we should be very aware of the dangers of laziness in the ways in which we choose our methods, wherein people simply use particular methods because they feel partial to them or because others have advised that they should use them. For example, researchers might choose to use qualitative research methods because they don't like or don't understand statistics. Or they may use grounded theory instead of hermeneutic phenomenology because their research supervisor has expertise in that area and not in others. Again, a person might choose a constructivist approach because she doesn't like the idea that authorities should have the power to determine what people should or should not think. Methodological laziness leads to uncritical naïveté about what methods reveal to us and how they impact upon our approach.

16. V. Corben, "Misusing Phenomenology in Nursing Research: Identifying the Is-

meaning onto a situation by extracting herself-as-herself from the interpretative process. But how (and why) would a Christian ethnographer desire to bracket off her beliefs? Why would she be comfortable with a phenomenological worldview that excludes theology as an interrogative category? What sense could she make of what was going on in the church or anything else within creation if she was successful in such a task? Precisely what do such Christians think she would *not* see if she looked at a situation through theological eyes? If she thought she would not see what is *actually* going on, that she might be blinded to the *real* psychological and social dynamics impacting the participants, then we have a problem. Why would looking at the situation from the perspective of psychology and sociology take precedence over theological looking? All these points may be answerable. My concern is whether or not such questions are even asked in the first place.

Methodological Deism

Brent Slife makes an interesting point with regard to the natural sciences' tendency to remove theology from research procedures. Even when Christians engage in scientific research, they tend to do so as Deists. "Natural science methods never require that investigators pray (or generally consult God or revelation) before designing or conducting a study. This requirement is omitted because God's current activities are presumed to be irrelevant to designing and conducting an effective investigation (though God's created order might be considered relevant to the results of the investigation)."[17] The temptation for the Christian ethnographer is that she drifts into some form of methodological Deism. For example, it is rare for prayer to be acknowledged as fundamental to the methods used and to be written into the methods section of a research report. Researchers may well pray before and during their research, but the fact that God's involvement in the research process is not publicly acknowledged and that the research can be presented perfectly well without any reference to God's action indicates

---

sues," *Nurse Researcher* 6, no. 3 (1999): 52-66; P. F. Colaizzi, "Psychological Research as the Phenomenologist Sees It," in *Existential Phenomenological Alternatives for Psychology*, ed. R. S. Valle and M. King (New York: Oxford University Press, 1978), pp. 48-71.

17. B. D. Slife, "Are the Natural Science Methods of Psychology Compatible with Theism?" in *Why Psychology Needs Theology: A Radical Reformation Perspective*, ed. Alvin Dueck and Cameron Lee (Grand Rapids: Eerdmans, 2005), pp. 172-84.

some form of implicit methodological Deism. Alternatively, it may simply reflect a desire to gain credibility within a professional or academic community that does not accept the legitimacy of theology as a valid mode of knowledge. Either way the possibility of the real, active presence of God within the research process is downplayed, psychologized, or withdrawn completely. Similarly, the suggestion that the Holy Spirit might *really* be at work within a particular instance of the church is not frequently reflected upon, primarily because it is difficult to observe and validate apart from particular behaviors that are embodied in people. Thus, there is a clear methodological clash. Because of our particular methodological choices and assumptions, the works of the Spirit can easily be implicitly and explicitly reduced to psychology and behavior.

It is a much more comfortable position to work with methods that enable us to observe behavior and reflect on beliefs[18] *as if* such behaviors and beliefs were nothing but the embodied actions of human beings. True, we might hint in a different direction during our analysis, but God is often absent from the immediate interpretations of our observations. However, you might ask, "How could you possibly measure or observe whether God is *really* at work in a community?" The answer, of course, is you probably can't! Except perhaps through the eyes of faith. But such an answer does not sit neatly with the claims made for ethnographic method, and it certainly doesn't sit well with peer reviewers and the editors of prestigious secular journals. And yet, faith: "confidence in what we hope for and assurance about what we do not see,"[19] is precisely what Christians are called to engage in at all times and in all places. This tension between the calling and expectations of the research community and the calling and expectations of God is not easily resolved. It is, however, important to notice that this tension is an issue of method and methodology, an issue of choice and preference.

18. Paul Griffiths makes the point that "secular universities now largely hold the view that religious preferences and their associated theological claims may have deep personal meaning but can have no cognitive significance and therefore ought not to be treated as if they had." "Theology as Knowledge," *First Things*, May 2006. The same point could be made for certain approaches within ethnography. Beliefs are assumed to be just objects of observation that reside purely within individuals and communities. Hence the claim that "this is true" makes no sense in terms of ethnographic proclamation.

19. Heb. 11:1.

Meaning and Interpretation

Another important aspect of Brewer's definition of ethnography is the claim that it is designed to capture the social meanings of situations. The assumption here is that meanings emerge from and are constructed by the participants within the particular context under scrutiny. The researcher's task is to familiarize herself with the situation through methods such as participant observation, interviews, reflexivity, and so forth. Observation is the primary means of data collection. She looks carefully at the situation and participates sensitively in it so these previously hidden meanings begin to emerge — previously hidden from the researcher, but also frequently hidden from the community. Thus in bringing these meanings to the attention of the community, she facilitates noticing, creates new theories, and offers the community insights that it may or may not have previously been aware of. The primary tool for capturing such meanings is the researcher herself. She is the research tool. Her task is not to stand back and objectify the situation but to take her methods into the situation; to immerse herself in the situation and from there to gain insight and an understanding of the meaning-generating processes within that community. Her methods allow her both to gather and to systematize the complex meanings within the situation and arrive at an understanding "from within," that is, an understanding that has not been imported into the situation by the researcher. Her task is simply to record what she sees without imposing alien meaning. That being so, the suggestion that theology should be a vital aspect of such observation seems methodologically inappropriate if not imperialistically oppressive. And yet, I want to suggest that *the importation of meaning is precisely what she should do.*

The Necessity of Bias

In making this point we need briefly to explore something of the nature of the hermeneutical enterprise that sits at the heart of ethnography. Ethnography is first and foremost an interpretative enterprise. The act of interpretation is necessarily value-laden. The only real question is whether or not the researcher recognizes this and seeks to work with it within the interpretative process, or pretends it doesn't exist and allows hidden biases to subliminally determine her interpretations. Hans-Georg Gadamer offers us a way of understanding the act of interpretation that opens up possibilities for understanding how theology might help expand the interpretative goals of the ethnographic process. In opposition to those who think that interpretation requires the removal of the interpreter from the process, Gadamer highlights the fact that the importation of external structures of meaning by the reader into interpretations of a text (text here meaning something written or performed) is not something to be avoided. Quite the opposite, such an importation of meaning is necessary for the act of interpretation; indeed, it is the only way we can make sense of anything. Gadamer argues that human beings are fundamentally interpretative creatures. "Our situatedness in history and time — is the precondition of truth, not an obstacle to it."[20] Hermeneutics is a basic human act and a significant way of being in the world. Central to the act of interpretation is what we already know. Our own embeddedness and historical situatedness not only deeply influences the way we interpret our world; it is the basic way we strive to make sense of anything in the world.[21]

Understanding cannot be done by separating subject from object in the way the natural sciences assume. Both subject and object are bound together and mediated by a common cultural and historical context: an *effective history* comprising personal experience and cultural traditions.[22] Gadamer refers to these preunderstandings as *prejudices*.[23] When one approaches a phenomenon, one inevitably does so with particular prejudices and preunderstandings that affect the process of interpretation. However, prejudice is not something that is negative or that we should try to eliminate. Prejudice is crucial for our emerging understanding of the world. Gadamer understands prejudice as a forestructure or a condition of knowledge in that it determines what we may find intelligible in any given situation.

It is therefore naive to believe that one can ever be truly detached from the object of interpretation. To understand a text we need what he describes as a fusion between the horizons of the world of the researcher/interpreter and the world of the text.[24] From this perspective, the task of the researcher is not to bracket off her prejudices, but to fuse her horizon with

20. S. Hekman, *Hermeneutics and the Sociology of Knowledge* (Cambridge: Polity Press, 1986), p. 117.

21. H.-G. Gadamer, *Truth and Method*, trans. J. Weinsheimer and D. G. Marshall, 2nd rev. ed. (New York: Crossroad, 1989).

22. Gadamer, *Truth and Method*, p. 273.

23. Gadamer, *Truth and Method*, pp. 266ff.

24. Gadamer, *Truth and Method*, p. 259.

the horizon of the research participants in a way that will deepen and clarify the meaning of the experience being explored. Horizons are closely connected with prejudice in that they contain an individual's and a society's underlying assumptions about the way the world is and how people and things should function within it. Thus, the task of the reader/researcher is to enter into a constructive, critical dialogue with the text within which a fusion of the two horizons is brought about. That being so, all ethnographic data is seen to be co-construction; a mutually constructed narrative that emerges from the merging of the researcher's horizon and the horizon of the text. If that is the case, rather than bracketing off theology from the process of looking and interpretation, the most authentic hermeneutical movement will be to draw it into the observation and analysis and allow its voice to enable clarity of vision and emerging understanding.

Ecclesiology and Ethnography

If Gadamer is correct, the task in investigating the meanings emerging from religious communities is not to bracket off our theology as if it were somehow possible to look at the situation without any need for it. Rather, it is necessary that we engage with our theology as a vital observational and analytical tool that has a voice throughout the whole of the research process. In other words, we don't just do ethnography in an apparently neutral fashion (if indeed such a thing was possible), and then theologize on our empirical results. In this approach, theology becomes a crucial part of the observation, analysis, and interpretation of the situation. It is as we bring our theological horizons into conversation with the methods of ethnography and the situation we are looking at that honest and faithful interpretation emerges.

Reflexivity

If this hermeneutical perspective is correct, in order for Christians to do ethnography faithfully they should develop a mode of reflexivity within which the theological is assumed as a normal and primary reflective dimension of the researcher's epistemological and methodological assumptions. Put simply, "reflexivity is the process of critical self-reflection carried out by the researcher throughout the research process that enables her to monitor and respond to her contribution to the proceedings."[25] Reflexivity is a mode of knowing that accepts the impossibility of the researcher standing outside of the research field and seeks to incorporate that knowledge creatively and effectively within the practice of interpretation. Willig notes that at a personal level it involves "reflecting upon the ways in which our own values, experiences, interests, beliefs, political commitments, wider aims in life and social identities have shaped the research. It also involves thinking about how the research may have affected and possibly changed us, as people and as researchers."[26] At this level it urges us to take seriously the suggestion that all research is, to an extent, autobiography. Reflexivity brings to the fore the fact mentioned previously that the creation and interpretation of texts is necessarily an act of co-creation.

At the level of epistemology, reflexivity encourages us to reflect on the assumptions (about the world and about the nature of knowledge) that we have made in the course of the research, and it helps us to think about the implications of such assumptions for the research and its findings.[27] Much more could be said about the importance of reflexivity for ethnography and the implications for the incorporation of theology, but for now the thing to notice is that from the perspectives of hermeneutics and reflexivity, that is, two of the primary methods within ethnography, the incorporation of theology-as-theology is far from ruled out. There is no inherent reason why the language of Trinity, cross, and resurrection should not form an important aspect of the data gathering and analytical process. Indeed, it may be that the honest methodological position from which Christians should begin their ethnographic practices is not neutrality but prayer.

Whom Is Your Research For?

Of course, the actual practice of introducing theological language into the research process in the way I have suggested is fraught and complex. An illustration will help to draw out this point. I recently attended a conference that was designed to teach hospital chaplains how to do research. The lec-

25. Swinton and Mowat, *Practical Theology,* p. 59.
26. C. Willig, *Qualitative Research in Psychology: A Practical Guide to Theory and Method* (Buckingham: Open University Press, 2001), p. 10.
27. Willig, *Qualitative Research in Psychology,* p. 10.

turer opened with a firm statement that impressed me: "I always begin the research project with prayer. I assume throughout that the Holy Spirit is integral to the research process and that he participates throughout." I thought this was an unusually bold statement. I asked her: "Do you write that into your research reports?" She seemed surprised by the question. "No, of course not! If I did I would never get published!" I asked her, "Are you then suggesting that chaplains should become social scientists rather than theologians?" She just smiled at me and said, "Needs must."

This brief encounter highlights a number of issues relating to the reflexive fusion of horizons between theology and ethnography that I am suggesting is vital for a Christian ethnography. Two things must be highlighted. Firstly, it was clear that the research being discussed made perfect sense without any direct reference to God. It was assumed that the methods that formed the ethnographic look enabled the researcher to see what was actually going on, and that that was enough. An atheist could read the research report and enjoy it without feeling threatened or challenged.[28] The Holy Spirit may have been working invisibly, but it was the empirical phenomenon revealed by the methods of ethnography that took primacy in terms of validity and interpretation.

Secondly, the primary criterion for the exclusion of theology seemed to be the predilections of secular journals that were looking for "unbiased" research findings that would apply to all people in all circumstances at all times. The particularities of Christianity were culturally inappropriate even if they might be true. Theology is there, but in terms of practice it becomes invisible; not because it has to, but because the context within which the research is being produced and the researcher's desired audience preclude its inclusion. The issue here is whether or not theology is considered an overt or a covert aspect of ethnographic method. The temptation to collapse theology into ethnography in order to please audiences beyond

---

28. This point, of course, relates to the generic nature of hospital chaplaincy. Chaplains work in a secular context within which they are called to minister to all faiths and none. Similarly as they strive to move toward the status of health care professionals, their emerging profession is required to participate in the evidence-based culture of the National Health Service. That being so, introducing theology to the research process in the ways I am suggesting is particularly difficult. However, the important thing to note is that it is not difficult because theology is necessarily irrelevant. It is difficult because the political expectations of society and the particular context in which chaplains minister make it so. That being so, a conscious decision to remove theology from the research process may be political or at least pragmatic rather than theological.

the church seems irresistible in terms of "relevance" and "effective communication" between church and world. But does it have to be that way?

One way practical theologians have sought to work with this tension is through the method of *mutual critical correlation.* Mutual critical correlation sees the practical theological task as bringing situations into dialectical conversation with insights from the Christian tradition and perspectives drawn from other sources of knowledge (primarily the social sciences). It is a model of integration that seeks to bring these dimensions together in a way that respects and gives an equal voice to each dialogue partner.[29] The vignette highlighted above reveals one of the problems with this approach: although the conversation appears to be mutual, in practice theology easily collapses into the social sciences.

The underlying methodological position within mutually critical correlative models is that theological truth is emergent and dialectical and as such requires partnering with other sources of knowledge that will enable clarity and revised ecclesial practices.[30] In this sense it stands opposed to positions that assume theology to be revealed and embodied in unchanging doctrines. Within the method of mutual critical correlation, the primary task is therefore to initiate a two-way conversation between the social sciences, in this case ethnography, and theology, with both partners open and willing to listen and respond to the insights gained from the other. The division of labor between the two is assumed to be more or less equal. Ethnography provides the empirical data about the church community which then becomes the locus for theological reflection. Out of this conversation emerge understanding and, if necessary, some form of retheologizing of the situation. At one level this seems fine. It opens up the opportunity to challenge aspects of Scripture and tradition that may have become distorted, forgotten, or deliberately overlooked. Likewise, it presents a space wherein ethnography (or at least the results of ethnographic investigation) can be critiqued in the light of theological assumptions and propositions.

There are, however, problems with this approach. Two questions will open this up. First: Who actually wants to correlate ethnography and theology? And second: In practice, how mutual are these conversations? Let us

---

29. Swinton and Mowat, *Practical Theology,* p. 78.

30. See, for example, the series of essays in section 2 of James Woodward and Stephen Pattison, eds., *The Blackwell Reader in Practical Theology and Pastoral Studies* (Oxford: Blackwell, 2000).

begin with the first question. As one reads through the mainstream ethnographic and sociological journals, one does not normally find an ethnographer who actively seeks to correlate her work with that of theologians, at least through sharing language that is specifically theological. I imagine that if one were to poll the members of the British or American sociological societies, few would actively seek dialogue with theology and genuinely integrate the critiques, insights, and challenges of theology into their day-to-day work using overt Christian language and concepts. If they did, where would they publish? The language of Spirit, cross, sanctification, salvation, and sin is not common parlance within the social scientific literature. And yet, as one peruses the literature produced by Christian theologians, the language of psychology and sociology seems to be completely at home. My point is this: mutual critical correlation is something that *theologians* seek, not ethnographers. Theology seems to want to have a mutually critical dialogue with a discipline that has absolutely no interest in dialoguing! That being so, unless the theologian is specifically trained in the field of ethnography or the social sciences, there is a danger that the conversation will end up being with her particular selective interpretation of a discipline within which she has no formal training and which is epistemologically problematic and perhaps contradictory to her theological training, goals, and beliefs. Of course, partnering with a social scientist might help to overcome this. Nevertheless, finding a social scientist that might be comfortable publishing an overtly theological piece of work may be more difficult.

The second question, whether the conversation is genuinely mutual, follows on from the first. Bearing in mind what has been already said about the value-laden nature of ethnographic method, it is difficult to see how or why theologians would be comfortable with a purely ethnographic description of an ecclesial situation. If, as I will suggest below, ethnography is both description and explanation, then this raises important questions for the mutuality of the relationship.

I am not suggesting that we should reject critical conversations between theology and ethnography. My point is quite simple: in terms of both method and methodology, theologians who desire to use ethnography as part of their theologizing should approach the issue as *theologians*. Ethnography should be perceived as occurring within a theological context, rather than theology speaking into a context that is already defined by ethnography. The danger with mutual critical correlation is that, because sociology has a broader and more culturally legitimate appeal, there is an inevitable temptation, sometimes for what appear to be good reasons, to privilege sociological descriptions and explanations of contexts over theological accounts. If theological reflection occurs *after* the event has been observed, recorded, interpreted, and explained, then theology becomes a second-order activity that is dependent on a particular account of the world that is generated via ethnographic methods that are far from neutral. This would mean that theology begins with an account of "reality" that is shaped by the methodological assumptions of ethnographic methods that do not require theology for their validation.

This point finds some resonance with aspects of John Milbank's critique of social theory: "Theology has frequently sought to borrow from elsewhere a fundamental account of society or history, and then to see what theological insights will cohere with it. But it has been shown that no such fundamental account, in the sense of something neutral, rational and universal, is really available. It is theology itself that will have to provide its own account of the final causes at work in human history, on the basis of its own particular, and historically specific faith."[31] I think Milbank's point is a strong one. His critique is aimed at the ways in which social theory provides explanations for what goes on in particular contexts according to causes (the market, social dislocation, anomie, liberal individualism, etc.) that lie outside theology. These explanations can easily take precedence over theological explanations, leading to theological explanations being excluded from the process of theorizing and practicing social theory. As Michael Baxter correctly observes:

> The problem, in Aristotelean-Thomistic terms, is that final and formal causes are ruled out of explanations altogether, in favour of efficient causes, deemed to be the only causes that meet scientific standards of empirical demonstration and verification. And for Milbank, the solution, in the same terms, is to retrieve this medieval vision of causality such that events and actions can be explained in terms of complex interrelationships of final, formal, and efficient causes, the overall operation of which is ultimately mysterious and can only be accounted for in traditional theological categories.[32]

31. John Milbank, *Theology and Social Theory: Beyond Secular Reason* (Cambridge, Mass.: Blackwell, 1990), p. 382.
32. Michael Horace Barnes, ed., *Theology and the Social Sciences* (New York: Orbis, 2001), p. 35.

The danger with a correlative approach is that it runs the risk of confusing efficient causes with final and formal causes. When this happens, history and experience become the focus of attention rather than eschatology and God. This confusion over final and efficient causes lies behind some of the methodological concerns I have highlighted thus far. When this occurs, the telos of the ethnographic enterprise takes on a particular shape and theology is forced into a role that reflects efficient rather than formal causes. Bearing in mind that theology, particularly practical theology, is about the recognition and description of final causes (i.e., the creative love of God) as they impinge upon and relate to current practices, this is no small issue.

Sanctifying Ethnography: Researching Faithfully

Ethnography need not be rejected as an appropriate tool of analysis for Christians who seek to look faithfully at churches. It does, however, require to be *sanctified.* Put slightly differently, we require a methodological framework that acknowledges that theology may have some first-order claims with regard to observation, knowledge creation, reflexivity, interpretation, analysis, and the "practices of looking" that are central to ethnography. I want to state that this knowledge, while always open to challenge and critical reflection, demands a central place within the research process.

By "sanctified" I simply mean that it must be blessed and set aside for a special purpose. It is true that one could argue that such a suggestion is unscientific and introduces a bias to ethnographic method that is unhelpful. However, we have already seen that such a bias is already there. If my suggestion that the need to correlate comes primarily from theologians rather than ethnographers, it is not unreasonable to presume that theology should be the primary frame of reference and the vital methodological underpinning for the research process. This, of course, opens up the question of what a "theological worldview" might look like. Theology is not a unified perspective and there are many theologies and different worldviews within Christianity. Some would be comfortable with simply correlating theology with other forms of knowledge, assuming that revelation is found in many different places and that it is right that theology and the social sciences should have an equal voice. Others might argue that revelation is quite specific and that that knowledge is deeply challenging to the basis of the ethnographic enterprise. This is an issue, but it is not unique to the use of ethnography.

My point is not that theology should pretend to be monolithic any more than I think ethnography should pretend to be monolithic. I am suggesting that, at a minimum, theology should assume the right to have a methodological voice that is deeply influential on the process of observation, the methods used, and the ways in which the Christian ethnographer's look is shaped, formed, and practiced. My primary point is this: whatever the theological position of the researcher might be, that position must be allowed to become integral to the ways in which the situation is looked at. "But," you might argue, "if there is no single theology, won't we just end up with a plurality of theologies all saying different things and all influencing analysis in different ways?" The answer to that question is of course yes! The form of a sanctified ethnography will inevitably be contextual and varied. But it was ever thus. Ethnographic methods have diverse and contradictory methodological bases: empiricism, postmodernism, social constructionism, critical realism, and so forth.[33] Ethnographers will look at the same thing from different positions and see different things. Ethnographers have to make a conscious choice as to which methods match their view of the world. If you don't believe that knowledge is socially constructed, you won't use constructivist methods. If you think that the observer can bracket off her beliefs in order to see the real phenomena, you will use phenomenology. These are not scientific decisions; they are personal preferences based on certain assumptions about the world. To suggest that having a plurality of theologies within our analytical practices that are based on particular worldview commitments seems no different from the way things already are. Ethnographers always have to make methodological decisions, and these decisions always depend on the way the ethnographer thinks/believes the world is. The ethnographic enterprise is based on faith and choice; recognizing a similar dynamic within our theologizing isn't unusual or, if Gadamer is correct, hermeneutically inappropriate. True, we will end up with Baptist, evangelical, fundamentalist, liberal, Catholic, Methodist, and Reformed ecclesial investigations. But this is not something new. Researchers from these traditions already explicitly or implicitly draw on their traditions for their interpretative initiatives. What is new is the suggestion that we should draw these theologies to the forefront and merge their horizons publicly in ways that are challenging, methodologically appropriate, and faithful. The key is to develop

---

33. For a useful overview of methods and methodologies, cf. J. McLeod, *Qualitative Research in Counselling and Psychotherapy* (London: Sage, 2001).

modes of reflexivity that ensure that while meaning is necessarily imported, it need not be imposed upon interpretations. If we are honest and reflexive about our prejudices, our interpretations will be much more faithful.

Of course, it could be objected that such a position would distance the ethnographer from her peer group; "social scientists would never buy it!" That may be true, although one would have to think long and hard about why that is the case and what statement that makes about the real mutuality of mutual critical correlation. Such a challenge simply calls the Christian ethnographer to a place of decision: Which audience does she seek to please? Which epistemological system does she desire to draw on for the legitimacy of her work? I stress again that my intention is *not* that theologians should close down their dialogue with the social scientific community; only that in their conversations they should first and foremost remain theologians. My question is whether or not there is actually a desire for dialogue within the social sciences if theology remains theology.

From Correlation to Hospitality

It could be argued that I have turned ethnography into a purely churchly discipline that excludes the ethnographer who does not belong to the church (broadly defined) and who simply wishes to look at the church as a social phenomenon. You might ask: "What if an atheist ethnographer wants to look at the church? Is she excluded by your criteria?" Not really. Anyone can look at the church. Churches are strange and fascinating places filled with love and dissonance, faithfulness and fallenness. As an object of purely sociological observation, they undoubtedly hold much attraction. But there is a difference between *looking at* and *living in.* Christian ethnographers cannot but engage in both practices, and that reflexive knowledge of "living in" makes a difference. The data produced by looking at and by living in will be similar, but those who *live in* the church inevitably work within a different methodology which means they will both look and see differently. Such modes of looking — looking at and living in — may complement one another, but they are not the same, nor are they inevitably or necessarily equal.

I will conclude by suggesting that the relationship between theology and the social sciences might be better summed up through the metaphor of *hospitality* than correlation. To correlate something is to indicate and work with the fact that the two things bear a reciprocal or mutual relation. However, reciprocity and relationship do not necessarily equate with equal ontological or epistemological weight. Hospitality functions in a different cadence. For me to be hospitable toward you, I need to respect you and to value your perspective and beliefs. If I have to pretend that I agree with you or if I have to dumb down my own views in order not to offend you, then we can never really have a meaningful conversation and we are unlikely to become friends. But if I respect your integrity and you respect mine, then we can engage in hospitable, friendly conversations. That might mean acknowledging that you know much more about certain issues than I do. But it might also mean that what I know is more foundational and more important for our journey together toward proper understanding.

This dynamic is apparent in the ministry of Jesus. Sometimes he was guest, sometimes he was host.[34] He seemed to move fluently from one role to the other. But he never ceased being Jesus, God incarnate who had a specific mission and who understood the world in terms that were often radically different from his hosts. If theology can work toward developing such an approach to the social sciences (and vice versa), then even the contentious issues may become avenues that reach toward creative friendships. My sense is that this might be the way we should begin to think through our methodological inclinations as well as the personal relationships between theologians and social scientists. Hospitality might be the key to bringing together those who fear the social sciences and wish to look at the church through the eyes of theology alone and those who have fallen in love with the social sciences and want to offer them too much creative power over theology. Hospitality might be the place to begin to help both to look and to see more clearly. Together, in hospitable relationships that recognize the importance of noticing that we are doing research in *creation,* theology and ethnography might just be able to help us begin to answer the questions with which we began: Where is this community you talk about? Where is your church? What does it look like?

34. Luke 24.

PART TWO

The Conversation

Charting the "Ethnographic Turn": Theologians and the Study of Christian Congregations

Elizabeth Phillips

It is a sunny, spring Sunday morning in the heartland of America. People are streaming into an enormous church building. They are serenaded by praise music played through speakers that line the walkways from the multiple parking lots. At the building's main entrance they pass a large fountain, above which a huge golden globe is suspended. Friendly church members meet them at every door with a handshake or a hug. As they enter the sanctuary they pass a large wall made of white stone imported from the Holy Land. Tall, black, metal letters are mounted on the wall reading "Pray for the Peace of Jerusalem." The sanctuary's 2,600 seats are steadily filling as a band, choir, and praise team lead worship. Everyone on stage is dressed in Israeli blue and white. Large video screens project words to the songs over a background image of the Western Wall of the Temple Mount. Everyone is singing in Hebrew, hands lifted high. "Meshiach! Meshiach! Meshiach!"

Today is this congregation's annual Israel Awareness Day. It is the culmination of a month of sermons and classes on topics related to biblical prophecy and current events in the Middle East. It is a day when the church's four worship services focus especially on the modern nation-state of Israel as the center of God's intentions for human history. The entire local community — particularly its Jewish members — are invited to come in the evening for an extravaganza of pro-Israel music, dance, drama, and prestigious speakers. Last year it was Israeli paratrooper Shaol Amir and Texas pastor John Hagee. Tonight it will be a local rabbi and former Israeli ambassador Dore Gold.

This morning's sermon is on Ezekiel's vision of the dry bones. Pastor George has some props on stage to drive the point home. The dry bones, he explains — standing next to and gesturing toward a pile of bones — is Israel scattered, the Diaspora. When the bones began to rattle, that was the rise of the Zionist movement. Pastor George unveils a classroom skeleton and says the bones began to come back together when Jews immigrated to the Holy Land in the 1940s. The skeleton received its muscles and flesh — it became a body — when Israel became a state. Then Pastor George tells the congregation what comes next.

He says, "Now . . . here's what's happening. Let me give you this picture so you can understand why we . . . stand with and support Israel as a nation and encourage our government to do the same, because . . . God says, 'I'm going to set watchmen [on the wall]. I'm gonna put people in position so that they would pray that the next step will happen to the nation of Israel.' What's the next step? The breath of God. God's spirit breathes on them and they come alive to accept their Messiah."

This was one Sunday morning in the Christian Zionist congregation I recently studied. As a Christian ethicist who has engaged in an "ethnographic"[1] study of a Christian congregation, I hope to make two contributions to the conversation represented by this volume. First, growing out of my own process of searching for reasons and ways to do this research, I hope to chart the wider conversations of which this one is a part, namely, the turn of theologians toward "ethnography" as well as concurrent and convergent shifts in anthropology and sociology. Second, I hope to relate this conversation to the discipline of theological ethics, illustrated by the ethnographic research I conducted in order to write a piece of theological ethics on the topic of American Christian Zionism, and to demonstrate why theologians (and theological ethicists in particular) should be studying Christian congregations.

A certain type of Christian Zionism is a formative influence — in widely varying degrees — for virtually all American Protestants who are anywhere right of center theologically. Many have concluded that the influence of Christian Zionism contributes significantly to Americans' misunderstandings of the Middle East and their support for foreign poli-

---

1. I am not entirely comfortable with theologians using the word "ethnography," but I will return to this below. For now I will allow it to stand as it does in the literature being discussed.

cies that have tragic consequences in that region. Moved by these realities and by desire for a just peace in the Middle East, I decided several years ago to study American Christian Zionism, but I was not sure how or where to begin. It was suggested to me that I read Randall Balmer's book *Mine Eyes Have Seen the Glory: A Journey into the Evangelical Subculture in America.*[2] Balmer is a professor of American Christianity at Columbia University, and his book narrates his visits to several evangelical and fundamentalist congregations, communities, and institutions across the United States. I found the book compelling, and the idea of spending time in a Christian Zionist congregation seemed to be the ideal way forward. However, it was immediately apparent to me that it would be a serious task to determine what it would mean for a theological ethicist to do this type of research.

This led me to an exploration of the ethnographic turn many theologians have been proposing, as well as to shifts in the social sciences that could make theological use of social-scientific methods somewhat less problematic and potentially more interesting across the divisions between the disciplines. I developed the following account of various sources and streams of the ethnographic conversation among theologians and how these relate to the social scientific disciplines as well as to existing theological disciplines of congregational studies.

In 1974 the American Baptist theologian James McClendon published *Biography as Theology*,[3] in which he argued that utilitarianism (and other forms of quandary-based or what he called "decisionistic" ethics), as well as Christian realism, had run their course and proved insufficient. He insisted that Christian practitioners of ethics should have intentionally theological methods, and he suggested that the task of theology is "investigation of the convictions of a convictional community," in which those convictions are discovered, interpreted, criticized, and if needed and possible, transformed. One task of theological ethics thus conceived should be reflection upon exemplary lives that embody the convictions of a community, which he called "biography as theology." As an illustration of this proposal, McClendon reflected upon instantiations of the doctrine of atonement in the lives of four individuals.[4] He was not suggesting that atonement (or any other doctrine)

2. Randall Balmer, *Mine Eyes Have Seen the Glory: A Journey into the Evangelical Subculture in America*, 3rd ed. (New York: Oxford University Press, 2000).

3. James Wm. McClendon Jr., *Biography as Theology: How Life Stories Can Remake Today's Theology* (Nashville: Abingdon, 1974; Philadelphia: Trinity, 1990).

4. Dag Hammarskjöld, Martin Luther King Jr., Clarence Jordan, and Charles Ives. In

is only "a motif embodied in contemporary life stories," but rather that while doctrines can be stated propositionally, such statements must be tested through "contact with lived experience."

One of McClendon's former students, Theophus Smith, who now teaches at Emory University and is an Episcopal priest, sought to widen the task from individual biography to ethnography of communities, and his work in African American Christianity has focused on the community as "socio-political performer of strategically selected biblical stories and images."[5] Smith was influenced in this work not only by McClendon, but also by other theologians who have been central to the ethnographic turn in America, including Roman Catholic scholar of missions and theology and culture, Robert Schreiter.[6] Chief among these, of course, is George Lindbeck and his argument in *The Nature of Doctrine* for a "cultural-linguistic model" of theology.[7] Lindbeck described the existing models of theology as (1) cognitive-propositional, which views religion as a cognitive enterprise and doctrines as propositional descriptions of objective truth, (2) experiential-expressive, which views religion as personal experience and doctrines as expressions of inward feelings, attitudes, or orientations, and (3) the combination of these two attempted especially by ecumenical Roman Catholics. Lindbeck offered his cultural-linguistic model as an alternative that, learning from contemporary anthropological, sociological, and philosophical literature, views religion as resembling cultures with languages and forms of life in which doctrines function as rules of discourse, attitude, and action.

McClendon was also influential for Stanley Hauerwas, who has advocated the narrative description of specific congregations as an important task for both theologians and congregations themselves. He has suggested that sociological and anthropological methods may be used fruitfully as long as congregations' stories are learned and told with nor-

---

the 1994 edition, McClendon's new preface described how feminism had since transformed his theology and how regrettable he now found it that he included only lives of men.

5. Theophus Smith, "Ethnography-as-Theology: Inscribing the African American Sacred Story," in *Theology without Foundations: Religious Practice and the Future of Theological Truth*, ed. Stanley Hauerwas, Nancey Murphy, and Mark Nation (Nashville: Abingdon, 1994), pp. 117-39. See also *Conjuring Culture: Biblical Formations of Black America* (New York: Oxford University Press, 1994).

6. Author of *Constructing Local Theologies* (New York: Orbis, 1985).

7. George Lindbeck, *The Nature of Doctrine: Religion and Theology in a Postliberal Age* (Philadelphia: Westminster, 1984).

mative, not merely descriptive, intentions. Hauerwas has emphasized that social-scientific methods are unhelpful to theologians only when they are employed so uncritically or rigorously as to "methodologically preclude the theological claims necessary for the church's intelligibility."[8]

Among British theologians, the work that parallels the widespread influence on this conversation that Lindbeck's *Nature of Doctrine* had previously, is of course Milbank's *Theology and Social Theory*.[9] Milbank argued that various forms of secular thought are actually pagan or heretical/heterodox in origin; they are not secular in the sense they claim to be (free from theology), but rather are countertheologies and quasi theologies in disguise. Both sociology (in particular the sociology of religion) and forms of theology that have been dependent upon the "ontology of violence" at the heart of so-called secular social theories must be dismantled by orthodox Christian theology. In their place, Milbank called for a "social theology" that grows out of an "ontology of peace."

The works of Lindbeck and Milbank have contributed to shifting the conversation away from whether and how theologians can use the social sciences, toward how theologians can deeply engage with and thickly describe social groups and realities — as social scientists have done — while not accepting the premises of social sciences, but allowing the research to be shaped by theological traditions and normative concerns.

Subsequently, British theologians and theological ethicists such as Nicholas Adams and Samuel Wells have also been calling for ethnographic research methods. In an article in 2000, Adams, along with Charles Elliott, proposed wedding insights from Barth and Foucault to produce "a form of description which acknowledges the dogmatics which is at work within it, but is liberated to attend to the practices of description themselves."[10] And in his book *Transforming Fate into Destiny*, Wells used description of the community of Le Chambon, where thousands of Jews were sheltered and rescued by Christians during World War II, to test Stanley Hauerwas's theological claims concerning community, narrative, virtue, and habit; the

8. Stanley Hauerwas, "The Ministry of a Congregation: Rethinking Christian Ethics for a Church-Centered Seminary," in *Christian Existence Today: Essays on Church, World, and Living in Between* (Durham: Labyrinth Press, 1988), pp. 111-31.

9. John Milbank, *Theology and Social Theory: Beyond Secular Reason* (Oxford: Blackwell, 1990 and 2006).

10. Nicholas Adams and Charles Elliott, "Ethnography Is Dogmatics: Making Description Central to Systematic Theology," *Scottish Journal of Theology* 53, no. 3 (2000): 339-64.

role of the stranger; and how nonviolence provokes a community's imagination and political activism.[11]

There is also a current movement among both British and American theologians, on which the present volume draws and to which it contributes, that is advocating the use of ethnographic research in congregations for the formation of ecclesiology. Perhaps the most full-bodied and well-known argument in this conversation is Nicholas Healy's *Church, World, and the Christian Life*,[12] which argues for "ecclesiological ethnography" as a method that can help theologians overcome both the disconnected idealism and the undermining of the church's distinctiveness that Healy identifies as the twin errors of modern ecclesiology.[13]

As is perhaps already clear, most of these theologians are talking about doing ethnography much more than doing ethnography. The work that is most often cited by scholars on both sides of the Atlantic as an actual example of successful theological ethnography is William Cavanaugh's *Torture and Eucharist*,[14] which describes the rise of Pinochet's torturing military dictatorship in Chile, how the church was at first powerless to resist the regime, and how the church eventually found its voice and the strength to stand up against torture. Just as thousands of Chileans had disappeared into the junta's torture chambers, their bodies invisible to the world, the church had disappeared into the "spiritual" sphere, becoming invisible as a social body. According to Cavanaugh, it was through eucharistic practices that some Christians in some places and times in Chile were able to reappear as the body of Christ.

Simultaneous to the turn among these theologians toward ethnography, there have been shifts in the social sciences that perhaps make the theological employment of social-scientific methodological insights slightly less problematic than some theologians may have previously assumed. In general, the social sciences have experienced a turn away from modern, structuralist, and positivist understandings of social science and social-scientific

11. Samuel Wells, *Transforming Fate into Destiny: The Theological Ethics of Stanley Hauerwas* (Carlisle, U.K.: Paternoster, 1998), pp. 134-40.

12. Nicholas M. Healy, *Church, World, and the Christian Life: Practical-Prophetic Ecclesiology* (Cambridge: Cambridge University Press, 2000).

13. Other key works in this conversation include Mary McClintock Fulkerson, *Places of Redemption: Theology for a Worldly Church* (Oxford: Oxford University Press, 2007), and Delwin Brown, *Converging on Culture* (Oxford: Oxford University Press, 2001).

14. William Cavanaugh, *Torture and Eucharist: Theology, Politics, and the Body of Christ* (Oxford: Blackwell, 1998).

objectivity toward post-structuralist, constructivist, and interpretivist understandings of the situatedness of the social sciences themselves as well as of the individuals who conduct social-scientific research.

One interesting outcome of this shift is the legitimization among some anthropologists of activist research. These anthropologists argue that it is not only possible, but sometimes even preferable, for a social scientist who is personally dedicated to a specific cause to conduct research that aims not only to better understand the issue, but also to work together with those affected by and involved in the issue to find solutions.[15]

Among anthropologists, there has also been a coming-to-grips with the postcolonial realities of their discipline. One of the widespread assumptions of early anthropologists, who conducted research in regions colonized by Europeans, was that Christianity and Christian congregations were not fit subjects of study because they were nonindigenous; they were imposed upon the natives by Europeans. As colonialism began to break down, the assumption was that this imported religion would disappear. As anthropologists have had to grapple not only with the inaccuracy of this prediction but also with the problematic nature of their discipline's founding assumptions, some have come to advocate and practice the anthropology of Christianity, performing in-depth anthropological analyses of specific Christian communities.[16]

Some anthropologists of Christianity are writing ethnographies of particular congregations and Christian cultures or subcultures. One early

---

15. See, for example, Charles R. Hale, "What Is Activist Research?" *Items and Issues* 2, nos. 1-2 (Summer 2001): 13-15. *Items and Issues* is a publication of the Social Science Research Council. Cited by Jamie Pitts, "Liberative and Congregational: An Anabaptist Social Theory for Practical Theology" (paper delivered at the American Academy of Religion Annual Conference, Chicago, November 2, 2008).

16. Tim Jenkins gives a concise introduction to and overview of this field in a recent conference paper, in which he said, "This approach centres around a few names, in particular, the work of Fenella Cannell and Joel Robbins. Each has published a programmatic article in a major journal, 'The Christianity of Anthropology' in the *JRAI* [*Journal of the Royal Anthropological Institute*] (Cannell 2005), and 'Continuity thinking and the problem of Christian culture,' in *Current Anthropology* (Robbins 2007). Cannell has edited a volume entitled *The Anthropology of Christianity* (Cannell 2006), with a focussed introduction, and Robbins edits a series of the same name with the University of California Press, the first two works in which are Webb Keane's *Christian Moderns* (Keane 2007) and Matthew Engelke's *A Problem of Presence* (Engelke 2007). Robbins has also published an ethnography, *Becoming Sinners* (Robbins 2004), and a number of relevant papers." Quoted from Jenkins's paper, "Anthropology of Christianity: Situation and Critique" (paper presented to a conference on the anthropology of Christianity, University of Copenhagen, April 2009).

and particularly noteworthy example of such work by an anthropologist of Christianity is Susan Friend Harding's *Book of Jerry Falwell,* a study of Falwell and his followers as they were transformed from separatist fundamentalists into political activists in the 1980s.[17] More recent is Joel Robbins's ethnography of the Christian culture of the Urapmin people of Papua New Guinea.[18]

Familiarity with these ethnographies should give theologians pause concerning their use of the term "ethnography." Anthropologists usually mean by the term something much more specific than do most theologians. An ethnography is an extraordinarily comprehensive and holistic study of a culture that usually requires several months, if not years, spent inside that culture. When theologians use the term to describe anything from a brief historical vignette to a theological case study, I fear they may be confusing matters more than clarifying. "Theological practices of thick description" does not roll off the tongue so easily as "ethnography," but perhaps it more accurately names what most theologians calling for and doing "theological ethnography" are actually discussing, as opposed to ethnography proper.

When theologians speak specifically of theological ethnography in relation to the study and description of particular congregations, we of course must also turn our attention toward those scholars who have been studying Christian congregations for quite some time. The discipline of congregational studies is self-consciously shaped by inheritances from anthropology, sociology, organizational studies, and theology. In the United States, the discipline has been decidedly more shaped by organizational studies, and the aims of studying a congregation are often to understand broad, institutional aspects of church life such as leadership, authority, and work flow in order to discern what is and is not "working" in a congregation and what changes need to be made. For many American practitioners of congregational studies, a primary goal has been church growth. By contrast, congregational studies in the United Kingdom have been formed more by sociology and anthropology, and practitioners have often focused on congregations as social systems simply to be understood on their own terms.

In both countries, those practitioners of congregational studies who

17. Susan Friend Harding, *The Book of Jerry Falwell: Fundamentalist Language and Politics* (Princeton: Princeton University Press, 2000).

18. Joel Robbins, *Becoming Sinners: Christianity and Moral Torment in a Papua New Guinea Society* (Berkeley: University of California Press, 2004).

have primarily theological, instead of organizational or sociological, interests are called "practical theologians." Their work resonates more with pastoral theology than with systematics, and often begins not with a research question formed by a scholar but with a congregational need. This type of congregational study often involves corporate approaches in which the members of the congregation actively engage in the research project and aim to make changes based on their findings. Some practical theologians more intentionally merge pastoral and systematic theology through the use of critical correlation, in which a particular theological doctrine is brought into dialogue with a contemporary congregation.[19]

It was with all this in mind that I went to visit Pastor George's church. I spent an academic term with this American Christian Zionist congregation, where I observed congregational life and conducted long, qualitative interviews. I sought to immerse myself in the pro-Israel culture of the congregation through attending worship services, Sunday school classes, prayer meetings, planning meetings, and large-scale events, reading the books that were being read and recommended by members, and exploring the Zionist organizations with which they are partners.

I was fortunate to be able to visit the congregation when their pro-Israel activism was at an annual peak. While I was there, the congregation prepared for and staged an extravagant evening program to honor Israel. Their pastor, whom everyone calls Pastor George, preached a five-week sermon series on Israel and the end times. Pastor George's wife, Cheryl, who is director of the congregation's Israel Outreach Ministry, prepared a group of young singers and dancers for their departure for their annual summer tour of performances at Israeli military bases, where their goal was to communicate God's love for and blessings upon Israeli troops. A large group of delegates also prepared to join thousands of Christian Zionists to lobby the United States government through the Washington, D.C., summit of Pastor John Hagee's organization, Christians United for Israel.

One of the main reasons I chose to study Pastor George's congregation is that they have provided support for an "adopted settlement" in the West Bank for nearly fifteen years, and this partnership and others like it have contributed significantly to the growth and stabilization of several

---

19. On congregational studies, see Helen Cameron et al., *Studying Local Churches: A Handbook* (London: SCM, 2005), and Matthew Guest, Karin Tusting, and Linda Woodhead, eds., *Congregational Studies in the UK: Christianity in a Post-Christian Context* (Aldershot: Ashgate, 2004).

settlements that will almost inevitably remain in Israeli hands should a two-state solution be reached. In other words, these American Christians have been helping Israeli settlers to establish facts on the ground. I was able to visit the settlement to see the fruits of this partnership firsthand and interview the settlers about their relationships with Christian Zionists.

I arrived with preformed theological questions about Christian Zionist eschatology and social ethics, and with a goal in mind to make normative claims about Christian theological ethics, but I had also learned a great deal about the openness to a community's own voice that is central to the anthropologist's practice of ethnography. This resulted in research that confirmed some of my preconceptions about Christian Zionism while troubling and disconfirming many others.

I concluded that the deeply problematic eschatology of Christian Zionism so alters their Christology and ecclesiology as to disconnect them from the christological and ecclesiological resources that are necessary for well-formed Christian social ethics. I may have been able to reach that conclusion through textual research alone. However, my further conclusion, which was entirely unexpected and which I feel sure I could not have reached without spending time with the congregation, listening to and observing the enactment of their theo-political discourse, is that their understanding of how eschatology relates to social ethics was surprisingly persuasive and even convicting.

Contrary to popular stereotypes that portray Christian Zionists as believing they can make Jesus return sooner through their pro-Israel activism, I found this congregation had rightly discerned that eschatology is not only a chronology of end-times events, but is also a doctrine of God's intentions for humanity and all creation, and of the status of those intentions in the time between the two advents of Jesus Christ. They believe they are engaging in the discernment of God's ultimate intentions for creation, discernment of God's ways of enacting these intentions in the world, and discernment of how they should best cooperate with God through participation in those purposes and those ways. I do not believe I could have been open to the complexity or the virtues of this understanding if I had not listened to and observed its enactment in person.

In my day-to-day interactions with Pastor George's congregation, there were long spans of time during which I was experiencing the lives of entirely average, middle-class Americans in an entirely mainstream evangelical megachurch. There were moments of sympathy and appreciation, moments of friendship and warmth. And there were moments of repugnance, shock, and dismay at certain beliefs, comments, and practices. This is the ambivalent reality of the human condition that is only fully experienced by entering into people's lives. I was not fully prepared for this ambivalence, and I quickly realized that I would not have been able to take Christian Zionists truly seriously as fellow Christians if my research had been only textual. This also taught me that the theologians practicing "ethnography" must take the complexity of human beings seriously enough neither to overstate the negative aspects of congregations that are deemed misguided in theology and ethics nor to understate the negative aspects of congregations that are deemed exemplary.

Theologians, and I would argue theological ethicists in particular, should intentionally and carefully attend to the complex realities of the actual people involved in the compelling theological and social issues of our day. Genuine attentiveness to people and genuine engagement with the complexities of their lives are only possible through research methods that take theologians beyond the desk and the library and into those lives. As we continue to discuss, explore, and develop such methods, we must be serious apprentices of sociologists, anthropologists, philosophers, and historians — all those who have long grappled with questions of how best to attend to the complexities of the human condition. However, in our apprenticeship to other disciplines, we must not lose sight of the crucial distinction that our task is first and foremost theological.

In one sense I am only saying what has already been said by many Christian ethicists in the last few decades: that it is in no way helpful to preserve the old distinction between theological ethics and social ethics, which has followed modern, scientific distinctions between so-called pure and applied research. However, I hope I am also saying more than this — more than just that Christian ethicists are theologians, not social scientists, and yet theologians should not be entirely dismissive of what we can learn from the social sciences. I am suggesting that more theologians who are writing on war and peace should spend time in war zones, with victims of war, with soldiers, with peacemakers. More theologians who are writing on the environment should visit sites of particular environmental concern, environmentalist groups, anti-environmentalist activists. And more theologians should spend time deeply engaging with the lives of particular Christian congregations.

As those who claim to be reflecting on the Christian life, theological ethicists in particular must seriously consider more frequent employment of research methods that involve encounter with actual Christians in the communities in which they are seeking to live the Christian life. These may be entirely average congregations, or particularly exemplary congregations, or (as in the case of my own research) congregations engaged in practices that the ethicist finds particularly problematic. For all those Christian ethicists who identify to any degree with the ecclesiological and ethnographic turns that theology and ethics have taken in the last few decades, the study of particular congregations should be a clear and pressing consideration in the formulation of research projects.

For all Christians studying congregations, attention to the complex admixture of faithful and flawed convictions and practices in other individuals and congregations can also helpfully draw attention to one's own unexamined assumptions, beliefs, and practices. This dynamic takes on a unique and important function when congregational research is done by a theologian for theological purposes — namely, that God is a recognized actor in the analytical process. The theologian can encounter the congregation not as subjects pinned under a microscope, but as persons held before God. And when persons are held before God that we might understand them better, their peculiarities for good or ill become prisms through which God's light allows us to see ourselves and our own peculiarities more clearly. When we enter into the lives of those we are researching, we must observe and question and listen as theologians. We are not scientists, and human beings are not our subjects. We are theologians, and we enter into the lives and struggles of fellow human beings because we need to hold them before God and for God to hold them before us so that we can see them as they are, and allow them to help us see ourselves anew for what we are.

CHAPTER 6

The Cultivation of Theological Vision:
Theological Attentiveness and
the Practice of Ministry

Alister E. McGrath

The current interest in the place and purpose of practical theology concerns more than the question of the relation of theology and ministry; it is more fundamentally about the nature of theology itself. In this paper, I want to set out and explore my fundamental conviction that Christian theology is seen at its best and at its most authentic when it engages and informs the life of the Christian community on the one hand, and is in turn engaged and informed by that life on the other. In short: theology is grounded in the life of a praying, worshiping, and reflecting community, which seeks to find the best manner of expressing that faith intellectually, and allows it to generate and inform its best practices. Theology does not create faith, but reflects a faith that is already present. Faith unquestionably seeks understanding;[1] it also seeks application.

This vision of theology is nothing new; after all, some such notions of theology can be argued to undergird the reflections and ministries of most classic theologians of the Christian church.[2] Yet it is a vision that needs to be recovered, revitalized, and reappropriated from time to time. This collection of essays seems an admirable and timely occasion to reflect afresh on this traditional theme, in the light of contemporary concerns and op-

---

1. The famous slogan *fides quaerens intellectum* (faith seeking understanding) of Anselm of Canterbury should be noted here: Marilyn McCord Adams, "*Fides Quaerens Intellectum:* St. Anselm's Method in Philosophical Theology," *Faith and Philosophy* 9 (1992): 409-35.

2. See Ellen T. Charry, *By the Renewing of Your Minds: The Pastoral Function of Christian Doctrine* (New York: Oxford University Press, 1997).

portunities. In this paper, I intend to reflect on the need to develop "theological attentiveness" as a means of safeguarding the distinctiveness of Christian ministry and social action, while at the same time giving it both depth and stability through grounding it in a theological vision of reality.

An essential part of that vision of reality is the creation of theological space for empirical space for the empirical study of Christian communities and their practices — not as an independent and unrelated matter, peripheral to the tasks of theology, but as an integral aspect of the theological enterprise, when properly conceived and understood. A theological understanding of the nature of the Christian community leads naturally into the empirical study of its forms and practices as a critical and positive means of enabling it to achieve its proper goals, and live out its proper identity.

The Church as an Interpretive Community

Part of the "discipleship of the mind" that arises from Christian faith has to do with the cultivation of a Christian "map of meaning"[3] — a distinctively Christian way of seeing things. At both the individual and the communal level, Christianity is nourished and sustained by a vision of reality, capable of impacting upon the mind, the emotions, and the imagination. This vision of reality is embodied in the Christian narrative, and celebrated and proclaimed in Christian worship. We are enabled to see the world and ourselves in a new light on account of the interpretative lens of the Christian tradition.

The Christian faith thus offers a way of seeing reality that brings about a transformation and a transvaluation of our understanding of the world, and our place within it. It strips away our delusions about reality, illuminating it and bringing it into sharp focus so that we may see it as it really is. The Christian church is a community that has been molded by this vision, and which in turn reflects it to the world through its core narrative, symbols, and sacramental actions.[4] It is thus a community of discernment, which sees the world in a way quite distinct from that of its secular and religious alternatives.

3. For this notion, see Jordan B. Peterson, *Maps of Meaning: The Architecture of Belief* (New York: Routledge, 1999), pp. 19-215.

4. For the relevance of this point to the postmodern cultural context, see Alister E. McGrath, "Erzählung, Gemeinschaft und Dogma: Reflexionen über das Zeugnis der Kirche in der Postmoderne," *Theologische Beiträge* 41, no. 1 (2010): 25-38.

The key point here is that we see things in a new way on account of faith, opening up new possibilities for perception and attention.[5] In one sense, practical theology can be considered as being about theologically attentive engagement with the tasks of ministry. The New Testament affirms the transformation of the human situation that results from the gospel. This renewal and regeneration is not restricted to moral and relational matters, but extends to an intellectual vision, summed up in Paul's great injunction to be actively "transformed by the renewal of your minds," rather than being passively "conformed to the world" (Rom. 12:2). The New Testament uses a wide range of images to describe this change, many of which suggest a change in the way in which we see things: our eyes are opened, and a veil is removed (Acts 9:9-19; 2 Cor. 3:13-16).

Through faith, Christians develop habits of engagement with reality that allow it to be seen, understood, and evaluated in new ways.[6] Such habits of thought are both generated and sustained by the Christian gospel, especially as this is proclaimed and embodied in the life of the church. The Christian church thus embodies a way of seeing the world that is proclaimed and sustained by its controlling words, images, and actions. We are thus called upon to see the world in its true light, by adopting a Christian *schema,* a "mental map" that enables the world to be illuminated and brought into focus, so that it may be seen as it really is. Stanley Hauerwas, writing from an Anabaptist perspective, thus rightly insists that "the church serves the world by giving the world the means to see itself truthfully."[7]

The Christian tradition thus offers us a framework or lens through which we may "see" the world of human behavior.[8] This is provided by sustained, detailed, extended reflection on the Christian narrative, which is articulated and enacted in the life and witness of the church. We might think of the church as an "interpretive community," to use Stanley Fish's

5. See further Alister E. McGrath, *The Open Secret: A New Vision for Natural Theology* (Oxford: Blackwell, 2008); Alister E. McGrath, "'Schläft ein Lied in allen Dingen'? Gedanken über die Zukunft der natürlichen Theologie," *Theologische Zeitschrift* 65, no. 3 (2009): 246-60.

6. For some useful reflections, see Stephen Pattison, *Seeing Things: Deepening Relations with Visual Artefacts* (London: SCM, 2007).

7. Stanley Hauerwas, *The Peaceable Kingdom: A Primer in Christian Ethics* (Notre Dame, Ind.: University of Notre Dame Press, 1983), pp. 101-2.

8. See Stanley Hauerwas, *Vision and Virtue: Essays in Christian Ethical Reflection* (Notre Dame, Ind.: University of Notre Dame Press, 1974).

luminous term,[9] which coalesces around and is characterized by a particular "point of view or way of organizing experience."[10] Fish developed the notion of the "interpretive community" primarily to account for a potential difficulty that emerged within postmodern explanations of the emergence of influential interpretations of texts, when no such interpretation could be regarded as "authoritative."[11] Ecclesiologically, this can be reformulated in terms of the crystallization of a community around what Rowan Williams styles "the one focal interpretive story of Jesus"[12] — a particular interpretation of the texts of Scripture, history, and nature, understood in terms of the life, death, and resurrection of Jesus Christ, or a Trinitarian economy of salvation of creation, redemption, and consummation. Faith thus entails that the community of faith sees the world in a manner that differs strikingly from what Charles Taylor termed the prevailing "social imaginaries."[13]

The essential point here is that we have to see the world and ourselves in a Christian way before we can minister faithfully and effectively. How we *act* is profoundly influenced by what we see, including how we see ourselves as active agents. The *practice* of ministry rests on a theologically grounded *vision* for ministry, which allows for critical reflection upon the actions of the church in the light of the gospel and the Christian tradition. Although the rise of theology as an academic discipline has sometimes led to a separation of its theoretical and practical aspects, this has been corrected in recent years through the rise of "practical theology."[14] Christian theology is capable of providing a vision that inspires and energizes the

9. Stanley Fish, *Is There a Text in This Class? The Authority of Interpretive Communities* (Cambridge: Harvard University Press, 1980), pp. 147-74.

10. Fish, *Is There a Text?* p. 141.

11. For reflections on the way in which the notion can be appropriated, see Michael Calvin McGee, "Text, Context, and the Fragmentation of Contemporary Culture," *Western Journal of Speech Communication* 54, no. 2 (1990): 274-89.

12. For the context of this phrase, see Rowan Williams, *Resurrection: Interpreting the Easter Gospel*, 2nd ed. (London: DLT, 2002), pp. 61-62.

13. Charles Taylor, *Modern Social Imaginaries* (Durham, N.C.: Duke University Press, 2002), p. 23.

14. See, for example, Don S. Browning, ed., *Practical Theology: The Emerging Field in Theology, Church, and World* (San Francisco: Harper and Row, 1983); Paul Ballard and John Pritchard, *Practical Theology in Action: Christian Thinking in the Service of Church and Society* (London: SPCK, 1996); Gerben Heitink, *Practical Theology: History, Theory, and Action Domains* (Grand Rapids: Eerdmans, 1999); Miroslav Volf and Dorothy C. Bass, *Practicing Theology: Beliefs and Practices in Christian Life* (Grand Rapids: Eerdmans, 2002).

pastoral tasks and ministry of the church, while enabling these to be scrutinized in the light of the gospel on the one hand, and related to the demands and challenges of the present day on the other.

So how is the community of faith to maintain its own distinctive way of seeing things, without losing touch with the world within which it must operate? At this point, I shall draw on the notion of "attentiveness" or "mindfulness" — in other words, the disciplined habit of developing ways of seeing or envisaging reality.[15] We begin by considering the notion of "attentiveness" as set out in the writings of Iris Murdoch (1919-90).

On Theological Attentiveness

Murdoch found the notion of "attentiveness" set out in the writings of Simone Weil (1909-43), especially her essay "Attention and Will."[16] In this paper, Weil used the French term *attention*, which has overtones of waiting, expectation, or longing.[17] To speak of attention in this way is fundamentally to distinguish between *looking* and *seeing*. For Weil, proper attention leads to a transformation of spiritual vision, opening up new ways of understanding the world and behaving within it. The idea is developed further by Murdoch, who defines it as "a just and loving gaze directed upon an individual reality."[18]

Murdoch's point is that the reality of the world is hidden from us, until we are enabled to see it properly. It is a point familiar from the New Testament, which is perhaps unexpectedly developed further in the writings of Murdoch, who emphasized the severe limitations of the human vision of reality. "By opening our eyes, we do not necessarily see what confronts us. . . . Our minds are continually active, fabricating an anx-

15. Kirk Warren Brown, Richard M. Ryan, and J. David Creswell, "Mindfulness: Theoretical Foundations and Evidence for Its Salutary Effects," *Psychological Inquiry* 18, no. 4 (2007): 211-37.

16. Simone Weil, "Attention and Will," in *Gravity and Grace* (New York: Putnam, 1952), pp. 169-76.

17. See the study of Martin Andic, "One Moment of Pure Attention Is Worth All the Works in the World," *Cahiers Simone Weil* 21, no. 4 (1998): 347-68. The translation of *attente de Dieu* as "waiting for God" rather misses this important point.

18. Iris Murdoch, *The Sovereignty of Good* (London: Macmillan, 1970), p. 34. For comment, see Charles Taylor, *Sources of the Self: The Making of the Modern Identity* (Cambridge: Harvard University Press, 1989), p. 96.

ious, usually self-preoccupied, often falsifying *veil* which partially conceals the world."[19]

To see things as they actually are thus requires the development of the skill of *discernment* as much as observational attentiveness. We do not come to know something fully simply by looking at it; we must "see" it at a deeper level. The development of this habit of principled "seeing" enables us, according to Murdoch, to "grow by looking."[20] Seeing things as they really are, penetrating beneath the surface of appearances, is both the goal and the outcome of the cultivation of perceptual attentiveness.

For Murdoch, it is "a *task* to come to see the world as it is."[21] When this is approached within a Christian framework, this transformation is to be seen as a work of divine grace and renewal, enabling us to see and act in ways that transcend both the empirical world and our own natural capacities. This is a significant point of divergence; nevertheless, Murdoch's analysis can still illuminate our reflections, by emphasizing the importance of principled reflection on the world. The person who deliberately and intentionally cultivates such habits of perception will see the world in a way that transcends the empirical, thus opening the way to moral action. The precondition for virtue is thus the capacity to see both the world and the self, as moral agent, as they really are. "Virtue is the attempt to pierce the veil of selfish consciousness and join the world as it really is."[22] As Lawrence Blum pointed out in his discerning analysis of her approach, Murdoch emphasizes that moral vision is something that must be worked at and developed. It builds on our past experiences, which help teach us "what to notice, how to care, what to be sensitive to, how to get beyond [our] own biases and narrowness of vision."[23]

Murdoch's ideal of "attention" as a compelling particularity of vision has much to say to a Christian "discipleship of the mind,"[24] which encour-

---

19. Murdoch, *The Sovereignty of Good*, p. 82.

20. Murdoch, *The Sovereignty of Good*, p. 30.

21. Murdoch, *The Sovereignty of Good*, p. 91.

22. Murdoch, *The Sovereignty of Good*, p. 93.

23. Lawrence Blum, "Particularity and Responsiveness," in *The Emergence of Morality in Young Children*, ed. Jerome Kagan and Sharon Lamb (Chicago: University of Chicago Press, 1987), pp. 306-37. See also Susan McDonough, "Iris Murdoch's Notion of Attention: Seeing the Moral Life in Teaching," in *Philosophy of Education Yearbook 2000*, ed. Lynda Stone (Urbana, Ill.: Philosophy of Education Society, 2000), pp. 217-25.

24. On this general theme, see Alister McGrath, *Mere Theology: Christian Faith and the Discipleship of the Mind* (London: SPCK, 2010).

ages a specifically and authentically Christian engagement with reality — such as the reading of texts,[25] or pastoral ministry. It has considerable potential for practical theology, as it emphasizes the need to bring a theological lens to bear upon the understanding and evaluation of both the pastoral situation and the pastoral agent. Theology has a genuine role to play in shaping and informing our "beholding" of pastoral tasks; yet it is incomplete without an empirical engagement with those tasks. We are offered a way of "seeing" capable of being refined and enhanced, and then *used* as we reflect on pastoral tasks and situations on the one hand, and on ourselves as pastoral agents on the other.

Murdoch's notion of "attentiveness" insists that particularity is to be respected, and not to be swallowed up in a generalized theory. Her first novel, *Under the Net* (1954), contains an extended reflection on the manner in which a "net of meaning" is necessary if particularities are to be described, while noting that it has the potential to conceal those particularities through its universalizing tendencies. As one of her characters comments, "The movement away from theory and generality is the movement toward truth. All theorizing is a fight. We must be ruled by the situation itself, and this is unutterably particular."[26] Practical theology brings a Christian "net of meaning" to particular situations — without in any way denying the specificity of that situation, or trying to convert it into something else. It is about being *attentive* to the specifics of a given situation — a given *place* — when seen through the lens of the Christian tradition.

So how might we cultivate this habit of theological attentiveness? How might we develop the committed, caring, and discerning theological gaze that permits us to strip away the shadows, dust, and prejudice that so often impair our spiritual vision? One obvious answer is to allow one's habits of sight and thought to be shaped by the Christian tradition. Stanley Hauerwas is an important representative of this approach. He rightly notes how immersion and participation in the corporate life of the church allow the formation and emergence of a theological vision, which is essential to ethical or pastoral reflection and action: "The primary task of Christian ethics involves an attempt to help us see. For we can only act within the world we can see, and we can only see the world

25. See, for example, Christophe Cobb, "Seeing 'That of God' in Texts: Christian Practices for Training in Perception," *Christianity and Literature* 58, no. 2 (2009): 243-51.
26. Iris Murdoch, *Under the Net* (London: Vintage, 2002), p. 91.

rightly by being trained to see. We do not come to see just by looking, but by disciplined skills developed through initiation into a narrative."[27] These "disciplined skills" arise from immersion in the Christian story, especially as this focuses on Jesus of Nazareth, noting the loving attentiveness toward individuals and communities that it both embodies and commends.

Hauerwas rightly emphasizes that this is a skill that is to be learned, not so much by reading textbooks, but through application and action — in short, through an apprenticeship to a master. Hauerwas — the son of a bricklayer — uses the art of laying bricks to illustrate this point. "To lay brick you must be initiated into the craft of bricklaying by a master craftsman."[28] Laying bricks is a skill located within a tradition, which is mastered through initiation and *practice*. "In order to lay brick you must hour after hour, day after day, lay brick." It is a skill that is learned through *doing* — through immersion in a craft, under the guidance of the wise and experienced — not a technique that is acquired through reading.

So how might such an approach illuminate practical theology? We may begin our reflections by considering the notion of "theological reflection," now deeply embedded in Western approaches to theological education and ministerial formation.

Theological Attentiveness and Theological Reflection

Practical theology involves the assessment of situations and ministerial possibilities, partly through observation. One of the most important themes in contemporary philosophy of science is that the process of observation is theory-laden.[29] We do not simply "see" things; we see them through a set of theoretical spectacles, which help us interpret and assess what we observe. To put this another way: we do not simply "see" or "experience" things; we see or experience them *as* something. An implicit process of interpretation and evaluation accompanies our engagement with reality. This point has important implications for natural theology, which

27. Stanley Hauerwas, "The Demands of a Truthful Story: Ethics and the Pastoral Task," *Chicago Studies* 21, no. 1 (1982): 59-71; quote at pp. 65-66.

28. Stanley Hauerwas, "Discipleship as a Craft, Church as a Disciplined Community," *Christian Century*, October 1991, pp. 881-84.

29. Matthias Adam, *Theoriebeladenheit und Objektivität. Zur Rolle von Beobachtungen in den Naturwissenschafte* (Frankfurt am Main: Ontos Verlag, 2002).

has not been properly appreciated until recently.[30] Christians cannot avoid "seeing" nature in a Christian manner, which subtly nuances and influences both what they actually observe and how they assess this.

Christians reflect theologically, whether they are aware of doing this or not. In many ways, the issue to be discussed is how to bring such implicit theological assumptions from the background to the foreground, so that they may be identified, interrogated, and critically applied. Yet many models of "theological reflection" in use within practical theology appear to assume that we "observe" or "experience" *before* we bring explicit theological presuppositions to bear on what is thus observed or experienced.

In 1990 Laurie Green proposed a "cycle of theological reflection" that he conceived as an "imaginative leap which sets up an interplay between the explored issue and the Christian faith tradition so that each is affected by the other."[31] This influential model emphasizes the importance of bridging the hermeneutical gap between practical experience and theological reflection: "Our reflective task is to find some way of bridging this cultural gap and seeing connections between the Christian heritage on one side and our present experience on the other — to hear resonances, to ring bells, to sense similarities, to sense opposition, to build up a whole range of sensitivities to the tradition so that we can draw upon it to check our present actions and understandings and see if our own story is part of the Jesus story, or not."[32] There is much to commend such an approach, in its original form or in later variants, such as that proposed by Stephen Pattison.[33] Yet it is important to appreciate that an implicit, intuitive process of theological reflection is already taking place in the processes of observation and reflection, in which the theological *schema* or "mental map" of the Christian observer subtly influences what is actually observed, and the action subsequently taken within that situation.

The primary task of practical theology is to enable us to see situations and individuals from the standpoint of the Christian tradition, so that we may evaluate them and behave toward them in an authentically Christian way. Such a process of theological reflection does not begin through a conscious decision to bring a Christian scheme to bear on the

---

30. This is a major theme in my own approach: see McGrath, *The Open Secret*, pp. 80-110, 171-216.

31. Laurie Green, *Let's Do Theology* (London: Continuum, 1990), p. 93.

32. Green, *Let's Do Theology*, p. 80.

33. Stephen Pattison, "Some Straw for Bricks: A Basic Introduction to Theological Reflection," in *The Blackwell Reader in Pastoral and Practical Theology*, ed. James Woodward and Stephen Pattison (Oxford: Blackwell, 2000), pp. 135-45.

neutral and objective process of observation. That process of interpretation and reflection is already under way, even if it is not fully articulated or completely understood. The Christian "map of reality" is already being absorbed through participation in the Christian community, in which the reading of Scripture, the inhabitation of liturgical forms, and exposure to preaching shape our outlooks. What is additionally required here is the *intentional* development of rigorous and principled habits of thought and action that enable such implicit reflection to be made explicit and principled. As Hauerwas rightly noted in relation to the shaping of ethical habits of thought, we need to be "trained to see" through "disciplined skills developed through initiation into a narrative."

This amounts to a reassertion of the primacy of theology, though not necessarily in its traditional dogmatic forms. Hauerwas's approach involves the recognition of the importance of community, tradition, and narrative in shaping the reflective mind, enabling the emergence and consolidation of specific ways of thinking and evaluating situations. Doctrines emerge as communities reflect on narratives,[34] and are best seen as secondary to the primary core of faith, articulated doxologically in worship and prayer. To speak of theological attentiveness is to highlight the importance of allowing the specifics of the Christian narrative to shape the way in which we understand the world and society, in order to better understand how to serve them.

In what follows, we shall develop this principle of theological attentiveness, and use it to illuminate and inform one important aspect of practical theology — the location of pastoral action.

Attentiveness to Pastoral Location: A Theology of Place

One of the most exciting works of theology that I read as a young man was T. F. Torrance's *Space, Time, and Incarnation*, first published in 1969, which I first read while I was a research student in Cambridge in 1979.[35] I found that it opened up new ways of thinking about the incarnation, and valued the

---

34. A point I emphasized in my 1990 Bampton Lectures: see Alister E. McGrath, *The Genesis of Doctrine: A Study in the Foundations of Doctrinal Criticism* (Oxford: Blackwell, 1990). See also Kevin J. Vanhoozer, *The Drama of Doctrine: A Canonical-Linguistic Approach to Christian Theology* (Louisville: Westminster John Knox, 2005).

35. Thomas Forsyth Torrance, *Space, Time, and Incarnation* (London: Oxford University Press, 1969).

stimulus that it brought to my own theological development. Yet I found myself uneasy about one aspect of this work. The doctrine of the incarnation was framed in terms of how God could enter into a world of space and time. At times, Torrance's analysis seemed to concern how a transcendent God could be positioned using the four coordinates x, y, z, and t. While this was undoubtedly theologically significant, it seemed to stand at a certain distance from a more biblical account of things. Here, the emphasis fell upon the expectation that God would enter into the lives and history of his people Israel. Where Torrance spoke of *space* and *time*, the Bible seemed much more concerned with *place* and *history*. Although I welcomed Torrance's conceptually rigorous account of the incarnation, and valued its intellectual integrity, I found it relatively difficult to use his approach in pastoral ministry.

Although I had yet to discover this, new insights were beginning to emerge that would enable me to make those connections more rigorously. In 1978, the noted Old Testament scholar Walter Brueggemann published his landmark work *The Land*.[36] Brueggemann argued that, to make sense of the theological concerns of ancient Israel, a fundamental distinction had to be made between "space" and "place." "Place is space which has historical meanings, where some things have happened which are now remembered and which provide continuity and identity across generations. Place is space in which important words have been spoken which have established identity, defined vocation, and envisioned destiny."[37]

There are obvious parallels here — sadly not noted by Brueggemann — with Simone Weil's notion of "rootedness" *(enracinement)*, which enables a "state" *(état)* to be seen as a "country" *(patrie* or *pays)*.[38] The same entity is observed in each case, but is *seen* in a very different way — leading to significantly different approaches to its political evaluation and engagement. Both Weil and Murdoch offer us intellectual frameworks for understanding how a *space* becomes a *place*.

Brueggemann's analysis of the history of Israel shifted scholarly discussion away from the abstract notions of space and time, and anchored it firmly to the realities of human existence, expressed in place and history. It rightly emphasized how *places* play a critically important place in human life, not least in that they function as anchor points for memory, identity,

---

36. Walter Brueggemann, *The Land: Place as Gift, Promise, and Challenge in Biblical Faith*, 2nd ed. (Philadelphia: Fortress, 2002).

37. Brueggemann, *The Land*, pp. 1-13, quote at p. 5.

38. Bertrand Saint-Sernin, *L'action politique selon Simone Weil* (Paris: Éditions du Cerf, 1988), p. 177.

and aspiration. Brueggemann's approach has considerable potential to illuminate Christian spirituality, particularly in relation to the role of pilgrimages to specific holy places. Yet for our purposes, it also has additional value in informing practical theology, by offering ways of engaging with some of the core questions of Christian ministry. How do I understand this place in which I minister? In which I live? What difference can I make?

This new interest in the specificities of place has, of course, been given new intellectual energy through the rise of postmodernism, which emphasizes the importance of local situations and narratives.[39] The approach can be taken further, making use of insights from contemporary sociology and anthropology. For example, the French anthropologist Marc Augé (b. 1935) draws a distinction between "place" *(lieu)*, which is associated with historical memories and able to sustain a meaningful social life, and what he calls "non-places" *(non-lieux)*, which are physical locations with no historical memories in which no meaningful social life is possible, such as airport departure lounges or supermarkets.[40] These, Augé argues, are ephemeral places of individual transition and passage, not places of habitation and communal significance.[41]

Theologians, especially those concerned with questions of pastoral ministry and spirituality, have realized the importance of these new developments.[42] On this approach, we must learn to speak of God entering, not just into space and time, but into *our place* and *our history.* The measure of God's involvement is no longer described *mathematically,* in terms of some abstract metaphysical trajectory, but *personally,* in terms of God's entering into and inhabiting the realities of human existence. To say that God enters into place and history is immediately to highlight the divine inhabitation of our world — not as a geometrical coordinate, but as a living human being, existing and acting under conditions that are manifestly ours.

---

39. See Edward S. Casey, *The Fate of Place: A Philosophical History* (Berkeley: University of California Press, 1998), pp. 285-330.

40. Marc Augé, *Non-lieux: Introduction à une anthropologie de la surmodernité* (Paris: Éditions du Seuil, 1992). See further the useful discussion in Emer O'Beirne, "Mapping the *Non-Lieu* in Marc Augé's Writings," *Forum for Modern Language Studies* 42, no. 1 (2006): 38-50.

41. Augé, *Non-lieux,* p. 101: "un monde. . . promis à l'individualité solitaire, au passage, au provisoire et à l'éphémère."

42. See, for example, Philip F. Sheldrake, *Spaces for the Sacred: Place, Memory, and Identity* (Baltimore: Johns Hopkins University Press, 2001); John Inge, *A Christian Theology of Place* (Aldershot: Ashgate, 2003), pp. 59-122; Mary McClintock Fulkerson, *Places of Redemption: Theology for a Worldly Church* (Oxford: Oxford University Press, 2007), pp. 231-52.

But my chief concern here is with issues of ministry — with the question of how a theological vision of reality shapes the life of the church and its ministers. More particularly, I wish to consider how such a theological approach creates conceptual space for the empirical investigation of communities and practices. To develop this, I suggest that we consider a model based on the wine industry — the *terroir*. This idea encapsulates the notion of a local identity, which is resistant to globalization or universalization, and must be understood in terms of its own distinct geography and culture.[43] The notion has become politically important in global trade negotiations, on account of the designation of certain "regions or localities" in which "a given quality, reputation or other characteristic of the good is essentially attributable to its geographical origin."[44]

The *terroir* designates a local region in which certain practices, qualities, and characteristics are socially embedded. *Terroir* is not simply a geographical designation; it is itself a social construction, designating cultural and professional values and practices.[45] The characteristics of the wine produced in a given *terroir* are shaped by the soil, the climate, the grape types, and the methods of production — all of which are specific to that given locality. The critical point here concerns respect, even reverence, for the specificities of place: "Terroir has become a buzz word in English language wine literature. This lighthearted use disregards reverence for the land which is a critical, invisible element of the term. The true concept is not easily grasped but includes physical elements of the vineyard habitat — the vine, subsoil, siting, drainage, and microclimate. Beyond the measurable ecosystem, there is an additional dimension — the spiritual aspect that recognizes the joys, the heartbreaks, the pride, the sweat, and the frustrations of its history."[46]

Some reject the importance of place in order to achieve homogeneity

43. Jonathan Murdoch, Terry Marsden, and Jo Banks, "Quality, Nature, and Embeddedness: Some Theoretical Considerations in the Context of the Food Sector," *Economic Geography* 76, no. 1 (2000): 107-25. The concept of *terroir* is also important in relation to olive oil, coffee, and tea.

44. See Elizabeth Barham, "Translating Terroir: The Global Challenge of French AOC Labeling," *Journal of Rural Studies* 19, no. 1 (2003): 127-38.

45. See especially Laurence Berard and Philippe Marchenay, "Lieux, temps et preuves: la construction sociale des produits de terroir," in *Terrain: Carnets du patrimoine ethnologique* (Paris: Ministère de la Culture, 1995), pp. 153-64.

46. James E. Wilson, *Terroir: The Role of Geology, Climate, and Culture in the Making of French Wines* (Berkeley: University of California Press, 1998), p. 55.

and consistency. Many large-scale wine producers in Australia and California blend wines made from grapes harvested across a wide geographical area in order to achieve uniformity of taste on a year-by-year basis. This is about the *abolition* of place, not its affirmation. Wines defined by their *terroir* make no such concessions. The wine is determined by a "defined place,"[47] which reflects the local climate, soil, and wine-making traditions.[48] Place is something to be celebrated, affirmed, and respected. It is shaped by local factors, varying from one year to another in response to the natural environment. There is no "typical" *terroir,* no universal template that can be applied to every situation.

There is an obvious and not unhelpful parallel between *terroir* and the parish church. Each is specific to its own distinct place. Each is shaped by the interaction of physical geography and human culture. And each is open to empirical investigation. Recognizing the importance of "place" demands that we treat it as a particularity, a distinct entity that cannot be reduced to a template or stereotype. A theology of place urges us to value the particular, identifying and appreciating its distinct characteristics, rather than rushing headlong to reduce it to another instance of a more general phenomenon or principle. When rightly understood, theory leads to a deeper engagement with particularities, rather than a retreat from them. Theology offers us a lens that brings things into sharper focus, and an illumination that allows the darker recesses of reality to be seen more clearly. It lays a foundation for an empirical engagement with reality, precisely because it allows us to "see" a place as significant and worthy of deeper engagement.

The affirmation of the importance of any given place leads naturally into an exploration of how that importance is informed, safeguarded, and developed through an understanding of the factors and forces that help to shape it. There is an obvious interaction between "place" and "understanding." As Timothy Gorringe points out, people initially "en-soul" and "en-story" places, whereas the passage of time leads to such places "en-souling" the people.[49] Empirical investigation can help us understand such processes, and redirect them toward achieving theologically and spiritually valuable outcomes.

---

47. Wilson, *Terroir,* p. 5.

48. Cornelis van Leeuwen and Gerard Seguin, "The Concept of Terroir in Viticulture," *Journal of Wine Research* 17, no. 1 (2006): 1-10.

49. Timothy J. Gorringe, *A Theology of the Built Environment: Justice, Empowerment, Redemption* (Cambridge: Cambridge University Press, 2002), p. 38.

Two characteristic features of *terroir* relate with equal ease and validity to a local pastoral context, such as a parish church.

1. The notion of "place" immediately identifies limitations and possibilities. It is not possible, for example, to produce the robust red wines of the southern Rhône Valley farther north in Alsace. These limitations often cannot be overcome, and in any case probably should not be overcome. Respect for place signals a willingness to work with the local situation, rather than trying to convert it into another place. Clergy who arrive in a new parish often bring with them the working assumptions and methods of their previous parish, often failing to realize how these practices and assumptions are embedded in the particularities of another place, and fail to connect adequately with their new situation.

2. The distinctives of a specific place are open to empirical study, which helps us understand its specific identity. For example, the factors affecting the ripening of grapes in specific *terroirs* are reasonably well understood, as are their implications for the distinct wines they produce.[50] Similarly, congregations can be studied empirically, helping their distinct identities to be appreciated and the implications of such findings for pastoral and evangelistic strategies to be determined.[51] Although most urban localities undergo rapid change, partly due to social mobility, such approaches nevertheless permit short-term planning to make the best possible use of the resources of any given place.

So important is this second point that it merits closer study.

The Empirical Study of Place

Let us return briefly to the notion of the *terroir,* of such critical importance to wine making. The concept of a *terroir* creates conceptual space for its empirical investigation. Its distinctiveness demands preservation — and, if it is to be preserved, it needs to be *understood.* How are its distinctive vintages shaped by climate? By the type of soil? By the type of grape prevalent

50. J. Duteau, M. Guilloux, and G. E. Seguis, "Influence des facteurs naturels sur la maturation du raisin, en 1979, à Pomerol et Saint-Emilion," *Connaissances de la Vigne et du Vin* 15, no. 1 (1981): 1-27.

51. For example, see Mathew Guest, Karin Tusting, and Linda Woodhead, *Congregational Studies in the UK: Christianity in a Post-Christian Context* (Aldershot: Ashgate, 2004); Paul R. Chambers, *Religion, Secularization, and Social Change in Wales: Congregational Studies in a Post-Christian Society* (Cardiff: University of Wales Press, 2005).

in the region? By the chemical composition of local water supplies? By specific wine-making practices, handed down from generation to generation?

The recognition of the importance of these factors has led to empirical studies that set out to identify what is distinct about each *terroir:* its soil chemistry, its microclimate, its irrigation, its types of grapes, the viticultural conventions, and so forth.[52] How do the geological, climatic, and cultural conventions of any given "defined place" fit into a greater picture? Ethnographic studies of *terroir* have illuminated the complex pattern of traditions that shape the distinctive "tastes" that emerge from each such place,[53] thus helping to maintain its distinct identity.

There is an immediate and obvious parallel with Christian communities. If the Christian church — I here use this term in a generic sense — does indeed possess a distinctive identity and mission, ethnographic descriptions and studies of the church are a legitimate tool of investigation as to how that distinct identity is embodied and operationalized. In other words, ecclesiology is not understood to be limited to theological reflection on the nature of the church, but to how this is expressed empirically — and whether such empirical expressions are indeed consistent with the theological realities they are held to embody.[54] The theologian must attend to what this community *does in practice,* rather than just what its theologians tell us it *is* or *ought to be.*

Just as importantly, the empirical study of Christian communities helps us understand how values, practices, and ideas whose origins lie outside the Christian faith shape their practices. It enables the question of "Christian distinctiveness" or "ecclesial identity" to be calibrated, not least in ascertaining the extent of ecclesial porosity to its cultural environment. It enables informed engagement with the question of how the church maintains its distinctiveness from society without losing its contact with society.[55] Ecclesiology is not a purely theoretical notion; all human com-

---

52. Wilson, *Terroir,* pp. 8-56.

53. An excellent example is found in Amy B. Trubek, *The Taste of Place: A Cultural Journey into Terroir* (Berkeley: University of California Press, 2009).

54. This raises some difficult questions, noted by Nicholas M. Healy, "Practices and the New Ecclesiology: Misplaced Concreteness?" *International Journal of Systematic Theology* 5 (2003): 287-308. Healy draws attention to some inconsistency in categorizing different types of Christian practices as *necessary* or *unnecessary to,* and *constitutive* or *not constitutive of,* the church, and further notes disagreement regarding whether sacraments should be grouped together with or separately from practices.

55. For the theoretical importance of this question, see Joon-Sik Park, *Missional*

munities, after all, are social realities, not theoretical abstractions. Rightly understood, empirical studies of Christian communities offer us the resources for exploring whether the church is indeed maintaining its distinct identity, while at the same time acting as "salt" and "light" to its cultural context. Perhaps more importantly, they might also point to certain corrective strategies when there turns out to be a fundamental misalignment between the Christian gospel and its institutional embodiments.

Conclusion

This chapter has argued for the deliberate cultivation of a habit of "seeing" the world in a Christian manner, deeply grounded in the narratives and values of the Christian tradition. This does not represent a lapse into a theology that merely echoes the habits and practices of religious communities.[56] I concede this danger, but wish to suggest that it may be avoided by the cultivation of precisely the "theological attentiveness" outlined in this essay. Such attentiveness leads into — not away from — empirical investigation of ecclesial structures, attitudes, and practices.

If the church is to remain an authentically and distinctively Christian community, it must be subjected to empirical study to ascertain whether its attitudes, values, and practices are indeed distinctive — and identify courses of action to ensure that its identity is safeguarded and appropriately embodied. The key to avoiding reducing theology to a "language of habit, practice, and virtue" lies not in denying the practical outworking of theology, but upon a recovery of its roots in the Christian tradition of life, thought, and worship — and above all by allowing ourselves to be shaped and inhabited by this distinctively Christian "map of meaning."

Ecclesiologies in Creative Tension: H. Richard Niebuhr and John Howard Yoder (New York: De Gruyter, 2007). For how it might be explored empirically, see Nicholas M. Healy, *Church, World, and the Christian Life: Practical-Prophetic Ecclesiology* (Cambridge: Cambridge University Press, 2000).

56. This is the concern of John Webster, whose critique of contemporary British systematic theology as "heavily ecclesial, strongly invested in the Gospel as social and moral reality, overly invested in the language of habit, practice and virtue, underdetermined by a theology of divine aseity" merits close attention. See John Webster, "Discovering Dogmatics," in *Shaping a Theological Mind: Theological Context and Methodology*, ed. Darren C. Marks (Aldershot: Ashgate, 2002), pp. 129-36.

CHAPTER 7

Interpreting a Situation:
When Is "Empirical" Also "Theological"?

Mary McClintock Fulkerson

Rethinking the Categories of a Discipline

"You go sit on a bench and nobody else sits on that bench. I'd say that's a very good clue" — a comment by a Kenyan, Njeroge, a black man, on his experience in U.S. churches. I would have thought that kind of behavior unusual, a relic of the old South, until my own experience as a participant observer in an interracial church, Good Samaritan United Methodist Church, to which Njeroge belonged, showed me otherwise. Good Samaritan, I should add, was an interracial church with regular attendants from group homes. After all, most white Americans have been saying for a number of years that they are in favor of racial integration and equal opportunity, or so reports Andrew Hacker.[1] To my surprise, however, when I first visited this church all eager to write about this great example of Christian faith, I discovered problems I had not anticipated. Arriving on a Sunday when most congregants in attendance were black, I felt hyperconscious of the whiteness of my skin and very uncomfortable being in the racial minority. Not only did the dominance of dark skin make me ill at ease, when I approached some of the people from group homes — a man with Down syndrome, another with a twisted body in a wheelchair — I became uncomfortable again, not knowing what to do with my own body. Which southern girl niceties should I display to these "grotesque" and pitiful peo-

---

1. Andrew Hacker, *Two Nations: Black and White, Separate, Hostile, Unequal* (New York: Scribner, 2003), p. 52. Of course, Hacker's point is to undermine this, as will be noted.

ple? I am not alone in my dis-ease, however. Despite what most white Americans say about race, "what has changed in recent years" really, says Hacker, is "the way people speak in public," not living patterns,[2] *or* the racial homogeneity of churches. Only 2.5 percent of mainline Protestant churches and 6 percent of evangelical churches are significantly interracial, that is, composed of no more than 80 percent of one race. And more educated and progressive-sounding whites are less likely to be in racially mixed churches or neighborhoods. People with "disabilities" are largely ghettoized, as well. Churches typically find them too disruptive and remain inaccessible to them.

My point? That there is a disjuncture between what we say and believe and what we do? But that is old news. What I want to ask is how a theologian can display the life of a faithful community in a way that takes this disjuncture seriously. In what follows I will trace my attempts to do this, indicating the role of so-called empirical studies and sketching out how I think of my work as theological. This disjuncture generated the need for other tools than those I had as someone trained in systematic theology. I simply had no categories that were adequate to make full theological sense of this community.[3] In short, theology *must* be shaped by empirical studies. A litmus test that relied solely on Christian belief turned out to be problematic in several ways. For example, I found white members who spoke enthusiastically of inclusiveness, that God's family consists of all kinds of diverse people, yet had aversive reactions to black bodies when the latter assumed positions of authority. The church's gracious inclusivity was not correlated to any kind of Christian orthodoxy; theological articulateness seemed almost inversely related to the gifts of overcoming what I will call aversions to the "other." Another problem with belief as a criterion: many of the people from the group homes did not even have the capacity to speak, much less be aware of Chalcedonian Christology or the Trinity.

I do not think that belief in a Christian version of diversity adequately accounts for the church's inclusiveness. I do not think that some good preaching or teaching that condemns racism and "able-ism" would fix the incompleteness of its transformation. Nor does it "cause" other churches to become inclusive. Categories of sin would eventually come to

---

2. Hacker, *Two Nations,* p. 52.

3. What I mean by "full theological sense" has to do, first of all, with recognition of the density of a situation, as I will explore, plus the way it is read with a logic of redemption.

matter in my analysis, but notions that sin is error, willful disobedience, malicious intent (racism, able-ism) — none of these could get at the complexities I found. Those who *could* understand the terms "racism" and "able-ism" did not think of themselves as racist or able-ist. There were others who would simply not know what these terms meant. Broken social structures or social sin understood as inherited biases and broken institutions does not account for enough either. While idolatry would ultimately be helpful, it could not be identified by a focus on cognitive belief. A Niebuhrian account of idolatry as *existential* self-securing in response to worldly threat would be more attuned to the prereflective character of anxiety that is a precondition to sin. However, it could not account for the very *different* racialized and "normate" responses. To display the complex sin and grace in this community required other tools or categories. In short, theology adequate to this community cannot be defined as a set of orthodox and systematic beliefs that members are simply not "up to."

One way to address my dilemma concerning the inadequacy of propositional theology for such complexity is to acknowledge that the task at hand was not properly the task of systematics. Defined as the theological interpretation of a particular contemporary faith situation, "practical theology," which "describes the critical reflection that is done about the meaning of faith and action in the world," was my real challenge.[4] In distinction from making systematic or philosophical judgments, the practical theological task has to do with the way Christian faith occurs as a contemporary situation.[5] With regard to this focus it is simply not helpful to ask only whether Good Samaritan UMC is "biblical" or to interrogate the systematic relations of its doctrinal loci. Instead, the complexity of Good Samaritan must be taken seriously as a "situation of faith" before even thinking about what a faithful mode of being biblical or doctrinal would look like. The group home members' nonsymbolic forms of communication, the racialized habituations of members, not to mention their cultural, regional, and religious shaping — all these complexities have to be factored into a theological reading of this faith community.

---

4. James N. Poling and Donald E. Miller, *Foundations for a Practical Theology of Ministry* (Nashville: Abingdon, 1985), p. 33.

5. David Tracy defines practical theology as "the mutually critical correlation of the interpreted theory and praxis of the Christian faith with the interpreted theory and praxis of the contemporary situation." David Tracy, "The Foundations of Practical Theology," in *Practical Theology: The Emerging Field in Theology, Church, and World*, ed. Don S. Browning (New York: Harper and Row, 1983), p. 76.

A problem of no small size, then, is the exercise of an analytical capacity to read a situation correctly. Here I prefer a definition that, although it sounds quite simple, provides a formal way to take a situation seriously. A situation is, according to Edward Farley, "the way various items, powers, and events in the environment gather to evoke responses from participants."[6] I favor this definition because it suggests a variety of elements — not just Scripture, not just culture, or racial or gendered markers, but a complexity of elements, including power — that *converge* relationally. That is, they *"evoke responses"* as opposed to unilaterally *causing* outcomes. I propose, then, that conceiving it as a "situation" helps image what needs to be foregrounded about Good Samaritan.[7]

The framing of any contemporary situation involves not only the question of "what to do," but equally what constitutes the relevant "items, powers, and events" and how to understand a contemporary environment as that which demands a response. What needs to be foregrounded in this particular situation of faith is a complexity involving racialized visceral, affective habituations and an environment shaped by institutional residuals of race (class, "normate" worldviews, etc.) from southern history. These residuals live on as part of "situations" not only as sociopolitical and economic structures, but also as "everyday practices" or racialized scripts, as Philomena Essed puts it.[8] Whatever role connections with origins or normative memory eventually play in a theological reading of this church, the impact of such "items" as various kinds of communicative abilities or the impact of racist and able-ist power structures cannot be ignored in determining that connection.[9]

---

6. Edward Farley, "Interpreting Situations: An Inquiry into the Nature of Practical Theology," in *Practicing Gospel: Unconventional Thoughts on the Church's Ministry* (Louisville: Westminster John Knox, 2003), p. 38.

7. The task of practical theology is to flesh out the frame of the "situational" character of lived faith. Theological education may be successful at teaching how to interpret texts, historical events, and doctrines, but continuation of its current fourfold structure problematically assumes that one can simply bring them to bear upon a context. As Farley puts it, this "bypasses most of the structural elements in the situation of the believer and, therefore, suppresses most of the acts in which communities interpret their own lives and situations." Farley, "Interpreting Situations," pp. 36, 38.

8. Philomena Essed, *Understanding Everyday Racism: An Interdisciplinary Theory* (London: Sage, 1991), pp. 48-49, 185-282.

9. And there are elements of the environment that I will not be able to take up here, like the relation of the everyday scripts to what Omi and Winant call political racial (and "normate") "projects" connected with the larger social-political realities. Michael Omi and

To define practical theology as a theological reading of contemporary situations is perhaps stating the obvious. Most accounts of academic theology assume that its ultimate end is contemporary lived faith (sometimes defined as "ethics"). However, by taking up the question of how "situation" is thematized, I make some distinctive moves in relation to various accounts of the theological task. Most obviously, this definition is an alternative to a frequently disavowed account that dominates the casual discourse of theological education known as the "trickle-down" theory of applied theology.[10] The notion that normative faith is something found in authoritative texts such as Scripture or doctrine and then "applied" in contemporary life situations is a popular pattern for thinking about what it means to do practical theology.[11] As I have implied, it is an unfortunate pattern that allows such crucial elements as social structures; the intersection of the cultural, economic, and political; the dialectic of individual agency with these structural constraints; and the distribution of power to be ignored or minimally addressed. Because such elements (despite the many theological versions of "world" as a compromising poison) have much to do with how anything "normative" becomes a situational reality, it is crucial to lay them out.[12]

To fill out this complex "situation" of Good Samaritan UMC, I appropriated a mixed bag of methods and theoretical frames beyond the historical, hermeneutical, and philosophical methods entailed in systematics. Most immediately, the tools of ethnography provided me with a way to approach communal faith as a subject matter. Engaging in around two and a

Howard Winant, *Racial Formation in the United States: From the 1960s to the 1990s,* 2nd ed. (New York: Routledge, 1994).

10. For examples of virtually unanimous rejection of this language in the 1980s, see Browning, *Practical Theology,* and Lewis Mudge and James Poling, eds., *Formation and Reflection: The Promise of Practical Theology* (Philadelphia: Fortress, 1987), pp. xxiv, xiii-xxxvi.

11. The dominant fourfold pattern, where three "fields" (Bible, church history, and theology/ethics) are considered the theoretical or "academic" disciplines that are then "applied" in a division typically characterized by the study of clerical practices, has been criticized, but helps keep this thinking alive. For the classic account of the fourfold, see Edward Farley, *Theologia: The Fragmentation and Unity of Theological Education* (Philadelphia: Fortress, 1983).

12. My attempt to do this raises a real question. Is the notion of elements of a situation a necessary prequestion to all other ways of reading a situation, or one option among others, such as pastoral care and counseling, Christian education, and other forms of what some associate with "practical theology"? These require other disciplines such as psychology and education theories, but some of the elements I am invoking can be relevant.

half years of participant observation in the church, I did interviews, collected documents, and engaged in worship and other church activities in order to get the benefit of one of the virtues of the case study. As one introduction to social science's empirical methods puts it: that virtue is the "grounding of observations and concepts about social action and social structures in natural settings studied at close hand."[13] The benefits of such work for the theologian are similar, namely, to get a sense of the density of lived faith, and to begin to see the importance of linkages between a thing of interest, such as racism or able-ism, and "the actual social world in which it is embedded and sustained or reproduced."[14] The implications of this move have already generated an implicit challenge for normative theology. To take this concern seriously means that historically normative texts should not be the primary "analytic object" for theological reflection. Theology's obsession with texts is now, at least in some quarters, being challenged and corrected in religious studies by a focus on lived religions and the appropriation of ethnography.[15] (Wesley Kort has characterized theology as texts-about-texts.)[16] The difference between a social, contextually defined subject "reading" Scripture and the blank-slate, bringing-no-eisegetical-self-interest-to-the-text interpreter that divinity schools frequently commend is quite important. And such attention to social worlds raises new questions about what counts as "normative" in the field. As an indirect way into those questions, let me point out some of the positives of ethnographic work.

The importance of the "nuanced and subtle set of interpretive categories" provided by ethnography, as one summary of qualitative method puts it, does not, of course, allow for causal or explanatory claims such as

13. Anthony M. Orum, Joe R. Feagin, and Gideon Sjoberg, "Introduction: The Nature of the Case Study," in *A Case for the Case Study*, ed. Joe R. Feagin, Anthony M. Orum, and Gideon Sjoberg (Chapel Hill: University of North Carolina Press, 1991), pp. 6-7.

14. David A. Snow and Leon Anderson, "Researching the Homeless: The Characteristic Features and Virtues of the Case Study," in *A Case for the Case Study*, p. 154.

15. For example, David D. Hall, *Lived Religion in America: Toward a History of Practice* (Princeton: Princeton University Press, 1997). The increasing significance of ethnography for theology is suggested by a conference at Yale Divinity School, "Ecclesiology and Ethnography: Exploring the Emerging Conversation between Theology and Congregational Studies," September 27-29, 2007, at which the original version of this paper was presented. Since then, however, a number of conferences have been sponsored both in the United States and in Europe on the topic, and three more are planned over the next several years.

16. Wesley A. Kort, *Bound to Differ: The Dynamics of Theological Discourses* (University Park: Pennsylvania State University Press, 1992).

are sought by quantitative procedures. Indeed, one of its limitations is that case studies are not generalizable in the way quantitative procedures might allow.[17] Clearly, however, a case study can provide important contextualization of belief in the instance of Christian faith and open to view important questions. For example, how do different beliefs converge? Which ones appear to matter most in different situations? What resonances do they have for differently classed, racialized, and gendered groups? Such questions inevitably nudge one toward normative issues. What are better ways to frame the circulation of preached and taught biblical and theological themes than the uni-directional causal models often implied by theological normative discourse? What about the powerful function of music that clearly has more significance than preaching for those who lack symbolizing abilities?

Such questions lead to one of the virtues claimed by case study literature for this contextualizing. Thick descriptions can be suggestive of needed alterations in theoretical approaches. Indeed, they can lead to changes in categorical frames used in empirical research.[18] Penny Edgell Becker and Nancy Eiesland themselves say that ethnography should function to "make us aware of the inadequacy of our most frequently used theoretical categories," giving the use of "liberal" and "conservative" as one of several examples of categories challenged by ethnographic studies.[19] On this point Eiesland's work is illustrative. In her recent book, *A Particular Place: Urban Restructuring and Religious Ecology in a Southern Exurb,* Eiesland makes an important case for the effects of an interinstitutional

17. Feagin, Orum, and Sjoberg, *Case,* p. 164. While the case study has a "presumed lack of generalizability," one author argues for a more intuitive, empirically grounded, context-specific generalization that he refers to as "naturalistic." The "data generated by case studies are often likely to resonate experientially or phenomenologically with a broad cross section of readers and thereby facilitate a greater understanding of the phenomenon in question. Although such an understanding may not facilitate prediction or control, it is still a kind of knowledge worth pursuing because, to borrow from Geertz, it puts 'us in touch with the lives of strangers' and thereby 'renders others accessible' and enlarges 'the universe of discourse.'" *Case,* p. 165.

18. According to Orum, Feagin, and Sjoberg, one of the virtues of the case study is the potential to generate theory by "suggesting new interpretations and concepts or reexamining earlier concepts and interpretations in major and innovative ways." *Case,* p. 13.

19. Penny Edgell Becker and Nancy L. Eiesland, "Developing Interpretations: Ethnography and the Restructuring of Knowledge in a Changing Field," in *Contemporary American Religion: An Ethnographic Reader,* ed. Penny Edgell Becker and Nancy L. Eiesland (Walnut Creek, Calif.: AltaMira Press, 1997), p. 19.

ecology on a faith community as well as that of the "residential and industrial urban deconcentration."[20] The important category of multilayered
habits of belonging that she found in her case study of an exurban religious ecology may suggest some implications for what appear now to be
acontextual theological notions of what it means to be a faithful Christian.
Multilayered loyalties could very well generate a reconsideration of overly
simplistic notions of "community" and community loyalty. I take Eiesland
and Becker's appeal to the "us" who need to pay attention to inadequate
categories to refer to sociologists of religion. However, such work should
also contribute to challenges to normative theological discourse.

My study of the interracial, multi-abled church thickened out the
context of Christian beliefs about welcoming communities and the inclusiveness of faith for me, but that very thickening leads me now to *question*
certain notions of tradition and catechesis. Important "elements" that
"converged" to make the situation of Good Samaritan were bodily interactions and communications. Taking these seriously prompted me to challenge accounts of tradition that fail to recognize what Paul Connerton calls
the bodily or incorporative practices that constitute a society's identity and
its traditions.[21] To be sure, theologians frequently intend traditioning to
refer to the full sense of habituation into Christian life, implying much
more than simply learning a written tradition. Christian tradition is "the
whole way of life of a people as it is transmitted from generation to generation," as J. P. Mackey puts it.[22] As a "way of life" and not simply the trans-
mission of belief, tradition is "best understood as an enduring practice or
set of practices including a vision (belief), attitudes (dispositions, affections), and patterns of actions," says Terry Tilley.[23] So you would think that
such a process would include bodily practices. Similarly, the popularity of
virtue ethics has given Alasdair MacIntyre's work considerable prominence, and his notion of practice would seem to include the full-bodied
character of lived faith. Relative to the issue of normativity, traditioning is
a practice, but not just any practice counts, says MacIntyre; it must en-

20. Nancy L. Eiesland, *A Particular Place: Urban Restructuring and Religious Ecology
in a Southern Exurb* (New Brunswick, N.J.: Rutgers University Press, 2000).

21. Paul Connerton, *How Societies Remember* (Cambridge: Cambridge University
Press, 1989).

22. J. P. Mackey, *Tradition and Change in the Church* (Dayton, Ohio: Pflaum Press,
1968), p. x.

23. Terrence W. Tilley, *Inventing Catholic Tradition* (Maryknoll, N.Y.: Orbis, 2000),
p. 45.

hance the internal goods of the tradition.[24] So we are not talking about *anything* that believers do, but rather those lived behaviors that enhance the goods of Christian faith. Despite these important recognitions by current accounts of tradition, however, my study of Good Samaritan surfaced two forms of communication that call the adequacy of even these practice-focused accounts of tradition into question. Good Samaritan UMC could not be made adequate sense of as a "situation" without attention to these communications.

To explain what I mean, I turn to definitions from Connerton's account of social identity. Societal identities constitute not only written and linguistic traditions, argues Connerton; also constitutive of a culture's identity and tradition are *incorporative* practices, the *bodily* communications characteristic of a group. Bodies do not simply express the meanings of practices of inscription; they communicate *distinctive* meanings. *Explicitly held ends and commitments and bodily knowledges cannot be collapsed into one another.*[25] My initial reaction of dis-ease to the "others" of the church exemplifies this; think of the gap between my intentions and my aversive reactions. Connerton identifies three kinds of bodily practices that make up tradition: ritual, techniques, and proprieties. Let me give examples of the second and third incorporative practices. Bodily *techniques* are special forms of communication that characterize different cultures, like talking with your hands; bodily *proprieties* are prereflective "wisdoms" regarding what it is *proper* to do with your kind of body. Such frames raise some new issues.

First, the issue of bodily techniques that have long gone unrecognized. When the only kind of communication theologians recognize is linguistic, then most of the people with intellectual disabilities from group homes become nonpersons, or, at best, objects of pity. However, much of their behavior previously thought to be disruptive — especially that of folks without language — is now recognized by educators as *communication.*[26] The twisted man in the wheelchair who made noises at certain times in the service was not simply making trouble. Rather, like many of the people from group homes, he was engaging in incorporative prac-

---

24. Alasdair MacIntyre, *After Virtue: A Study in Moral Theory,* 2nd ed. (Notre Dame, Ind.: Notre Dame University Press, 1984), pp. 187, 191, 204-25.

25. Connerton, *How Societies Remember,* pp. 72-73.

26. Ellin Siegel and Amy Wetherby, "Enhancing Nonsymbolic Communication," in *Instruction of Students with Severe Disabilities,* ed. Martha E. Snell and Freeda Brown, 5th ed. (Upper Saddle River, N.J.: Prentice-Hall, 2000).

tices, bodily communications (in Connerton's terms, techniques). So-called normate people need to be habituated into the skill of understanding and communicating with such folks.[27] On the basis of this, I concluded that if all members of Good Samaritan are to be considered practitioners of the faith, such bodily "wisdom" or communication is crucial to theological concepts of practice and, inevitably, tradition if, that is, we are to regard all as potential *contributors to* and not simply *passive objects of* traditioning.

A second issue is bodily *proprieties*. This refers to the bodily "knowledges" into which persons are habituated about what is *proper;* they typically signal gender, class, race, and other markers of status. A young Saudi Arabian girl, for example, knows without having to reflect upon the matter where she can place herself in relation to males in her society; likewise, African American slaves knew where to put their bodies and what postures to assume around the white master class. An African American in a white-owned store today will have internalized racialized bodily proprieties so as not to be surprised when white clerks follow him around. Indeed, my sense is that most African Americans have much sharper awareness of racialized bodily proprieties than do whites; theirs I called proprieties of hypervigilance (connected to Du Bois's notion of double-consciousness/twoness). As for the whites in the community — however unaware or oblivious they may be — most are traditioned into what my colleague William Hart terms bodily proprieties of "ownership of space."[28]

Nancy Eiesland invokes socially produced affective practices similar to these bodily proprieties that were central in Good Samaritan. She refers to the "aversions and biases" the "normate" have toward people with disabilities. It is not simply prejudice at work in these encounters, but "revulsion" — a revulsion that is "endemic in society."[29] And this problem can be

---

27. It can result from the attentive presence of a parent or teacher to a child who lacks symbolic capabilities. The adult can develop an acute sensibility that becomes a *habitus* of "being aware and receptive to the subtle cues" of the child, from her use of conventional movements such as pointing to her subtle facial expressions. Developing such a disposition includes reflective reasoning, but is fundamentally a bodily skill as well, enabling the parent to know when to wait, when to augment, when to intervene, and thereby to solicit new communication.

28. I thank my former Duke colleague, Prof. William Hart, for this concept.

29. Nancy L. Eiesland, *The Disabled God: Toward a Liberatory Theology of Disability* (Nashville: Abingdon, 1994).

attended to not only by changing language/symbols and practices of those of us who are church, but also by requiring a theologian to have the ability to read what she calls a "body language": "The body practices of the church are a physical language — the routines, rules, and practices of the body, conscious and unconscious. In the church, the body practices are the physical discourse of inclusion and exclusion. These practices reveal the hidden 'membership roll,' those whose bodies matter in the shaping of liturgies and services."[30]

My reading of Good Samaritan, in other words, surfaced the concern for more complex categories for knowledge and communication, categories that include bodies. Already moving into the reading of material culture, of space and architecture, and not confining themselves to written material or oral communications, ethnographers might find the categories of incorporative practices useful. Theology, with its concern for normative traditioning, would certainly need to rethink some issues if these forms of communication are to be taken seriously. Cultural anthropologist Sherry Ortner argues that, while it was important that her field moved to a study of practices, the challenge to cultural anthropology was that it needed a "practice-theorized *history*" as well, in order to break up its static notion of culture. Theology with *its* laudable move to practices needs something similar.[31] Corporate memory is borne in inscribed or storable memory, primarily taking the form of written traditions such as Scripture and ecclesiastical traditions; we know that and have a history of texts as a result. Corporate memory is also borne in incorporative practices, where the messages *are* bodily performances, and potential sites for visceral reactions to the other.[32] These proprieties and techniques are *who we are* as a society; they are part of our social identity; and we need a history of bodily practices as well as inscripted practices. As much as we would like to consider that peripheral — Christian communities maintain a faithful identity by "remembering Jesus," right? — we need recognition of different modes of *performing* Jesus, as well. And this may require more reading and communicative skills than we typically get in the highly text-focused divinity education. What is more, the harm effected by racialized proprieties of our traditions has certainly not gone away.

---

30. Eiesland, *The Disabled God*, p. 112.

31. Sherry B. Ortner, *Anthropology and Social Theory: Culture, Power, and the Acting Subject* (Durham, N.C.: Duke University Press, 2006), p. 9.

32. MacIntyre's account of tradition is most explicitly about inscribed memory.

Such knowledges are found in every culture, and they are constructive. Take examples such as Bourdieu's of the sense of honor in fencing or boxing. A kind of wisdom, the cultural *habitus* of fencing accumulates as "a permanent disposition, embedded in the agents' very bodies in the form of mental disposition, schemes of perception and thought . . . which enables each agent to engender all the practices consistent with the logic of challenge and riposte."[33] A boxer can constantly read and react to every move of his or her opponent, even before it is complete — a "reading" that is not the rapid mental selection of the proper response to fit each of the opponent's responses, but "a knowledge and a remembering in the hands and in the body," as Connerton puts it.[34] Not confined to explicitly learned skills, a *habitus* can emerge from the requirements of polite conversation, for example, skills of "unceasing vigilance" for proper participation in the game, such as "the art of playing on the equivocations, innuendoes and unspoken implications of gestural or verbal symbolism . . . required, whenever the right objective distance is in question."[35]

My point in this section has been to illustrate how an ethnographic study generated for me the need to rethink some categories of my discipline. It may be obvious already that it also led me beyond what would be considered closely monitored empirical research. I found the gap between what people said and what they did the kind of disconnect that led me to use other theories. My own sense of dis-ease, described earlier, my bodily discomfort with being a racial minority and with being around persons with disabilities, was key in generating these theoretical frames. I not only turned to Paul Connerton's theory of social memory/tradition (in *How Societies Remember*) to enhance Bourdieu's concept of bodily *habitus*, but I also drew upon Erving Goffman's theories of stigma to indicate marked bodies and to elaborate the categories of aversion and desire.[36] I used postmodern place theory to get at the permeable boundaries of "community" and other forms of signifying that, despite their hybrid, impure, "enculturated" character, effected what I would call faithful practices. All

33. Claudia Strauss and Naomi Quinn, *A Cognitive Theory of Cultural Meaning* (Cambridge: Cambridge University Press, 1997), p. 15.

34. Connerton, *How Societies Remember*, p. 95.

35. Pierre Bourdieu, *The Logic of Practice*, trans. Richard Nice (Stanford: Stanford University Press, 1980), pp. 80-81.

36. Erving Goffman, *Stigma: Notes on the Management of Spoiled Identity* (Englewood Cliff, N.J.: Prentice-Hall, 1963).

these theoretical frames helped me expand the experiential and social-political, power-connected dimensions of what I saw and heard. I can say that mine are not quantitative procedures that look for uniformities of social life and render them into precise, numeric forms that can easily lend themselves to the testing of hypotheses. I cannot prove these connections between the elements of bodied and cognitive experience I have identified.[37] The legitimacy of my account may be somewhat akin to the argument that unproveable case studies "are [however] often likely to resonate experientially or phenomenologically" with readers.[38] But I am certainly guilty of what cultural anthropologist James Clifford claims about ethnography: it is "always caught up in the invention, not the representation, of cultures."[39]

Theology as Creative Reflection Generated by a Wound

So, given that such virtues as thickness, complexity, and the challenging of dominant theories are good things for sociologists, cultural anthropologists, and religious studies scholars, what has this to do with being "theological"? All I have suggested as *theological* cover for my work thus far is an appeal to practical theology, taking its definition to require that I complicate the way a contemporary situation is defined. My account, however, is not much different from a postmodern version of cultural anthropology's notion of ethnography. So what is the justification for calling my reading theological? Especially since I have not identified any goods internal to the practices I studied, as Alasdair MacIntyre would require, or a telos for practical theology's reading of a situation. What is the good served by faithful practices, once they've been properly complexified with bodies and desire, and context? And what is the end of my reading of the situation?

37. I am drawing on brief phrases that describe quantitative research from Orum, Feagin, and Sjoberg, "Introduction," pp. 1-26, 17.

38. Snow and Anderson, "Researching the Homeless," p. 165. But maybe not, given all the theory I use.

39. By that he means an ethnography that moves into practices and power, and thus includes all the theory stuff, à la Said, Jameson, Bourdieu, de Certeau, and Raymond Williams. James Clifford, introduction to *Writing Culture: The Poetics and Politics of Ethnography,* ed. James Clifford and George E. Marcus (Berkeley: University of California Press, 1986), pp. 2-3.

My attempt to answer these questions brings me to a final way in which I read my analysis as theological; that has to do with its *logic*. In other words, it has to do with what caught my attention and why, what I pursued, and how I interpreted it — and, finally, how I brought these together. It is a logic that displays what I judge to be the telos of practical theology's reading of a situation. My analysis not only drew upon theories that complexified the situation to signify affective, bodily, power-related, and other elements as they thickened out belief. It also traced the community's practices through a *logic of transformation*. In short, I read the situation as one of harm that demanded redress.

Theological reflection does not begin with a doctrine, a theme (biblical or otherwise) to be applied, as that old problematic yet persistent myth of practical theology implies. Rather, the reflection is generated by sensibilities shaped by a plethora of factors, including but not limited to Christian discourse. The particular role and form of these factors are typically both inchoate and conscious-reflective. Creative thinking, someone has said, originates at the site of a wound. A dilemma is perceived (or felt) that generates new thinking, takes on the tradition, and develops new configurations and convergences of insight and reality. To make sense of the church, then, I began with the notion of a *wound*, a wound signified by, but not confined to, this community.

One form of theology that has been prominent for proceeding from a site of woundedness is liberation theology. Liberationists initiate theology from "wounds" that are connected to deep social harms; they require a hermeneutics of suspicion aimed at both the contemporary social realities and the Christian tradition. Just such liberation thinking characterizes Nancy Eiesland's work in *The Disabled God*, where she identifies a serious wound and offers it as a site that generates an important and productive kind of theology. As she puts it in another article, "liberatory theology is driven by the need to *lament* the social conditions under which we live and to work to transform societies that oppress us."[40] Following the liberation logic, *The Disabled God* traces uses of Christian tradition through the lens of a group that has been ignored/oppressed by the tradition and its accompanying cultures. It surfaces biblical and other traditions that do harm to those with disabilities *and to the so-called nondisabled* as well (from the

---

40. Nancy L. Eiesland, "Things Not Seen: Women with Physical Disabilities, Oppression and Practical Theology," in *Liberating Faith Practices: Feminist Practical Theologies in Context*, ed. Denise Ackermann (Leuven: Peeters, 1998), p. 120, emphasis added.

identification of disabilities with sin, to Jesus' physical healings as norma-tive for redemption) — ideological valences that can only be seen from this newly recognized subject position and its symbols. The wound of able-ism, then, generates new readings of Christian faith and new accounts of who we all are. As Eiesland says, "(p)ersons with disabilities must gain access to the social-symbolic life of the church, and the church must gain access to the social-symbolic lives of people with disabilities."[41]

So I mapped the community with a logic of transformation. I at-tempted to trace out the appearance of certain harms, their perpetuation, and the ways in which they were in the process of being transformed. I used categories that expand the harms of racism and able-ism beyond in-tentional acts of malice — including Omi and Winant's notion of a racial formation — which in turn led to a proposal of terms for harm that oc-curred in everyday practices at the prereflective level: bodily practices of white ownership of space and black hypervigilance.[42] Part of the harm for whites (and the "normate") was obliviousness — obliviousness to a group's aversions and unconscious habits and dispositions constitutive of "othering." For those designated "black," harms included self-hatred, fear, and distrust, among other things, but obliviousness only when it came to people with disabilities. What counted as transformative *change* I labeled the creation of a "place to appear," a phrase that trades on Hannah Arendt's concept for the creation of a sociality/public where persons can fully see, recognize, and honor the other.[43] What counted as transforma-tional in my mapping of the community were practices that had to do with the alterations of these attitudes. Such changes, I argued, required physical face-to-face presencing and acknowledgment. Whites had to be in the presence of and recognize blacks in leadership positions; they had to listen to and empathize with one another's stories. Habituations into comfort, empathy, recognition, and respect for the other had to at least have *begun* to occur, so that whites could become more aware of the wounds and blacks could begin to trust and humanize whites. (This obvi-ously would take time, and my temptation was to overread success, with what a social scientist would probably consider minimal evidential con-nections.) Often the language of Christian faith was key in the disclosure/

---

41. Eiesland, *The Disabled God*, p. 20.

42. Omi and Winant, *Racial Formation in the United States*.

43. See Kimberley Curtis, *Our Sense of the Real: Aesthetic Experience and Arendtian Politics* (Ithaca, N.Y.: Cornell University Press, 1999).

interpretation of these activities, but it was never enough. Thus I found that practices such as what I called "homemaking" practices and money-making projects were often as significant if not more so in transforming habituations than the explicitly "religious" practices such as worship and Bible reading.

With the identification of ends such as "a place to appear," I have addressed one aspect of the normative character of my theological task, Mac-Intyre's insistence that practices have ends that generate internal goods. Given this logic of redemption, however, one still might ask, so what accounts for liberation/redemption? What distinguishes these accounts from being simply functional, for example — people start paying attention and their improved behavior causes improved racial conditions? How is *my* reading normatively *theological*? It is here that I took another step in my analysis, which is too complicated to rehash in full, but will have to suffice for my conclusion.

Briefly, a classic sense of theology is *theologia*, wisdom in divine things — a pursuit of "reality" by means of a transformed *habitus*. The telos of *theologia* is discernment of the theonomy or God-dependence of a situation, a discernment enabled by habituation into a communal memory that does somehow claim to mediate transformation. On the basis of this definition, a worry about whether the use of empirical cultural analysis alone is adequately theological might have some legitimacy. By this I do not mean to suggest, however, that an analysis is theological simply by fulfilling the criterion of "Christianness," that is, reproducing the specificities of the tradition itself.[44] That, it seems to me, would be analogous to a mere descriptive task that any social scientist could do, that is, discern whether a social entity is properly reproducing its historical identity. Such a definition of "theological" would basically collapse the God-referent of *theologia* into a finite museum piece. While having some account of the shape of the tradition, its logic, its "essence," or its central themes is unavoidably part of the theological task, I am saying that something else might be more vital than simply the reproduction of the tradition or the tracing of change with which any other discipline could concur.

Of the many different experiences of the world that might motivate people to attribute reality to God (e.g., as an entity that explains the world

---

44. Of course, liberal (revisionist modern) theologies are guilty of this, too, insofar as they use a criterion of "appropriateness." But I may contradict myself soon, since I want to appropriate something like what Farley calls a "portrait."

metaphysically, as a source for aid, or as compensatory being), I propose the most salient are those that display a move out of bondage, a bondage that, according to the tradition, only a transcendent/eternal reality can relieve or redeem. I take the fulfillment of the theological task, then, as one of discerning and testifying to redemptive alterations of contemporary reality. In positing "redemptive alteration" as key to judging a contemporary practice/discernment as theological, I borrow from theologian Edward Farley's way of granting the primacy of an ecclesial redemptive sociality as mediator or as *appresentor* of transcendence. God is never "present" as a referent or cause of redemption in the way in which other realities are present to consciousness; the theological task is not study of God (nor is it study of the experience of God). "What we human beings do experience and subject to reflection is always discrete, a focused content limited by or to entities and events, or to strata and qualities of events," says Farley. "Such things may serve as theophanies, occasions of worship, or signs of sacred power. They are never the presented God."[45]

This subject matter for theology — "occasions of worship . . . signs of sacred power," as he puts it — is, in my project, defined according to a central way in which the confession of God's reality occurs, namely, when people experience transformation in the direction of an ultimate good: redemption. There is, of course, no one way of defining that good — redemption — but let me quickly review the logic I have employed. Creatures defined as *imago Dei*, desiring God as proper end, are sinners — sinners who respond to the threats of the world with substitution of that which is not God (true end); such creatures are only freed for nonidolatrous love of the world insofar as that end is somehow real, as in, founding. What *is* present, then, when the harms we call sin are diminished (given that God is not), are the intersubjectively and sociopolitically mediated realities of redemption. The shape that takes is the diminishing of the need to be secured by worldly (finite) entities, accompanied by the increased capacity to care for, forgive, and be in accountable relation to the neighbor. It

45. Edward Farley, *Divine Empathy: A Theology of God* (Minneapolis: Fortress, 1996), p. 54. He continues: "As nonpresentational God is at the same time nonintentional; that is, unavailable to direct acts of meaning. We human beings move through everyday life by way of multiple kinds of acts directed toward specifically meant contents: friends, physical objects, and abstractions like love or numbers. Unable to referentially mean God, we are in a cognitive quandary when we would summon evidences for God, even in the form of reasons for our worship. What sort of evidences does one muster for what one cannot directly mean or have in view?"

is filled out by traditions of law, covenant, agape, justice, conversion-repentance, iconoclasm, and a host of communal and social narratives of faithful life. This is to say that I must read my analysis of the diminishing of obliviousness and of hypervigilance with its aversions as places to appear *through the logic of creation-sin-redemption.*

My brief description is inadequate, but it depends upon a set of traditions that fill out the good for human being as that which is not finite, that which secures in a way that enhances the capacity to be for the neighbor — enhances ontological courage — the capacity to flourish in spite of the threats and harms of finitude. In sum, if there is a key logic here, it is that when the freedom to bypass the self occurs, its condition must be that which is never fully presented, namely, God, because that "end" of creatures is the only thing that could relieve the desire for (ultimate/true) security.

Read with this "theo-logic," then, Good Samaritan's practices can be seen in three ways: first, to signify the pursuit of created, finite goods, displaying desire for God's world as well as for God. Desire for survival, for well-being, pleasure, joy, and communion with others — all these define what it means to be a creature of God.[46] My expansion of relevant categories from belief, to *habitus,* to bodied communications, and the larger social formation has been a way to honor the fullness of creatureliness. The importance of relations to the neighbor was seen in the community's attempts to be inclusive, to welcome "those who are not like us." Read theologically, these practices attempted to reconcile groups divided by sins of racism and able-ism, the second dimension of the logic. With the move to such categories as sin, however, analysis becomes more difficult and complex.

According to a theo-centric view of human being, where desire for God's finitely good world is fundamental, broken social relations are signs of deformed desire. Yet identifying the broken relations in the community was quite a challenge.[47] Since no one engaged in explicit acts of malice, I had to develop classic symbols of sin in relation to *unintentional* practices of populations who were very differently habituated. Whites were deformed by virtue of participation in racist structures that habituated them into postures of obliviousness to the continued harm of racism; African

46. Most explicitly seen in the aesthetic and bodily joy experienced in the community's worship and the pleasures of activities and relationships, worldly desires were all a faithful honoring of the creation as finitely good.

47. My turn to signs of redemption as an alternative to "unaccommodated discourse" as normative sign does not mean the former are not ambiguous, a topic needing more discussion than I can give it.

Americans were deformed into postures of distrust, self-hatred, and fear. Those of Africans were even more complex. As the feminist critique of classic theological focus on pride has long insisted, pride is inadequate as a way to define the deformation of subjugated groups. Victimization is typically followed by defensive responses and the sedimentation of these harms — both internally and in larger social inheritances. While all are deformed by these forms of brokenness, not all participate in the same way. Niebuhr's existentialist accounts of anxiety as precondition for sin moved out of the sin as error or sheer malice problem, but were inadequate for the differently marked groups. So I expanded traditional concepts of sin by incorporating bodies and social structures as part of human brokenness. The particular wounds — obliviousness of the whites, hypervigilance of those designated "black," and the discomfort of the so-called normates with people from group homes — were read through the grammar of sin (sin as the distortion of *finitely good creatures*); these defamations of social relations were also read as the effects of idolatry (however indirect), the classic way to name our theonomous nature.

I turn now to the third moment in this reading. I had interpreted the practices of the community, as I said, with an eye to whether they created places to appear, which included physical comfort as part of the many elements of enhanced recognition and respect. As the desired end of these practices, these places to appear needed to be interpreted as a display of redemption (the indirect appresence of the Transcendent). This process of production of new free social spaces amounted to an incessant widening — an extension of sociality, of social space to appear. However, it was not simply tolerance, or inclusion; it came with change of persons (diminishing of obliviousness on the part of whites and enhanced safety and capacity to trust on the part of blacks). Read in explicit theological terms, it is grounded in ontological courage (and has political analogues).

To summarize this brief review of my mapping of the community's life, I have said that my very choice of framing categories and events was ordered by tracing a wound and practices that (partially) altered it. The theological character of my account was most explicit when I read bodied practices, their deformation by racism, and able-ism, and relief by places to appear through the lenses of creation, sin, and redemption. However, the appropriation of such categories to begin with came from the theological impulse to foreground the thickness and complexity of created existence. A number of dilemmas remain. First, what is at stake in my boundary blurring? I say that my theological and "empirical" choices and lenses are shaping each other. However, is this not simply an add-on of explicitly theological categories to an ethnographic and theory-laden account? A reason to say it is not is that I take the bodied practices to be as constitutive of the site of faithfulness/faithlessness as the expressed beliefs. However, I have not based my account of what is redemptive on what the *participants* say is redemptive. I have brought my own categories to bear upon that judgment.

One issue generated by my possible imposing of foreign theological categories would suggest a rethinking of normative tradition as an important next step. When it comes to the people with disabilities, I find my traditional categories challenged. *Whether my framing of brokenness is completely linkable to something resembling idolatry is a real question.* Idolatry did not, in the end, seem a category adequate to persons with perlocutionary nonsymbolic skills, thus leaving me with the question of the adequacy of traditional notions of sin and whether they exclude certain subjects from the category of human being/*imago Dei*. It may be that the work of other theories, such as object relations theory, might be preferable to my use of the category of desire. If some people with disabilities cannot "desire" or order desire, have I implicitly suggested that they are not fully human?

In closing, I wonder if this rendition of the community is, perhaps, something like what Clifford calls the allegorical character of ethnography.[48] This story about Good Samaritan is, in reality, a story about something else. You might say, then, that what I wrote was in effect a testimony, albeit *my* testimony, not simply that of the participants. It was an account of a kind of sociality that indirectly testifies to a redeeming God who sustains the displays of courage in the church. More than that it can never be. This reciprocity is not "experience of God," but somehow it is a display of a movement into freedom that, on the logic of a theological anthropology, testifies to a sustaining by That Alone Which Can Sustain. A final question, then, would be if I have transgressed the claim that the only thing we have access to is human products. But even then, as Richard Fenn says, the boundaries between sociology and cultural anthropology, even between these approaches and theology, are getting more complicated to define.[49]

48. James Clifford, "On Ethnographic Allegory," in *Writing Culture*, pp. 98-121.
49. Richard K. Fenn, "Editorial Commentary: Looking for the Boundaries of the Field; Social Anthropology, Theology, and Ethnography," in *The Blackwell Companion to Sociology of Religion*, ed. Richard K. Fenn (Oxford: Blackwell, 2001), pp. 363-70.

In that vein I conclude that just as cultural anthropologists (and sociologists) offer larger interpretations than what is reducible to individual intent, as a theologian, so do I.[50]

50. I am not able to speak to what theology might have to contribute to these social science approaches. See Kieran Flanagan's argument to this effect. Although, he says, sociology would typically reject association with theology, it is "implicated in theology" and theology offers the good of a vision of life's meaning that sociology cannot supply. Kieran Flanagan, "The Return of Theology: Sociology's Distant Relative," in *The Blackwell Companion to Sociology of Religion*, pp. 432-44.

CHAPTER 8

Generating Christian Political Theory and the Uses of Ethnography

Luke Bretherton

Introduction: Politics, Ethnography, and the Theological Turn to Practice

On November 25, 2009, in the midst of anxiety about the financial crisis and the scandal over MPs' expenses, two thousand people gathered at the Barbican in London for an assembly of London Citizens. The event that evening opened with the following scenario to explain what London Citizens was and what the event was about. After two female members from the Pentecostal New Testament Church of God sang "Lean on Me" followed by a performance by a street dance troupe called Visionz, Sr Una McLeash, a former head teacher of a Catholic girls school in East London and trustee of London Citizens, introduced the panel of chairs (of which I was one) and sought approval from everyone in the room for the authority of chairs to govern the assembly. This consisted of asking the two thousand participants (the total capacity of the Barbican) to say "Aye" and wave their programs if they agreed. It was difficult to see if there were any dissenters as the rest of the auditorium was darkened, while lights shone directly on the platform, creating something of a gulf between the stage and the seating area. However, the overwhelming impression was of a mass rustling of paper and a chorus of "Aye's." As Sr Una did this, five religious leaders, in clerical dress, took to the stage to sit, positioned like a panel of judges, at the back of the platform. These leaders came from nonestablishment traditions. They were the Roman Catholic vicar-general of East London, the head of the Muslim Council of Britain, the head of the Salvation Army, the senior rabbi of the Masorti synagogues, and the leading bishop of the New Testament Church of God. After Sr Una had finished, two young, black comedians and children's television presenters named Ashley J and Tee-J bounded to the front of the stage while I stood at the lectern behind them. I was there as a representative "leader" from a local church in membership who had been involved in helping to organize the event.

Ashley J began the dialogue, which was mostly scripted on my part and largely improvised on theirs. Tee-J started by asking who we were and how we came to the proposals to be discussed that evening. My response, agreed to and edited with other organizers at a Sunday evening rehearsal three days previous, was the following:

> We are 2,000 people gathered here in this place tonight, who represent over 150 institutions, and that itself represents 50,000 people from across London. And we are schools, synagogues, churches, trade unions, university departments, and other civil society institutions from across this city. And we are people who take responsibility for ourselves, for our families and for the communities where we live. And we expect others to do the same, whether they be our neighbours, whether they be bankers, or whether they be politicians. So that's who we are.[1]

"I like, I like," responded Tee-J, who went on, "So what is London Citizens' response to the economic crisis?" My agreed-on explanation was as follows:

> So given who we are, we've been working with low paid workers from across the capital for about ten years on the issue of getting them a living wage. And from that experience when the recession came we were listening to people in our institutions, in our communities and in our workplace and we spent time listening to what the impact of the recession was on them through one-on-ones, we had over a thousand of them and had over a hundred house group meetings and a whole range of different ways in which we listened to people. And from that experience of listening to the experience of ordinary people we began to formulate these proposals. . . . That process came together in September when about a hundred different leaders from our institutions came together and debated and formulated the five proposals as you

---

1. Transcribed from video recording of the event filmed by London Citizens, November 25, 2009.

have them. They were then taken to three assemblies from across London and over 700 people voted on those proposals and that is what we are bringing here tonight. These proposals were not born out of any prior political programme or ideology, they were not born out of the need to keep vested powers in power. They were born out of listening to the experiences of ordinary people and how the recession was impacting them and a commitment to working together for the common good.[2]

Ashley cut in: "Tee-J, you look a bit confused. Did you understand that? There were a lot of words that were more than four letters long." To which Tee-J responded: "Yeah, there's a few things I didn't catch. But I'm wondering if you can break it down for me." So Ashley said: "I'll break it down for you East London stylie. Right. Basically everyone here tonight is coming together and they have put their trust back in a democracy: getting people to come together and decide what they want to happen and creating a proposal and putting that towards the people who have the powers that be to change these things." "Ah, makes sense now," replied Tee-J.

The reality of how the proposals came together was a less linear and more multilateral process than the one depicted. However, Ashley's summation was accurate: the gathering was testimony to a renewed trust in democracy as a way of gaining some power to determine what was happening in our city. The event was also a singularly important instance of the intersection of religion and the performance of democratic citizenship within urban politics.

My involvement in the event was both as a participant and as an observer, for London Citizens, and its umbrella organization, CitizensUK, was the subject of a three-year research project I was leading. My investigation of London Citizens focused on whether broad-based community organizing represented a practice through which churches might develop a critical yet constructive relationship with the state and market while at the same time forging a common life with those of other faiths and of no faith. However, the aim of the research was theoretical and not simply descriptive: I was interested in how ethnographic methods might be used to excavate particular practices as part of theory generation. This research can be situated within an ongoing conversation about the relationship between theological ethics and practice and the nature of theology as a practice.

---

2. Transcribed from video recording of the event.

Central to this turn to practice are political concerns manifested in both a focus on Christian political engagement and the production, distribution, and consumption of theology as a culturally constructed and contested mode of discourse.[3] This is partly a legacy of liberation theology, and is illustrated by liberation theology. Liberation theology grew out of political concerns about what constitutes faithful witness in a context of oppression and at the same time called into question how theology was done. Gustavo Gutiérrez's *Theology of Liberation* exemplifies this with its call for attention to praxis over theory as the beginning point for theological reflection and its call for solidarity with the oppressed expressed through involvement in the class struggle. Similarly, the critique of liberation theology by John Milbank, William Cavanaugh, and others simultaneously raises both methodological and political concerns. For Cavanaugh and Milbank, liberation theology uncritically accepted the role of the state in delivering social justice and failed to take seriously enough the church and its practices as sources of social analysis. For these theologians, the church is itself a polity or *res publica* that forms and socializes human bodies in ways that are very different to those of the modern nation-state and either a capitalist or a centrally planned economy.[4] Cavanaugh's work points to how the church is the primary community for Christians whose pattern of citizenship constitutes a truly public form of life.[5] Milbank's critique of liberation theology, and in particular its conceptualization of the relationship between theology and social science, not only pushes theology to pay attention to the practices of the church as themselves generative of social theory but also problematizes how to study these practices without falling prey to the antitheological bias inherent in much social science.[6] The exploration of the relationship between ecclesiology and ethnography represents an emerging response to the dual problematic Milbank poses. Nicholas Healy's advocacy of "ecclesiological ethnography," Christian Scharen's "ethnography as ecclesiology," and Nicholas Adams and Charles Elliott's account of ethnography as a dogmatic task all represent attempts

---

3. Examples of the latter are Kathryn Tanner, *Theories of Culture: A New Agenda for Theology* (Minneapolis: Fortress, 1997), and Graham Ward, *Cultural Transformation and Religious Practice* (Cambridge: Cambridge University Press, 2005).

4. William Cavanaugh, *Theopolitical Imagination: Discovering the Liturgy as a Political Act in an Age of Global Consumerism* (Edinburgh: T. & T. Clark, 2002), p. 83.

5. Cavanaugh, *Theopolitical Imagination,* p. 84.

6. John Milbank, *Theology and Social Theory: Beyond Secular Reason* (Oxford: Blackwell, 1993), p. 380.

to give a theological account of the church that draws on historical and social scientific accounts while being mindful of and not capitulating to the methodological atheism that often undergirds such research.[7]

A related development within theological ethics intersects with and feeds into the exploration of the relationship between ecclesiology and ethnography: that is, the emergence of virtue ethics. Again, methodological issues were intertwined with concerns about the nature and practice of Christian witness in the world. The work of Stanley Hauerwas is both representative of and catalytic in this parallel development. As Hauerwas makes clear in his autobiography — both in what it says and in how it constitutes a form of "biography as theology" — a central thematic in his work is the interrelationship between the ability to think rightly and live well, and the communities that form us.[8] For Hauerwas, description and narrative are central to any account of the truth. For example, Hauerwas's descriptions of bricklaying and stonemasons are examples of his thick descriptions that in themselves explain as descriptions what his conception of ethics is and how we come to be virtuous.[9] Such descriptions pay attention to the symbiosis of theory and practice in ways much systematic theology often fails to. As Hauerwas comments, while owing a great debt to Karl Barth, his work is born out of a worry that "Barth may have given an account of Christian doctrine in which the material conditions necessary to make doctrine intelligible were not accounted for sufficiently."[10] Adams and Elliott point out that in his recent work Hauerwas has "struggled against what he sees as the twin temptations of presenting Christian

7. Nicholas Healy, *Church, World, and the Christian Life: Practical-Prophetic Ecclesiology* (Cambridge: Cambridge University Press, 2000), pp. 154-85; Christian Batalden Scharen, "'Judicious Narratives,' or Ethnography as Ecclesiology," *Scottish Journal of Theology* 58, no. 2 (2005): 125-42; Nicholas Adams and Charles Elliott, "Ethnography Is Dogmatics: Making Description Central to Systematic Theology," *Scottish Journal of Theology* 53 (2000): 339-64.

8. The term "biography as theology" is taken from James McClendon's work of the same name that Hauerwas cites as influential in the development of his own thinking. James William McClendon, *Biography as Theology: How Life Stories Can Remake Today's Theology* (Nashville: Abingdon, 1974).

9. Stanley Hauerwas, "The Politics of Church: How We Lay Bricks and Make Disciples," in Stanley Hauerwas, *After Christendom? How the Church Is to Behave If Freedom, Justice, and a Christian Nation Are Bad Ideas* (Nashville: Abingdon, 1991), chapter 4; "Carving Stone or Learning to Speak Christian," in Stanley Hauerwas, *The State of the University: Academic Knowledges and the Knowledge of God* (Oxford: Blackwell, 2007), chapter 7.

10. Stanley Hauerwas, *Hannah's Child* (London: SCM, 2010), p. 87.

thought as a disembodied system of ideas and doing 'Durkheim with an ecclesial twist.'"[11] Hauerwas's conception of politics and his critique of liberalism directly follow on from these concerns. As he puts it: "My criticism of liberal political presumptions is based in my presumption that politics, like laying brick, is a wisdom-determined activity. Liberalism too often is the attempt to have concrete replace stone in an effort to avoid the necessary existence of a people with wisdom."[12] What he means by this is that politics, as a "wisdom-determined activity," requires being apprenticed into a particular form of life and way of seeing the world that enable one to make right judgments about how to act appropriately. Like Milbank, Hauerwas's work directs theology toward paying attention to the practices of the church and offers description as a way of paying attention. An ethnographic perspective suggests itself as one way to offer such descriptions of the "material conditions necessary to make doctrine intelligible."

There is something more going on in Hauerwas, Milbank, and liberation theology than either the attempt to make doctrine intelligible or simply the recognition that Christian belief is inherently contextual. There is an epistemological claim that knowledge of the good is dependent on participation in the good. Right thinking (and thence theory) is dependent on and subsequent to participation in good practice, and practice is itself theory-laden: that is, normative conceptualizations require the identification of and participation in social relationships that embody them. Or to put it another way, there is a symbiosis between orthodoxy and orthopraxy. What follows is one attempt to develop an account of how to draw on ethnographic modes of research in the development of normative Christian political conceptualizations of the conditions and possibilities of faithful witness within contemporary politics. This account is developed in relation to my research on the relationship between Christianity and broad-based community organizing (BBCO).

Broad-Based Community Organizing and the Necessity of Apprenticeship

To research CitizensUK, my research colleague, Maurice Glasman, and I drew on ethnographic approaches so as to pay close attention to the peo-

---

11. Adams and Elliott, "Ethnography Is Dogmatics," p. 362.
12. Hauerwas, *Hannah's Child*, pp. 36-37.

ple, institutions, practices, and processes involved in community organizing. We became embedded within CitizensUK in order to excavate how those involved acted and conceptualized their involvement and what discourses and practices they drew on in doing so. The primary point of data collection was through being participant observers from 2008 to 2011 at over a hundred events and meetings; this represents hundreds of hours and innumerable conversations in and around these gatherings. These meetings and events ranged in focus from local to citywide to national to international. They included internal organizational meetings, large public actions, training events (including the CitizensUK five-day training program), seminars, day retreats, private meetings among CitizensUK participants, and meetings between representatives from CitizensUK and political or business leaders. In addition to those meetings and events specifically organized by CitizensUK, we attended numerous meetings put on by other institutions that leaders and organizers from CitizensUK attended as representatives of the organization. To supplement this process of observation we undertook thirty in-depth interviews with key leaders, organizers, and critics of CitizensUK's work and organizers from the Industrial Areas Foundation (IAF) in the United States, the German Institute for Community Organizing (DICO), and Sydney Alliance. The information and reflections based on this process of participant observation and the interviews were then triangulated by reference to archive material (both from CitizensUK's records and the IAF archive held by the University of Illinois in Chicago), the mainstream media and blogosphere's coverage of the work, other academic studies of community organizing in the United Kingdom and United States, and checking the emerging conclusions with both long-established organizers and commentators on community organizing external to the IAF network and organizers and leaders within the IAF network.[13]

We focused on the work of CitizensUK because it was the only form of community organizing immediately available to us in London. Since CitizensUK is affiliated with the IAF in the United States, this led to an inevitable focus on the history and context of the IAF. This twin focus turned out to be providential. CitizensUK is a particularly generative ex-

---

13. I am extremely grateful for the conversation, patient feedback, and comments on the research from those outside the IAF, in particular Richard Woods, Mark Warren, Marshall Ganz, Mike Miller, Harry Boyte, and Heidi Swarts; and those within the IAF, in particular Neil Jameson, Matthew Bolton, Jonathan Lange, Leo Penta, Michael Gecan, and Amanda Tattersall.

ample of community organizing within the context of a global city. Moreover, the financial crises that unfolded from 2008 onward, along with the 2010 general election, resulted in a hugely significant moment in the history of the organization: one that launched it onto the national stage in the United Kingdom. The IAF is the stem root of community organizing, as it is the organization founded by Saul Alinsky, widely recognized as the "dean" of community organizing worldwide. For historical reasons alone its significance is important. Added to that, its leadership training program and practices form the prototype that the great majority of other contemporary community-organizing networks build on. This does not necessarily make it the best or most effective. But it does mean the IAF has a plausible claim to be counted as paradigmatic for community organizing in general.

At the outset of the research we negotiated access to the work of CitizensUK with Neil Jameson, its lead organizer. The agreement we reached was that access was conditional on commitment and involvement in the organization as "leaders": hence my involvement on the stage at the Barbican event on November 25. To be a leader we had to be a member of an institution in membership. My own church was already a member of London Citizens, so I took part in events and meetings as one of its representatives. For my colleague, being a leader entailed bringing his university department into membership (which he did); subsequently he brokered the Masorti synagogues, of which he was a member, coming into membership of London Citizens. However, it was made explicit that while we would seek the good of CitizensUK and actively take part in and contribute to the work to the best of our abilities, we would be critical and use the research process to suggest changes in practice where this seemed appropriate. What we were aiming for was a reciprocal, noninstrumental relationship, one that honored the particular but intertwined interests of each party and where we as researchers made a real contribution to the organization while at the same time the organization actively contributed to and engaged with our research. Negotiating this insider-outsider status required a constantly evolving combination of rapport, trust building, identification, and critical distance. However, far from being innovative, such an approach fits an interpretive and participatory research method where the line between researcher and research is fluid and there is a commitment to work collaboratively with those researched to generate knowledge that is useful and transformative of their practice. Our method was also consistent with key practices of community organizing that train people to identify their mutual interests and form a common work around the pursuit of that shared interest, critically evaluating everything that is done in that common work and engaging in constant learning and education in order to improve practice and deepen insight. Finally, given the goals of the study, which was the development of a constructive political and theological framework for conceptualizing democratic citizenship within the contemporary context, the reciprocal and participatory approach undertaken was the most appropriate as the process embodied the desired outcome.

Another factor in adopting the approach outlined here was epistemological and echoes Hauerwas's reflections on bricklaying and the place of apprenticeship in learning to see the world rightly. Understanding the practice of community organizing was not possible simply through interviews and observation. Susan Harding notes that in her study of Jerry Falwell and the Christian Right she could not understand this movement without direct participation and "becoming one's own informant."[14] She describes her own "conversion" to the language world that Jerry Falwell inhabited without this entailing her becoming an "insider." She states: "There is no such thing as a neutral position, no place for an ethnographer who seeks 'information.' Either you are lost, or you are saved."[15] My experience with CitizensUK was similar. I began on the outside looking in, and found it difficult to understand. At some point I became an insider and was looking from the inside out and had inhabited as tacit the knowledge of community organizing. My experience was corroborated by other participants, who commented on how difficult it was to explain community organizing to outsiders. The language of conversion was repeatedly used to explain the process of getting involved. This was an analogy rather than a literal description, but it captured for participants the way in which learning came by doing and involvement and how it was difficult to verbalize or describe community organizing in explicit terms. This is partly explained by the unfamiliarity with BBCO in the United Kingdom in contrast to the United States. But it is also partly explained by the nature of BBCO as a form of craft knowledge as against a rationally explicable technique that can be set out in a manual. To learn a craft one has to be apprenticed in its ways and means, but acquiring this knowledge is no guarantee of being able to give a theoretical account of it to the uninitiated. Apprentices or

14. Susan Friend Harding, *The Book of Jerry Falwell: Fundamentalist Language and Politics* (Princeton: Princeton University Press, 2000), p. 39.

15. Harding, *Book of Jerry Falwell*, p. 39.

even master carpenters cannot necessarily give a theoretical account of what they are doing and its rationale, but that does not mean they are not good at what they do. Participation was key to understanding BBCO, but not sufficient for explaining it. To explain it, broader theoretical frameworks, engagement with its intellectual history, and comparison with other case studies were needed to bring the craft knowledge to speech.

As a craft that requires entry into the "guild" as a full-orbed participant, BBCO points to the limits of interviews and observation as ways of gaining understanding. This is something that is increasingly recognized in broader methodological discussions. For example, Charles Briggs describes how, in his research on traditional religious wood carving in the Spanish-speaking community in northern New Mexico, the cultural norms and communicative repertoires of the community made the interviews he attempted inappropriate and largely useless as means of gaining insight. This situation forced him to discover the culturally appropriate way to learn about this topic, which was by apprenticeship.[16] Timothy Jenkins echoes Briggs's reflection in his own account of the relationship between fieldwork and knowledge generation: "Knowledge of everyday life is not available to the disinterested gaze of an inquirer; rather, fieldwork is an apprenticeship of signs, the process of entry into a particular world, governed by a variety of factors, including the situation and previous experience of the anthropologist. During an apprenticeship, as well as skills and perceptions, memories and desires are altered, so that every actor, indigenous or ethnographer, is engaged in a personal and experiential capacity."[17] Jenkins goes on to note that knowledge gained through such a process of apprenticeship is theoretically rich, equivalent to what he calls "moral knowledge": it gives order and yet is revisable; it provides the basis for both action and understanding and reflection on action.[18]

Apprenticeship as a form of learning suggests a different epistemological relationship to the subject of study than a positivist-empirical one. Rather than autonomous distance and observation, it demands immersion and commitment to do the work well and to seek the best for the practice at all times. Through apprenticeship in what is studied and through practicing, and even demonstrating flair at its proper practice — being judged

16. Charles Briggs, *Learning How to Ask: A Sociolinguistic Appraisal of the Role of Interview in Social Science Research* (Cambridge: Cambridge University Press, 1986).

17. Timothy Jenkins, "Fieldwork and the Perception of Everyday Life," *Man* 29, no. 2 (1994): 445.

18. Jenkins, "Fieldwork," p. 452.

a good practitioner by acknowledged masters in the craft — one can check whether one has understood the practice properly. Such learning may generate new ideas, but the primary aim in relation to the study of community organizing was learning new possibilities for forging a common life. In apprenticeship we learn through mimesis of other practitioners; but akin to Alasdair MacIntyre's conception of a tradition as an argument over time about what constitutes the good, this does not imply uncritical acceptance of the norms and behavioral processes embedded within the practice. Rather, it entails listening and doing what one is told as well as argumentative collaboration. Broader validation of the personal perspective gained as constituting something of the "common sense" of the practice studied is enabled through triangulating one's own perspective with others, comparing it with other formal studies, reading archive material to gain a historical perspective, and engaging with criticisms of the work and the observations of those external to it.

Apprenticeship is particularly important for getting at the "theory-in-use" of the participants in community organizing. In any project there is a need to move beyond the standard descriptions and accounts reported by participants because these tend to draw on narrow definitions, a limited range of language available, and distorted pictures of the practice under study. In community organizing this is particularly acute as interviewees often commented on how difficult it was to explain community organizing as a practice to others. The communicative disjuncture experienced by interviewees provides an important clue to the kind of knowledge community organizing embodies. As a form of political action it is focused on practices, sequences learned and bodily employed. Mastery is transmitted in and through practice, without necessarily requiring a high level of conscious verbalization or rational deliberation — despite plenty of words being used in the formulation and outworking of the practice. Rather than cognitive recognition and verbal articulation, what is important in community organizing is the sequence of things and the skillful deployment of a repertoire of actions in order to provoke the desired reaction: one-on-ones, caucusing, assemblies, power analysis, evaluations, and inventive forms of contention are the ingredients of a successful sequence. Community organizing as a sequence of actions that constitute a public or common work can be distinguished from the formal campaigns that are run. The formal campaigns — to promote a living wage, to stop the detention of the children of asylum seekers, or to introduce a cap on interest rates — require cognitive and conscious assent to the issues. Without bringing about a new understanding in those one is addressing — changing hearts and minds — the campaign fails. Consciousness raising and education are key to such work: people need to understand the issues. However, the focus or primary desired outcome of BBCO as distinct from its campaigns is organized people, leadership development, and "reweaving civil society." It is the artful deployment of a repertoire of actions to form a particular sequence within a distinct context amid a unique set of circumstances and among particular people that enables the identification and training of leaders, the building of relational power, and the reweaving of civil society. Although winning a campaign is an important part of what makes a sequence good or not, it is not the primary aim of BBCO. Apprenticeship and the tacit knowledge it engenders are the only way to learn how to make judgments about what constitutes a well-executed or poorly executed sequence.

Practical Reason and the Generation of Judgment

The account of apprenticeship as a way of coming to understand and make judgments upon a particular form of political practice accords with broader accounts of practical reason and its role in the generation of political theory. Drawing on the Aristotelian distinction between *sophia* (theoretical wisdom) and *phronēsis* (practical wisdom), we can say that the former has dominated political philosophy and theology.[19] However, overly theoretical accounts of politics fail to reckon with the nature of politics itself. Politics is, as Machiavelli discerned, about action in time and as such it involves questions of power (the ability to act) and historicity (the temporal and temporary nature of action).[20] The unpredictable and unstable nature of political life directs attention away from universal principles and

19. This is not to suggest an opposition between the two. They are mutually dependent but distinct modes of reasoning. However, *sophia* strives to rise above common sense and subsumes the particular to the universal, whereas *phronesis* is rooted in common sense and responds to the particular. Judgment, as an outcome of *phronesis*, does not seek universal validity. Rather, it appeals to those participating and present within a public realm where the situation or objects to be judged appear.

20. "In my view, he who conforms his course of action to the quality of the times will fare well, and conversely he whose course of action clashes with the times will fare badly." Niccolo Machiavelli, *The Prince*, trans. Peter Constantine, paperback edition (New York: Modern Library, 2008), p. 116. The quote comes from chapter 25 where Machiavelli discusses the need for prudence in identifying the right course of action in relation to the changing of Fortune's wheel; that is, the contingency and flux of history.

general historical patterns "towards the peculiar features of singular and discrete events and institutions located in particular historical settings."[21] The need to act in a way appropriate to the time, and hence the need for judgments about what is best for these people, in this place, at this time, applies to the pastoral intervention of the priest as much as to the political intervention of the prince, for both are forms of public action within a particular kind of polis. As action in time, politics requires a means of coming to judgment suited to the needs and vicissitudes of the political world. *Phronēsis* is that means.

Following Hannah Arendt, we can say that political theory (as against political philosophy) attempts to develop conceptions of politics derived from *phronēsis*.[22] Its task is not to work from first principles but to reflect on already established practices and the presuppositions that inform them in order to develop an account of what is the case and theorize out of that to generate wider prescriptions and criteria of evaluation.[23] The patriarch of such an approach is Aristotle, not Plato. Where rational humans for Plato are moved by the cosmic order, for Aristotle they are moved by a sense of the proper order among the ends we pursue. This sense cannot be articulated in terms of theoretical axioms, but rather, is grasped by *phronēsis*. Aristotle links the study of politics and *phronēsis* (*Nichomachean Ethics* 1141b8-b27).[24] This is necessary for Aristotle because the nature of politics means it cannot be reduced to questions of *epistēmē* (politics is always particular and contextual) or *technē* (politics as the pursuit of a common life always concerns questions of morality rather than simply questions of technique or skill).[25] It is my contention that the generation of Christian political theory demands a similar attention to developing *phronēsis* through apprenticeship in particular kinds of practice

21. Peter Steinberger, *The Concept of Political Judgment* (Chicago: University of Chicago Press, 1993), p. 14.

22. Such a distinction is of course heuristic, as hard-and-fast lines between political theory and political philosophy are notoriously difficult to demarcate when discussing most significant political thinkers (with the exception perhaps of Plato).

23. Whether Arendt's own account of political judgment really does this is another matter.

24. For a critique of Aristotle's conception of *phronēsis* and how this problematizes an account of political judgment based on an Aristotelian conception, see Steinberger, *Concept of Political Judgment*, pp. 106-27.

25. Bent Flyvbjerg, *Making Social Science Matter: Why Social Inquiry Fails and How It Can Succeed Again*, trans. Steven Sampson (Cambridge: Cambridge University Press, 2001), p. 59.

through which churches negotiate a shared political life with others (as distinct from specifically ecclesial modes of witness).

Practical Reason and Research Methods

The key to generating judgments on the basis of *phronēsis* is to identify case studies within which assessment of practices can take place. These must possess what Arendt called an "exemplary validity"; that is, while retaining their particularity, and without reducing or subsuming them to expressions of a prior universal (whether it be a Platonic ideal or a Kantian *schema*), the cases provide insight into the generality that otherwise could not be discerned by us as those who are participants in the very context under scrutiny.[26] What Bent Flyvbjerg calls "phronetic" research necessarily focuses on case studies, precedents, and exemplars.[27] "Practical rationality and judgment evolve and operate primarily by virtue of deep-going case experiences. Practical rationality, therefore, is best understood through cases — experienced or narrated — just as judgment is best cultivated and communicated via the exposition of cases."[28] However, as David Thacher points out, such empirical cases are different from the hypothetical case studies much loved by moral philosophers that are both too tenuously related to real dilemmas of judgment to be of any practical value in guiding future judgment, and fail to confront the unfamiliar and unnoticed nature of experience generated, as they grow out of the philosophers' own introspection.[29] Flyvbjerg notes that in both philosophy and social science, empirical cases have generated key conceptual insights, and he gives the examples of Foucault's panopticon and Freud's "Wolfman" as having strategic importance in the development of these thinkers' work.[30] However, in terms of political life such an approach is

---

26. Hannah Arendt, *Lectures on Kant's Political Philosophy,* ed. Ronald Beiner (Chicago: University of Chicago Press, 1982), pp. 76-77.

27. Flyvbjerg is himself building on the work of Robert Bellah, who first proposed reconceptualizing social science as a form of *phronēsis*. Robert Bellah, "Social Science as Practical Reason," in *Ethics, Social Sciences, and Policy Analysis,* ed. Daniel Callahan and Bruce Jennings (New York: Plenum Press, 1983), pp. 37-64.

28. Flyvbjerg, *Making Social Science Matter,* p. 135.

29. David Thacher, "The Normative Case Study," *American Journal of Sociology* 111, no. 6 (2006): 1661.

30. Likewise, Thacher, in his parallel account of what he calls the "normative case

best exemplified by Tocqueville, for whom observation of the dynamics and interrelation of political and social life forms the basis of generating conceptual categories and normative accounts of political life and action within a particular context of study. The case study method enables the formulation of normative judgments in dialogue with the concerns and practices of ordinary people and their judgments about what is meaningful and important. Ethnographic modes of attention (interview, participant observation, archive research, etc.) are vital for generating conceptual refinement and development in relation to lived practices as the political life of ordinary people occurs not in texts but in contingent interactions among persons and groups. Ethnographic modes of investigation represent one way of doing this and constitute a way that not only puts narrative and participation at the center of the method of study but can also serve the ability of a community — whether political or ecclesial — to come to judgment. This of course raises the question of how to proceed using a case study method. The work of Michael Burawoy is helpful in this regard as it is richly suggestive of a way to relate the study of the empirical to the generation of theoretical conceptions.

The Extended Case Study Method

Michael Burawoy is an anthropologist whose approach is directly relevant to the study of political engagement, forged as it was through his own ethnographic studies of union and other labor struggles in different contexts such as Zambia and Russia. He has developed what he calls the extended case study method, an approach that seeks, on the one hand, to avoid the positivism that reduces social science to a natural science model and that seeks to minimize "bias," and, on the other hand, to avoid a reductive postmodernism that suppresses any scientific dimension at all, reducing social science to dialogue between insider and outsider aimed at mutual self-understanding without any attempt at explanation.[31] For Burawoy, the very methods of investigation deployed in ethnography point the way beyond the impasse of positivism and postmodernism. For

---

study," gives a long array of other such examples. Thacher, "The Normative Case Study," pp. 1638-46.

31. Michael Burawoy, *Ethnography Unbound: Power and Resistance in the Modern Metropolis* (Berkeley: University of California Press, 1991), p. 3.

example, he values participant observation because it enables dialogue between the participant who calls for understanding and the observer who seeks causal explanation. This dialogic encounter involves neither distance nor immersion. Rather, as Burawoy puts it: "The purpose of fieldwork is not to strip ourselves of biases, for that is an illusory goal, nor to celebrate those biases as the authorial voice of the ethnographer, but rather to discover and perhaps change our biases through interaction with others."[32]

Burawoy contrasts his approach with that of Clifford Geertz, a figure of not inconsiderable influence in theology. For Burawoy, Geertz subsumes the particular to the universal. He states: "The *interpretive case method* [of Geertz] regards the micro-context as a setting in which a particular 'macro' principle, such as commodification, rationalization, or male domination, reveals itself. The uniqueness of each situation is then lost as it becomes an expression of the whole, or of some essential defining feature of the totality."[33] Geertz's famous account of the Balinese cockfight as a "paradigmatic event" is an example of this process of subsumption. For Geertz, the cockfight is a symbolic expression of broader social processes and discourses. It functions as a key to interpreting Balinese society rather than having intrinsic value in itself. Burawoy comments: "The differences between the interpretive and extended case methods become clearer on re-examination of Geertz's Balinese cockfight. Whereas Geertz regards it as a 'paradigmatic event' that displays the social organization of Balinese society, the extended case method would examine the specificity of the cockfight — how it varies from place to place, how it has changed over time — as a vehicle for comprehending the forces shaping Balinese society."[34]

Burawoy's extended case study method seeks to examine the macroworld through the way it shapes and in turn is shaped and conditioned by the microworld, the everyday world of face-to-face interaction. Macro and micro are in a relation of codetermination rather than the micro simply being a paradigm or expression of the macro. My own work on community organizing in London bears this out. It would be easy to interpret the conditions of organizing in London as paradigmatic of wider forces of economic globalization. However, this would be to miss how the structures of economic globalization are themselves affected by the partic-

32. Burawoy, *Ethnography Unbound*, p. 4.
33. Burawoy, *Ethnography Unbound*, p. 6.
34. Burawoy, *Ethnography Unbound*, p. 278.

ular constellation of banking and politics in London and how community organizing in London is able to act upon place-based banks and regulatory authorities that in turn feed into broader global networks and flows. As Saskia Sassen notes, locality is a "microenvironment with global span."[35] A city is a proliferation of these microenvironments with multiple and overlapping global circuits that run between them. Urban local politics in a global city is always then operating in a number of registers — micro, local (meso), and global (macro) — with global and nonlocal political dynamics impacting a particular locality and local politics affecting or being imbricated in global or transnational political dynamics. This is especially so in a city like London that is a major generator of cultural production and a crucial node of global capitalism, and has myriad diaspora and transnational communities. The broader point to draw out for the relationship between ethnography, ecclesiology, and political theory is that the church cannot be read as simply a microcosm of broader political processes and structural forces: it has its own integrity. Yet neither can an analysis of the church be separated from how it is in a relationship of codetermination (and at times co-construction) with its political environment. What I mean by codetermination is illustrated by Charles Taylor's account of how secularity is the result not of external processes of modernization acting upon belief and practice (i.e., wherein the political environment determines the nature of belief and practice) nor of the internal logic of Christianity, but results from how belief and unbelief are themselves constantly interacting and changing (i.e., belief and unbelief codetermine and mutually constitute each other in an ongoing way).[36]

In addition to contrasting his approach to that of Geertz, Burawoy also distinguishes his approach from the influential method of grounded theory first elaborated by Barney Glaser and Anselm Strauss but already present in outline in the origins of urban sociology in the work of Park and Burgess.[37] Like Geertz, Burawoy believes grounded theory subsumes the

35. Saskia Sassen, "Making Public Interventions in Today's Massive Cities," *Static* 4 (2006): 6.

36. Charles Taylor, *A Secular Age* (Cambridge: Harvard University Press, 2007).

37. Barney Glaser and Anselm Strauss, *Discovery of Grounded Theory: Strategies for Qualitative Research* (Mill Valley, Calif.: Sociology Press, 1967). Since the publication of their original work, Glaser and Strauss have diverged in what they understand grounded theory to be. Burawoy's criticism more accurately applies to Glaser's development of the approach, which emphasizes the creation of generalized theories, than it does Strauss's. This is not something that Burawoy acknowledges.

particular to the universal. In grounded theory the particular becomes a resource from which to derive generalizations.[38] He characterizes the difference between grounded theory and his approach as that between a *genetic* and a *generic* approach, stating, "Grounded theory's inductive strategy leads to generic explanations, which take the form of invariant laws. . . . The extended case method constructs *genetic* explanations, that is, explanations of particular outcomes. . . . A generic strategy looks for similarities among disparate cases, whereas the genetic strategy focuses on differences between similar cases. The goal of the first is to seek abstract laws or formal theory, whereas the goal of the second is historically specific causality."[39]

Burawoy's approach can also be contrasted with the dominant approaches in practical theology that, analogously to grounded theory, seek to develop models of practice that subordinate the particular to the universal. Although there are direct parallels between the approach to practical reason and attention to the theory-laden nature of practice set out here, and that put forward by Don Browning, the relationship between the universal and the particular is a key point of differentiation.[40] While alert to the tradition-constituted nature of practical reason, Browning is at pains to argue for the tradition-transcending nature of practical reason. Against MacIntyre, Browning argues that Christianity "adds very important ingredients" to practical reason but does not in itself give rise to a distinct rationality.[41] Within Browning's "hermeneutically conceived understanding of practical reason," practical reason does not form the basis of a *sensus communis* within which public judgments can be made, but rather, the judgments of any community must be verified and interpreted against broader principles that claim universal validity (albeit a universality that is a "socially achieved objectivity" rather than an "absolute objectivity").[42] For Browning, case studies are used to generate an interaction between a

38. Burawoy, *Ethnography Unbound*, pp. 275-76. Burawoy's criticism can be directed at many approaches to case study research. For example, Robert Yin's standard account sees the purpose of the case study approach as enabling the creation of "analytic generalization." Robert K. Yin, *Case Study Research: Design and Methods*, 2nd ed. (London: Sage, 1994), p. 30.

39. Burawoy, *Ethnography Unbound*, pp. 280-81.

40. What is said here is an amplification and corrective to the half-formed and underdeveloped evaluation given on Browning's approach in my previous work. Luke Bretherton, *Christianity and Contemporary Politics* (Oxford: Wiley-Blackwell, 2010), pp. 29-30 n. 73.

41. Don Browning, *A Fundamental Practical Theology: Descriptive and Strategic Proposals* (Minneapolis: Fortress, 1991), p. 194.

42. Browning, *A Fundamental Practical Theology*, p. 183.

particular tradition of beliefs and practices and both a broader range of autonomous discourses and what he calls "brute experience" in order to generate "publically valid" interpretations of action that can then regenerate existing practice. The contrast with Burawoy is one of emphasis. For Browning theory regenerates practice with case studies subordinated to the validation of universal principles; whereas for Burawoy, practice presents a crisis to theory, which must then be reformulated and repaired in the light of insights derived from the case study.

In contrast to the kinds of generic approaches outlined above, Burawoy's genetic approach looks for what is anomalous, not what is typical or representative. It seeks the unexpected, not the sample. Through attention to anomaly the relationship between theory and practice can be critically examined and new theoretical insights generated. Of course, the importance of anomaly to generate new theoretical insights has been a central feature in the development of Christian doctrine that is constantly working with paradox and contradictory tensions as measures of faithfulness in questions of belief and practice: the Chalcedonian conception of Jesus Christ as fully God and fully human, the Trinitarian conception of God as three in one, and the Pentecostal principle of translating the Scriptures wherein the one word of God is only truly heard in one's local tongue are just a few examples.

For Burawoy, theory is central to the process of analysis. It not only guides the focus of a study, but also locates particular social processes in their wider context of determination.[43] However, instead of a given theory being confirmed or refuted by attention to a case study, the ways in which a case violates or presents a crisis of the theory — and so the more anomalous the case the better — are the means by which the theory is strengthened and developed. As Burawoy notes: "The shortcomings of the theory become grounds for a reconstruction that locates the social situation in its historically specific context of determination. . . . Rather than treating the social situation as the confirmation of some theory, we regard it as the failure of the theory. But failure leads not to rejection but to rebuilding theory."[44] Burawoy contends that such an approach follows Karl Popper's logic of scientific discovery with its emphasis on processes of conjecture

43. Michael Burawoy, "The Extended Case Method," *Sociological Theory* 16, no. 1 (1998): 21. See also Michael Burawoy, "Revisits: An Outline of a Theory of Reflexive Ethnography," *American Sociological Review* 68 (2003): 645-79.

44. Burawoy, *Ethnography Unbound*, p. 9.

and refutation. However, it differs from Popper because "instead of proving a theory by corroboration or forsaking their theory because it faces falsification, our preferred approach is to improve theories by turning anomalies into exemplars. In a sense we take Popper to his logical conclusion. Instead of abandoning theory when it faces refutation, we try to 'refute the refutation' by making our theory stronger."[45] The researcher thus works with a prior body of theory (in my case this entailed a combination of political theology and political theory), but it is one that is continually evolving through attention to concrete cases that themselves generate the conceptual resources for the repair and reformulation of the prior body of theory. Burawoy calls such an approach a "reflexive science," stating: "Reflexive science starts out from dialogue, virtual or real, between observer and participants, embeds such dialogue within a second dialogue between local processes and extralocal forces that in turn can only be comprehended through a third, expanding dialogue of theory with itself. Objectivity is not measured by procedures that assure an accurate mapping of the world but by the growth of knowledge; that is, the imaginative and parsimonious reconstruction of theory to accommodate anomalies."[46]

At this point a connection with Flyvbjerg's "phronetic" approach can be made. Both draw on *phronēsis* as the key mode of reason that generates organizing concepts and "genetic," historically alert explanations. As with the contextually located judgments arising within a particular *sensus communis,* knowledge generated from Burawoy's extended case method has what he calls an "embedded objectivity." Burawoy comments: "Here we have a craft mode of knowledge production in which *the product governs the process. . . .* Theory and research are inextricable. The extended case method is thus a form of craft production of knowledge wherein the conceiver of research is simultaneously the executor."[47] Burawoy's extended case study method points to how particular and often anomalous case studies can help enrich and develop conceptualizations of the interrelationship between Christianity and politics through ethnographic research. There is not the space to outline it here, but for many reasons BBCO represented an anomaly to many standard accounts of the relationship between Christianity and liberal democracy developed within political theory and political theology.

---

45. Burawoy, *Ethnography Unbound,* p. 10.
46. Burawoy, "The Extended Case Method," p. 5.
47. Burawoy, "The Extended Case Method," p. 28.

Conclusion

The extended case study method raises the question not only of how to conduct research but also of what the purpose of such research is. Geertz's approach identifies interpretation as the aim of his method, with interpretation arising out of "thick description." Interpretation is understood to be an articulation of the meanings practitioners ascribe to their actions. However, I contend that the purpose of research is not simply interpretation but judgment leading to further action. The focus on judgment is not meant to exclude interpretation. Interpretation is a key part of coming to judgments that enable better action. Theologically, politics is a way to act truly in the world and, following Augustine, however corrupt, it is a form of peaceableness that derives its truth from how far it conforms to the truly peaceable kingdom established by Christ. Faithful research is not afraid of moving beyond interpretation to judgment, and such judgment enables and recommends better action. Research leading to judgment thus contributes to what O'Donovan identifies as the twofold aspect of good judgment: discrimination and decision. For O'Donovan, right judgment has a retrospective element (as an act of discrimination it pronounces upon an existent state of affairs), and as a decision it has a prospective dimension (it is effective in establishing or clearing a space for a common field of meaning and action in which moral relations are possible).[48]

Recourse to ethnographic methods is not simply in order to describe practices and interpret their meanings. Rather, on my account, theology involves constructive judgments and can utilize ethnographic modes of attention as ways of engaging not in abstract judgments but listening up close and participating so as to make judgments based on practical reason. Such judgments are in the service of better — that is, more faithful — action. This kind of approach does not presume a coherent whole of which the rules or grammar can be uncovered through thick description. Theology is not simply the explication and articulation of a preexisting set of meanings waiting to be uncovered. Rather, making judgments requires dialogic encounter with practice and the ways preexisting theological judgments fail to connect with practice, and practice challenges existing theological frames of reference. Flux and multiplicity become occasions for refinement and further specificity in theology as judgment on practice.

48. Oliver O'Donovan, *The Ways of Judgment* (Grand Rapids: Eerdmans, 2005), pp. 7-12.

Such judgments are themselves contextual, but, as in the extended case method, that does not make them relativistic. Rather, they are part of the ongoing argument within a tradition about the good. In the case of political engagement, it is the political import of the good of Christianity that is at stake.

CHAPTER 9

Practical Ecclesiology:
What Counts as Theology in Studying the Church?

Clare Watkins (with Deborah Bhatti, Helen Cameron, Catherine Duce, and James Sweeney)

Introduction: The Whole Problem with Ecclesiology . . .

This chapter is written from the perspective of someone whose working life has been taken up — in one way or another — by concern for the church. It has been a concern expressed both through pastoral work and through academic research and teaching, reflecting a perennial anxiety about what ecclesiology has to do with how ordinary Christians get on with living the church "on the ground." The tension — even wound — that is often uncovered here is the motivation for an attempt to develop and describe a fresh way of speaking effectively and transformatively about church, a way that speaks into practice *and* systematics with equal authenticity.

This concern is hardly new, nor is it rare among practitioners and academics. Those of us involved in the training of people for ministry, and in

---

The multiple authorship of this paper reflects the paper's origin in team-based research through the project Action Research — Church and Society (ARCS). The nature of this project — a collaboration between Heythrop College, University of London, and the Oxford Centre for Ecclesiology and Practical Theology (OxCEPT), Ripon College Cuddesdon — requires that recognition be given to all members of the team, as the significant insights and language of the research have been generated largely through shared conversation and mutual learning. For more about the ARCS project, see Helen Cameron, Deborah Bhatti, Catherine Duce, James Sweeney, and Clare Watkins, *Talking about God in Practice: Theological Action Research and Practical Theology* (London: SCM, 2010).

ongoing formation for clergy, will be familiar with the frustrations felt when what has been learned in the ecclesiological textbooks and courses seems an impossible mismatch with the realities of pastoral work. The academy, likewise, is increasingly aware of the conceptual, linguistic, and interdisciplinary challenges that face the ecclesiologist, as she struggles to find ways of speaking *both* of the church as described in the Christian tradition *and* of the real, lived experience of Christian communal life and work.[1] In all this the need presents itself for an "authentic ecclesiology" — one that is able to speak truthfully about concrete realities, and faithfully about the historical and present promise of the work of the Spirit, enlivening what we understand to be "the body of Christ," the church.

The length of this chapter does not allow for a detailed account of the various attempts that have been — and are being — made to address this perennial difficulty with ecclesiology. In modern times, with the growing sense of fragmentation of religion and society, such work has intensified, and is bearing some real and exciting fruits. The thoughts of this chapter are indebted to this corpus of work, while offering a critical and constructive response and a distinctive way forward for fresh work to be done in this area. For, even given the insights of interdisciplinary ecclesiologies,[2] missiological approaches,[3] and social science readings of the church[4] — all of which are essential for an authentic ecclesiology of the

---

1. This concern lies behind Nicholas M. Healy, *Church, World, and the Christian Life: Practical-Prophetic Ecclesiology* (Cambridge: Cambridge University Press, 2000), which persuasively argues for a greater attention to the "concrete" reality of church in ecclesiology. Another vivid example of this concern is Johannes A. Van der Ven, *Ecclesiology in Context* (Grand Rapids: Eerdmans, 1993).

2. There has been a trickle of such attempts at inner-disciplinary ecclesiology since Dietrich Bonhoeffer took on the subject in the 1920s: Dietrich Bonhoeffer, *Sanctorum Communio: A Dogmatic Enquiry into the Sociology of the Church* (ET: London: Collins, 1963; original German, 1927). Most recently I would refer to Richard H. Roberts, *Religion, Theology, and Human Sciences* (Cambridge: Cambridge University Press, 2002); John Swinton and H. Mowat, *Practical Theology and Qualitative Research* (London: SCM, 2006). For something of a survey of earlier material in the field, see Clare Watkins, "Organizing the People of God: Social Science Theories of Organization in Ecclesiology," *Theological Studies* 52, no. 4 (December 1991): 689-711.

3. For example, see Helen Cameron, *Resourcing Mission: Practical Theology for Changing Churches* (London: SCM, 2010); Stephen B. Bevans and R. P. Schroeder, *Constants in Context: A Theology of Mission for Today* (Maryknoll, N.Y.: Orbis, 2004); David J. Bosch, *Transforming Mission: Paradigm Shift in Theology of Mission* (Maryknoll, N.Y.: Orbis, 1991).

4. Sociological accounts of the cultural contexts of church life are especially important for contemporary ecclesiology. For example, Callum G. Brown, *Religion and Society in*

kind needed — there remains a stubborn difficulty: *how actual practices are given their proper place within the theological discourse of church.*

The team behind the thoughts and processes described in this chapter fiercely believe in the indispensable place that the voices of Christian practice must have in ecclesiology. These practices describe the reality of the church's mystery, as embodied in particular contexts and groups; they both disclose proper questions for the theology of church and — we believe — present an essential locus for the discovery of fresh responses to those questions. Such commitment to practice as a place of true theology for the church has led our research to work extensively with detailed accounts of particular Christian practice.[5] However, such accounts of practice in themselves could remain on the level of sociological analysis or observation; in particular, they can be presented as examples of action research. We wish to go further than these kinds of descriptions, valuable as they are; our concern has been to develop an ecclesiology in which we are enabled to recognize practices as themselves "bearers of theology."[6] In this work practice *must* count as theology in our development of an authentic ecclesiology. The challenge, then, is to create a methodology and a process that better enable such a counting in of the reality of practice in our faithful thinking about church. This chapter argues for one way in which this challenge has been responded to.

Twentieth Century Britain (Harlow, U.K.: Longman, 2006); Grace Davie, *Religion in Britain Since 1945: Believing without Belonging* (Oxford: Blackwell, 1994); Paul Heelas et al., *The Spiritual Revolution: Why Religion Is Giving Way to Spirituality* (Oxford: Blackwell, 2005); David Martin, *On Secularization: Towards a Revised General Theory* (Aldershot: Ashgate, 2005); Charles Taylor, *A Secular Age* (Cambridge: Harvard University Press, 2007).

5. Some account of this can be found in our research report: Deborah Bhatti, Helen Cameron, Catherine Duce, James Sweeney, and Clare Watkins, *Living Church in the Global City: Theology in Practice* (2008), available for download at: http://www.rcc.ac.uk/downloads/pdf_files/ARCS%2520Report%25202008.pdf; as well as in the recent book, Helen Cameron et al., *Talking about God in Practice*. The full list of the eleven practitioner groups worked with is as follows: CaFE (Catholic Faith Exploration); Youth 2000; Housing Justice (UNLEASH); Roman Catholic Diocese of Portsmouth; Roman Catholic Diocese of Westminster's Agency for Evangelisation; Church of England Diocese of Southwark's Social Responsibility Network; Roman Catholic Diocese of Westminster's Justice and Peace Commission; Church of England Parish of St. Mary's Battersea; London Jesuit Volunteers; CAFOD (Catholic Agency for Overseas Development); Messy Church, Croydon.

6. *Living Church,* p. 25.

Ecclesiology Called by Practice

One possible starting place for practical ecclesiology is the body of academic literature that reflects on the various questions raised by the bringing together of abstract and concrete approaches to church. This would be a fairly standard way of looking at the question posed. However, in what follows a practical ecclesiological methodology is developed from a primary reflection on the practices of church, in the belief that such practical realities are *already,* in some way, a theological voice — even authority. By making this our starting point we are not simply privileging practice, in a way consonant with wider practical theology; we are also seeking to articulate the specifically *theological* meaning expressed in the ways in which church is lived out. The things Christians do together, to express their faith, are examples of "faith seeking understanding." To listen to these practices is to listen to works of theology. They are embodied works of theology that call ecclesiology into making room for them.

In this section I want simply to name some of the challenges and gifts to ecclesiology that attention to the voices of practice has yielded. There is a risk in referring, without detailed case studies, to examples of practice in the way this section will have to do. Inevitably such general observations as can be made in so limited a space are not, on their own, persuasive: an element of trusting the researchers' accounts is called for. I take this risk, however, as the price paid for the necessary articulating of *something* of the voices of church practice that have been so vividly speaking into our development of a practical ecclesiological approach over the last six years of research. My hope is that even just these echoes from our detailed, long, and sometimes painful conversations with the ecclesiology borne by practices will be sufficient to ground the subsequent argument for a way of doing ecclesiology that counts practices in.

The practical research that grounds this chapter has extended over six years and been conducted with eleven practitioner groups, both Roman Catholic and Anglican.[7] As such it has given rise to a vast amount of complex and rich data, only a small section of which can be referred to here. The ecclesiological "calls" on our attention are, inevitably, many and varied, and have involved us in reflecting on questions of ecclesial pedagogy, the theology of orders and ministry, the nature of ecclesial struc-

---

7. For a fuller account see Cameron et al., *Talking about God in Practice,* and the report *Living Church.*

tures, sacramentality, and the ecclesiological significance of different readings of tradition. Any one of these might be chosen as a lens through which to explore the possibilities for practical ecclesiology as we have developed it. In what follows particular attention will be given to certain pervasive missiological themes, centering on the relation of "church-and-world," the *ad intra* and *ad extra* readings of church.

The groups worked with were all — in different ways — involved in outreach work, in *evangelization*.[8] As such they can all be seen as embodying theologies of church-and-world, testifying both to powerful insights and to problematic tendencies.

One very prevalent problematic, identified early in our work, has been the tendency for agencies concerned ostensibly with *evangelization/mission* to end up, in practice, being agencies of *renewal/adult faith formation*. CaFE,[9] an agency originally committed to bring people from a position of no faith to a living faith as members of the church, increasingly saw their work as offering educational and inspirational resources to those who already belonged to the church, to enable them better to evangelize. Such a shift in emphasis was an intelligent and sensitive response to the reality experienced by the practitioner group: that most of the church members they sought to work with were at best ambivalent to the idea of evangelization, and generally neither confident nor informed enough to be able to respond to the call to mission *ad extra*. At the same time, this move, in practice, tended to frustrate the evangelizing intentions of the group, as the meetings for faith formation often seemed to become ends in themselves for those who attended — pleasant, often uplifting evenings, which clearly fed a number of people's spiritual and personal lives, but which generally failed to help them make the move from maintenance to mission. It is significant that, of the resources provided by CaFE, those on social justice seemed the least positively received by regular users of the materials. The question presented itself whether what had actually been achieved had more to do with establishing parish groups — albeit often lively and interesting ones — than with shifting attention from the parish to the world beyond.

---

8. The language of evangelization is adopted in our work in a way continuous with its use in recent Roman Catholic thinking — for example, see Paul VI's Apostolic Exhortation, *Evangelii Nuntiandi* (1975). The meaning here includes both the evangelizing of individual women and men, and the "evangelization of culture," which includes works of social justice, media activities, and outreach to sectors of wider society.

9. Catholic Faith Exploration (CaFE): www.faithcafe.org. For an outline of their work and the research carried out, see *Living Church,* appendix 4.

Similar stories could be told from elsewhere. In diocesan programs, in particular, the language of mission was frequently responded to by practices of education, renewal, and the development of *ad intra* ministries. The remarkable and fruitful stewardship program of the Roman Catholic Diocese of Portsmouth[10] was clearly set in the context of the call to be a more deeply missiological church. At the same time, the data on practice, gathered through our research, disclosed a marked tendency to consider the gifts and talents of church people in terms of how they might contribute to maintenance ministries, rather than overt encouragement to see them with respect to outreach, social action, or bringing people outside the church to faith in Christ. Another Roman Catholic diocese's Agency for Evangelisation turned out, through reflection on the descriptions of their actual practice, to be entirely concerned with catechesis and adult education.[11] While in both cases intelligent and thoughtful reasons could be given for this emphasis on *ad intra* renewal, at the expense of *ad extra* focus, the frustration and sense of something being fractured here were often vividly evident: "You know, like, in our talks and our small communities and our catechetical groups and so on, and I find that a bit frustrating on one level because I like to think of us as being, you know, out there getting souls for Christ, and that kind of imagery, but knowing that . . . but feeling torn because I know there's, or feel, or institutionally we are told, or in terms of the church's documents being told there's *prima facie* work to be done internally, as it were."[12] In fact, one of the learning points for our research across the eleven groups we have worked with is the sheer difficulty, *in practice*, of keeping outreach initiatives focused on the *ad extra*. Repeatedly the *ad intra* makes itself felt, as missionary moves are caught up in questions of church polity, order, and authority. For the church traditions we have been working with, the role of the clergy is especially striking here: the ability of evangelizing movements — whether initiated from dioceses or agencies — is almost universally dependent on the person and theology of the parish priest: "We have tried to sort of understand what the parishes want and tried to respond to [it], but it is not necessarily very easy to get parishes and parish priests to respond to what they see as coming from

10. Roman Catholic Diocese of Portsmouth: www.portsmouthdiocese.org.uk. In particular, looking at the diocesan pastoral plan and the stewardship scheme formed an important focus for the research.

11. Roman Catholic Archdiocese of Westminster (www.rcdow.org.uk), Agency for Evangelisation, www.rcdow.org.uk/evangelisation/default.asp?library_ref=26.

12. Westminster Agency for Evangelisation, Agency Focus Group, session 1.

central services."[13] "Until the priest feels comfortable with it [stewardship] it cannot really flourish."[14]

This exercise of power, with which, we should note, laypeople generally collude heartily, tends to pull descriptions of *ad extra* ecclesial practices back into the *ad intra* sphere, as the enabling and disabling factors lead those reading the data from practice to necessary consideration of internal church structures and hierarchies.

What is clear even from these brief accounts of church practice is that there is a *problem* being voiced in the embodied theology of church: even where there is "a heart for mission," there are real, and considerable, obstacles for many people and communities in moving from the place of maintenance to the work of mission. In practical ecclesiology there is a default position that focuses attention on the church *ad intra* — a tendency completely coherent with a large part of traditional academic ecclesiology. What the voice of practice speaks of, however, is not simply this well-recognized tendency, but also the damage of this tendency to the life of a church urgently in need of missionary impetus, and the possibilities for where we might look to identify what is making the move from maintenance to mission so difficult, both in practice and conceptually.

So, we can see already how the practices referred to have — with others — led to a clearer picture of how the complexities of power in clergy-lay relations need exploring if effective *ad extra* practices are to be established in the groups we have worked with. But other insights can also be gleaned. One is the ways in which many practitioners committed to outreach practices of church have — more or less consciously — adopted aspects of prevailing societal and contextual cultures so as to speak more effectively into "the world." The Anglican parish of St. Mary's, Battersea, arguably reflects dominant social values in its emphasis on inclusivity and community for all comers,[15] while Youth 2000 has developed successful "retreats" for young people, which bear a striking resemblance, sociologically, to the phenomenon of "the big event" in youth culture, with its large gatherings, use of contemporary worship, and strong sense of identity through clear formation in distinctively Catholic traditions and practices.[16] In their own ways, too, the

13. Westminster Agency for Evangelisation, interview with director.

14. Portsmouth Diocese, comment from Clergy Workshop.

15. St. Mary's Parish Church, Battersea: www.stmarysbattersea.org.uk. The research was focused initially on the parish's experience of running its own Alpha course.

16. Youth 2000: www.youth2000.org. This is a Roman Catholic national initiative, aimed at developing youth events for young people.

Portsmouth diocesan adoption of the stewardship theme, CaFE's package of DVDs and a "café-style" setting, and Messy Church's[17] use of extracurricular educational practices for children signify a sensitivity to "the world" and a readiness to learn from it how different groups in society are best spoken to. Clearly there is an embodied theology of a proper ecclesial being *in* the world that needs to be recognized.

At the same time, all those initiatives that use such "worldly wisdom" sooner or later come up against some difficult questions. In part, these questions have to do with an appropriately critical, or discerning, adoption of cultural practices. For example, the actual experience of St. Mary's parish of a culture of inclusivity, their desire to be a parish where *everybody* is welcome, led them to a deeper questioning of whether in fact being a member of church ultimately required something in the nature of a "discipline," or a commitment beyond being a perpetually welcomed *guest,* and toward being *hosts* who were able to welcome new people. Reflection on data from involved parishioners enabled the leadership team to recognize this difficulty as an unintended result of adopting a culturally extremely attractive understanding of inclusivity that, at the same time, wasn't *quite* identical with the Christian sense of being welcomed *into* something new, with new demands and responsibilities. The difficulty here — and for our other practitioners in relation to cultural practices — was how to recognize and respond to *both* what is similar and consonant between the gospel message and culture, *and* what is radically (though often subtly) different between them. This difficulty is a real and practical place of the asking of a sharp ecclesiological question: How is the church a place of *discernment* of culture, a community in which both grace and sin can be seen, named, and appropriately responded to in ways that enable the gospel to be heard in particular contexts?

This is an extremely complex and difficult question to answer, not least because it is framed in such a way that "church" and "culture" are held distinct from one another. What is vividly clear from the practices we have encountered is the reality that — of course — such distinction is not true, at least in any clear or separated way. Church members are themselves thoroughly embedded in and formed by prevailing cultures; it is this that both enables them instinctively to "borrow" from wider society in the ways described, and makes it hard, sometimes, to know how to discern critically

17. Messy Church, a Fresh Expressions movement, working with parents and children: www.messychurch.org.uk.

and humbly what is being taken on in such borrowing. So, then, we see faithful Christian volunteers working with the homeless who are deliberately resistant to using any explicit faith language to describe — even to themselves — the nature of that work.[18] The volunteers show themselves sensitive to a certain social "incorrectness" of such public naming of faith, particularly in relation to their own good works; this cultural formation becomes a factor in their lack of sense of connection between the grace of table sharing with the homeless and the grace of their regular celebration of Eucharist. The voices of ecclesial practice speak of the reality of the church as made up of communities of people in whose hearts and minds the assumptions of dominant culture are inextricably entwined with faith and its practices. Here there is no room for a nonhyphenated sense of church-and-world; here what is being called for is not so much a theology of church and culture as a practical ecclesiology of enabling and better understanding Christian discernment, as a necessary part of a complete ecclesiology — one as attentive to the church *ad extra* as traditionally academic ecclesiology has been to the church *ad intra*.

The real live voices behind these observations from practice have been "flattened out" in this presentation, as — systematic theologian that I am — I have codified and thematized from the data on practice, to present theological questions and ideas. In doing this I have in fact broken with the practice and philosophy of the ARCS research itself, which, in its own processes, works to keep the particularity of the practical voices distinct. However, this treatment of practice may be a start for a practical theology; but it cannot be simply the pastoral beginnings of a systematic approach to church. Rather, what is called for is a new method that goes deeper than such generalizations and enables the particularity of practical voices to be heard within the conversations of an authentic ecclesiology.

Ecclesiology Called into Practice

This chapter is concerned with making the case for the essential inclusion of ecclesial practices in any discourse about church claiming to be an authentic ecclesiology. This is not simply a case for including practical observations from church life; but, more particularly, it argues that such practices

---

18. This was the experience in working with volunteers in Housing Justice, a homelessness charity supporting winter night shelter work in parishes. www.housingjustice.org.uk.

are themselves properly theological, bearers of an emerging ecclesiology. To support this argument I have referred — inadequately, for sure — to the ways in which Christian practitioners are constantly working with and responding to thoroughly theological questions in their living of church in the world. This voice of practice must be heard, for it is spoken from the heart of the church itself. In this second section I want to develop the case for such a practical theological voice by demonstrating how it can be appropriately heard and its proper authority enabled through a particular methodological approach — an approach the ARCS research team, whose work underpins this chapter, refers to as "theology in four voices."[19]

The four-voices methodology arises out of the question of how the voices of practice can be given their proper place in theological discourse about the church. The temptation of much systematic theology, when confronted with the questions and challenges of practice, is simply to respond by articulating what seem (to academics) to be pertinent aspects of traditional ecclesiology, in the belief that this will better enable practice. Such an approach may, of course, be genuinely helpful; but it tends to assume that the places of practice are the loci of problems and that the theological tradition is a treasure trove of answers, which can be more or less readily applied to contemporary questions. Of course, described in this way few would agree with such a position; but it is worth presenting the dynamic of practice and academic theology this starkly, so as to make clear what might be needed for a more effective discourse for and about the whole church. In reality, church practitioner groups find the insights of the academy often strange or irrelevant, and systematic theologians feel unsure how to incorporate practices into their work and remain academically "respectable."

For all that, it is clear, even from the reflections on practice offered in this chapter, that the ecclesial realities Christians work in and with have thematic resonances with academic ecclesiology: the concern for the relation of church and world, the problematic of church ordering and polity, the questions of culture and intended and unintended inculturation — all this can be explored through extensive bibliographies of contemporary ecclesiology. The tragedy is, of course, that — in the main — the discourse of the bibliographies and the conversations of practice are notoriously difficult to integrate. This is what ARCS has tried to respond to methodologically and procedurally.

---

19. For a full account of "the four voices of theology," see chapter 4 of Cameron et al., *Talking about God in Practice*.

A fundamental starting place is the central conviction that has appeared as a kind of refrain throughout this chapter: *that practices are bearers of theology.* To say this is to recognize that, from the start, and all through the action-research style of data gathering, we are involved in a work that is properly theological. Our first step — to converse with practitioner groups and identify a research question with them — is itself a kind of theological work of discernment, as the question of faith regarding what is being practiced is identified and formulated. We seek, with practitioners, to ask a *theological* question of the practices under discussion; for example, "How are we making disciples?" (Messy Church), or "What are the implicit and explicit values in the 'reflective talking' that takes place?" (London Jesuit Volunteers).

The next steps in the process are also properly theological. In transcribing data from interviews, focus groups, participant reflections, and observations, we see ourselves as collecting witnesses not only to what happens and what people think about it, but simultaneously, and necessarily, to an embodied theology, and to the workings of grace, the Spirit — and sin — in what is happening.

To recognize in this way that practices are themselves properly theological requires some careful thinking. For these embodied theologies are not, by their nature, verbally articulate; nor is how they are described or intellectually understood by the practitioners the only account of the theology they bear. In fact, in keeping with classic action-research findings, it is clear that the *espoused* theology of practitioners — what they say they are about theologically — is generally in some tension with their *operant* theology — the theology suggested by and embodied in the practices themselves. A simple example would be the recognition that a diocesan Agency for Evangelisation, whose members are clearly there because they are committed to the *ad extra* work of the church, has an espoused theology that is in some tension with the operant theology of its actual practice, which is focused, *ad intra,* on catechesis, adult education courses, and so forth. The focus on practice introduces the first two of our four voices of theology: the espoused and the operant voices.

Enabling these voices to be heard is a first concern of our practical ecclesiological approach. In setting up the research, practitioners — often with some difficulty — name the theology that describes what they understand themselves to be about; and in gathering data from practice, we begin to give a complex, often conversational, voice to the operant theology. Already this is a useful process for practitioners — a classic action-research process. However, the recognition of the operant and espoused voices as properly theological demands that we go beyond a simple action-research approach, and develop a *theological action-research* process. This necessitates that the conversation must be widened to include (at least)[20] two other theological voices — that of normative and formal theologies.

The widening of the conversation in this way takes place through reflective conversations in the ARCS reflection team and the insider practitioner reflection team, and then between reflection teams. In this way both practitioners and those external to the practice are able to reflect on how the operant and espoused theologies relate (and fail to relate), *and* on how the questions that arise relate to normative and formal theological voices. For many the normative voice will be embodied in Scripture and liturgy, with a particular emphasis for our Roman Catholic partners on church teaching. The formal voice is more difficult to locate in the reflections, and depends, in large part, on the theological expertise present in the reflection groups. Part of what the outsider team of ARCS can offer is a link to the formal voices of the academy and tradition, which can be introduced through appropriate conversation springing from real practices.

This last point draws attention to our methods as essentially *conversational,* and is an important one. For what is essential for an effective practical ecclesiology is that it is properly respectful of and engaged with the voices of practice in its account of formal ecclesiology. Too often formal theology, in genuinely trying to respond to church life, addresses, in reality, the academy, or the theologically fluent, at least; our conversational, reflective methods ensure that formal theology finds its proper place as one voice in an ongoing conversation, in which all voices, in their distinct and proper ways, are understood as theological. In particular, the power of this practical ecclesiological method lies in its locating of the conversations of the four voices around the table set by church practices, as the operant-espoused tension opens up the possibility of effective engagement beyond particular practice to the wider traditions and thinking of the normative and formal voices.

A number of claims can be made for this practical ecclesiological method. First, we can recognize in it a coherent fundamental theology of

20. While the ARCS team has developed its thinking in relation to four voices of theology in conversation, we recognize the possibility and potential usefulness of identifying other theological voices for enriching this conversation. We welcome developments here from others using this methodology.

church and revelation. For both Anglican and Roman Catholic traditions with which we have worked, there is a recognition that God speaks to the church and world in a variety of ways; formally this has to do with the loci of revelation and authoritative sources for theology. So, the Anglican tradition broadly recognizes Scripture, tradition, reason, and experience as, together, sources of revelation, places where we can expect to hear God's word. In contemporary Roman Catholic thought there is a similar recognition of a variety of "voices" at play in the revelation of God's word to us. Indeed, the Second Vatican Council goes so far as to describe a "progress" or "development" of the tradition, taking place in a variety of places and activities within the church:

> This tradition which comes from the Apostles develops [*proficit*] in the Church with the help of the Holy Spirit. For there is a growth in the understanding of the realities and the words which have been handed down. This happens through the contemplation and study made by believers, who treasure these things in their hearts (see Luke, 2:19, 51) through a penetrating understanding of the spiritual realities which they experience, and through the preaching of those who have received through Episcopal succession the sure gift of truth. For as the centuries succeed one another, the Church constantly moves forward toward the fullness of divine truth until the words of God reach their complete fulfillment in her.[21]

This is an account of apostolic tradition that clearly and necessarily includes not only episcopal teaching, but also the day-to-day "hidden" reflections and insights of praying, practicing believers. It is the contention of this chapter that the presence of such multivoiced understandings of revelation in the Christian tradition demands that theological methodology be similarly framed, and that this challenges us to develop appropriate processes to enable such conversational theology. The ARCS methodology and process for practical ecclesiology can properly be presented, then, not only as an effective piece of interdisciplinary practical theology, but also as a serious attempt to embody the very premises of Christian understanding of the complexity of divine revelation — a complexity that demands the bringing together of different theological voices.

The theological integrity of the approach we are arguing for can also

---

21. Second Vatican Council, Dogmatic Constitution on Divine Revelation, *Dei Verbum*, no. 8. Translation by Vatican Web site.

be understood in terms of pneumatology. It is striking that the quote from *Dei Verbum* just cited names the work of the Holy Spirit in describing the "progress" of apostolic tradition. The troubling doctrine of the Spirit, affirming as it does both the promise of the Spirit's guidance to the church and the Spirit's radical freedom as God, seems further to require a theological articulation that has more in common with the pedagogy of conversation than with the monologues of the academy, or of the magisterium, or of practice itself. For the church to be charismatic it must be multivoiced.

What all this suggests is that the practical ecclesiology we are suggesting is one that, not only in practice but also in principle, requires ongoing conversation as the appropriate pattern of theology. Here "faith seeking understanding" is embodied through a recognition of ecclesial faith as something necessarily communal, discursive. The truth we seek — the truth that is our redemption in Christ — is always disclosed through the coming together of the various formal and normative voices of Christian thinking with those of experience, of practice. Again, the Second Vatican Council describes the human search for truth in exactly such a conversational way, in which not only expertise and certainty have their place, but also searchings, wonderings, and mistakes: "Truth, however, is to be sought after in a manner proper to the dignity of the human person and his social nature. The inquiry is to be free, carried on with the aid of teaching or instruction, communication and dialogue, in the course of which men explain to one another the truth they have discovered, or think they have discovered, in order thus to assist one another in the quest for truth. Moreover, as the truth is discovered, it is by a personal assent that men are to adhere to it."[22]

The point of describing these theological underpinnings of the four-voices approach to practical ecclesiology is to make clear that the methods used are, themselves, thoroughly theological. More than that, we might also reasonably claim that these methods, which so centrally attend to the voices of practice, enable a fullness of theological perspective, an integrity of ecclesiological understanding, which approaches that are unable thoroughly to include practical voices cannot. In the light of what we believe about revelation, the work of the Spirit in the church, and the nature of theology as a conversational searching, how can we, in fact, dare to speak of church apart from the voices that are heard in the heart of church life, the voices of Christian practice?

---

22. Second Vatican Council, Declaration on Religious Liberty, *Dignitatis Humanae,* no. 3. Translation by Vatican Web site.

A second set of claims can also be made, we believe, in relation to this interdisciplinary approach as a practically transformative ecclesiology. The locating of the center of gravity for our practical ecclesiology in the reflective conversations of practitioners and academics together can be seen as an effective pedagogy, formative of all involved. All participants in the process, whether members of the ARCS team or the practitioners with whom we have worked, can witness to personal "epiphanies" in which conversations and reflections on the four voices have led to fresh insights, fresh understandings. In particular, the ability of the process to enable an effective engagement for practitioners with formal and normative theologies, through a pedagogy that begins with their own realities, should be warmly recognized. Attentiveness to what is received and challenged here can provide important — even chastening — insights for the academic ecclesiologist.

To Finish: Hopes for a Practical Ecclesiology

The testing of the claims made in the previous section can be fully made only through more detailed attention to case studies. This is a work that the ARCS team is now concentrating on, with a publication of a detailed study planned for 2012. Nonetheless, this chapter can stand as an opening statement for what we believe can be achieved by a theological action-research approach for a practical ecclesiology. It is an approach that has proved accessible to and welcomed by practitioners in the field, and is deeply rooted in fundamentals of Christian theology. What is harder to grasp is the full and potential impact of such an ecclesiology: in part, its results are always ongoing, often embedded in practices and particular groups, and — as this chapter demonstrates — difficult to summarize as systematic "results." This should not, we believe, be disheartening, nor should it undermine the endeavor; rather it strikes a note of authenticity as practical ecclesiology finds its fullest expression, in conclusion, not in a simple, single voice, but in the dynamism of ongoing conversation and multivoiced reflections. It is here that the truth about church will be disclosed.

CHAPTER 10

Ecclesiology, Ethnography, and God: An Interplay of Reality Descriptions

Nicholas M. Healy

In the introduction to his book *On Christian Theology*, Rowan Williams talks about what he terms his "methodological starting point." He "assumes," he says, that theological inquiry is "always beginning in the middle of things," amidst "a practice of common life and language already there, a practice that defines a specific shared way of interpreting human life as lived in relation to God." This assumption yields a fundamental methodological principle: "The meanings of the word 'God' are to be discovered by watching what this community does," not only when what it does is conceptual reflection but also "when it is acting, educating or 'inducting,' imagining and worshipping."[1]

Williams's principle and the background beliefs that warrant it clearly reflect both the modern turn to the subject and the later turn to language, forms of life, and praxis. Among other things, his principle indicates that Christian doctrines are not revealed directly from heaven, as it were, but are shaped over time within the lived experience of the church. Here Williams shares something with the founder of modern theology, Friedrich Schleiermacher. For Schleiermacher, the theological "subject" — Williams's "this community" — is the church as a "communion"[2] *(Gemeinschaft)*,[3] that body of people that, as a "moral Person" *(eine moralische Person)*, has,

---

1. Rowan Williams, *On Christian Theology* (Oxford: Blackwell, 2000), p. xii.
2. Friedrich Schleiermacher, *The Christian Faith* (Edinburgh: T. & T. Clark, 1976), p. 206.
3. Friedrich Schleiermacher, *Der Christliche Glaube* (Berlin: De Gruyter, 1999), p. 141.

as he puts it, "a genuine individual life" *(wahrhaftes Einzelleben).*[4] God makes God known to us, and we experience God, in and through the beliefs and practices of the community.

In this chapter I have two main aims. The broader one is to draw upon ethnographic descriptions of the churches to suggest that if we watch the details, complexities, and messiness of their "common life and language," we will find it rather more difficult to discern "this community" than Williams seems to suggest, and thus harder to learn its understanding of God than perhaps he assumes in his introduction. I want to propose that ethnographic studies of the churches should create some unease about modern theological method, whether it be a critical correlationist or a cultural-linguistic approach, or indeed any method that begins with the church.

My second, more specifically ecclesiological aim will be to argue that ethnographic descriptions of the church should prompt revisions of traditional claims the church makes about itself, theological claims as well as empirical. Theologians as different as John Webster and Edward Schillebeeckx have argued, in the latter's words, that "we need a bit of *negative ecclesiology,* church theology in a minor key."[5] I want to say that ethnography supports and to some extent guides such a chastening of the church's doctrinal self-understanding.

We can begin by looking a little more at Williams's principle. To follow it, the theologian must make decisions about the "what" and the "how." That is, we must decide just *what* "this community" is that we are to watch: Is it the church as a whole or just a part of it; if a part, which part? Second, we must decide *how* we should watch it, with what agenda in mind and with what approach: data-driven, social-theoretical, historical, religious-theoretical, doctrinal, or some combination?

For Schleiermacher himself, the church he watches is identified by eliminating "everything that is heretical" as well as "such propositions as are the elements of the Science of Christian Morals."[6] He admits that it may seem very "uncertain" to discern what is heretical. However, he contends that "the distinctive essence of Christianity" permits us to distinguish between heretical and orthodox doctrine. He then indicates how he watches this community. Since the essence of Christianity cannot be "dis-

---

4. Schleiermacher, *The Christian Faith,* p. 95; *Der Christliche Glaube,* p. 127.

5. Edward Schillebeeckx, *The Church: The Human Story of God* (New York: Crossroad, 1990), p. xix. John Webster refers to Schillebeeckx's call in his *Word and Church* (Edinburgh: T. & T. Clark, 2001), p. 214.

6. Schleiermacher, *The Christian Faith,* p. 111.

covered by a merely empirical method,"[7] our explication of it should be guided by "the facts of the religious self-consciousness" as these are developed in his phenomenology.[8]

Not surprisingly, Williams does something rather different in his *On Christian Theology.* Despite his stated principle, he spends very little time watching what most people would think of as "what this community does." He attends instead to the written forms of a very limited group of Christians — saints and theologians — using them constructively to help our contemporary "common life and language" be more Christian. Other contemporary theologians also adopt something like the same principle but make rather different decisions about the "what" and the "how." In his magisterial three-volume ecclesiology,[9] Roger Haight takes a very broad view of the church, watching its history with the help of social theory in order to draw out commonalities and principles that should constitute a contemporary transdenominational ecclesiology. Stanley Hauerwas has turned in a big way to practices as constitutive of the church's life, very much in line with Williams's principle. He, too, selects what he watches, often, it seems, on the principle that the church's practices should be different from those of the world, and especially from those he considers to be the dominant practices of the USA. This is most evident, perhaps, in his portrayal of the church as a nonviolent community.

I will return to these examples later. Here I want only to make an initial and obvious point: that no one simply watches the community in order to "discover the meanings of the word 'God.'" Everyone makes prior decisions as to what is significant and how to look at it. Williams's principle, and more broadly the turn to the collective Christian subject in modern theological inquiry, requires one to make a contestable construal as to what "this community" or this collective subject is that one is going to watch, and decide from a range of reasonable choices how one should watch it. The question, then, is, what guides these decisions?

7. Schleiermacher, *The Christian Faith,* p. 105.

8. Schleiermacher, *The Christian Faith,* p. 123.

9. Roger Haight, S.J., *Christian Community in History,* 3 vols. (New York and London: Continuum, 2004-8).

Ethnographic Watching

Before I address that question, though, let's look at what can happen when we apply Williams's principle more empirically. And rather than follow Haight and consider the church broadly and in the full reach of its history, let us "watch" "this community" ethnographically, as it is found in congregations and parishes. The advantage of the ethnographic view is that, if you so choose, you can watch the church without theological or institutional agendas and, possibly, with less theoretical baggage than with other methods. Thus, for example, you can avoid theological assumptions — whether derived from Christianity or elsewhere — about what "religion" might be, and what might constitute "a religious community."[10] But they go against the general consensus, initiated by theorists like Wilfrid Cantwell Smith and restated recently by the ethnographer Timothy Jenkins: "the category of religion . . . is not a good one for sociological purposes, for there is no homogeneous bounded phenomenon that can be so labelled a priori and thus isolated for analysis. Further, to claim that there is, . . . is unconsciously to take up a position within the field under consideration, to adopt certain tactics and stakes."[11] Ethnography thus takes us a long way from Schleiermacher's nonempirical way of watching the community.

Here I will generalize from empirical studies to note three main elements of what, for convenience, I will call "the ethnographic view," though I am fully aware that there is no such single thing and that what I say is necessarily selective and constructive. First, and most obviously, congregational studies show that congregations differ, often quite intensely and extensively, in their "life and language" and in what they do, and thus in their understanding of "the meanings of the word 'God.'" To say this is not merely to make the obvious point that the local Methodist church does things differently than the high Anglican church round the corner. Within the same denomination and in similar localities, congregations usually differ substantially, each having its own, often easily recognizable, style. Jerome Baggett's study, for example, describes the substantial differences

10. Among ethnographers, scholars such as M. D. Stringer are significant exceptions to this, of course. M. D. Stringer, *Contemporary Western Ethnography and the Definition of Religion* (New York: Continuum, 2008). Fall into the trap of binary oppositions, and expect the critique of John Milbank.

11. Timothy Jenkins, *Religion in English Everyday Life: An Ethnographic Approach* (New York and Oxford: Berghahn, 1999), p. 70.

among six Roman Catholic parishes in the San Francisco Bay region.[12] One is a largely gay congregation, another is centered on the Latin Mass; one is oriented toward supporting suburban families, another is mostly Latino, and so on. Certainly all six share some characteristics, but each congregation's life, language, and what it does indicate a substantially different understanding of Christianity from the other five. The beliefs, practices, and attitudes of the six congregations are not sufficiently held in common or "shared" such that together they form a single community, as in, say, "the Bay Area Roman Catholic community."

Furthermore, second, participant observation and extensive interviews with individual members of congregations indicate far fewer commonalities *within* each congregation than one might expect. While data tables may point usefully to certain beliefs held by most members of a particular congregation, there are always people who disagree with the majority, often in remarkably counterintuitive ways. Baggett records, for example, that even in a Catholic congregation clearly identifying itself as having very traditionalist beliefs, 8 percent of its members think you can be a good Catholic without believing that Jesus physically rose from the dead, or without believing in the real presence, and 13 percent without following the magisterium teaching on abortion.[13] And it's not merely a question of beliefs, of course. Most American Roman Catholics are familiar with the large suburban parishes that require multiple services, where the Saturday evening service is loud and excited, with clap-alongs and guitars, while the 7:30 Sunday morning Mass is contemplative and virtually silent, and the 9:30 is family-oriented and noisy in a different way. Many people who usually go to one of these services would not go happily to any of the others.

Although the word "ethnography" suggests a written account of a group having readily discernible distinguishing characteristics, some ethnographers have noted how difficult, even personally disturbing, it can be to describe a congregation's character or identity. One can reasonably attempt to describe a particular congregation's style, its configuration of central practices, and its set of typically held beliefs and attitudes. But to go further to try to define its distinctive identity raises questions about the ethnographer's role and perspective, about the role of dominant members

12. Jerome P. Baggett, *Sense of the Faithful: How American Catholics Live Their Faith* (Oxford: Oxford University Press, 2009).

13. Baggett, *Sense of the Faithful,* p. 105, table 4.2.

of the congregation and why they are dominant, and about how to address and, as it were, *place* that which is present but is not typical of the congregation more generally. Ethnography is difficult, as Frances Ward remarks, because writing up your notes into their final "textual order" is to a significant extent an imposition upon what is concretely confused and messy, a construction that involves "deleting some voices, some perspectives, in favour of others."[14] I don't mean to suggest that we should therefore give up the attempt. I only want to point out how ethnographic study can reveal how congregations are too complex to be described without some degree of distortion.[15]

Third, and partly by way of explanation, the diversity of belief and practice between and within congregations seems not simply to be disagreement about the meaning of the word "God" or, more broadly, the meaning of Christianity and its practice. Both what is diverse and what is shared are as much the product of non-Christian influences. The conclusion of some studies[16] can be generalized to say that the life and language of a particular congregation can be understood adequately only in light of its place within the particularities of its host society. It may have some influence on that larger society, but the congregation itself is also as it were a Christian expression of the town or region in which it is located, rather than something separate built on another foundation. If so, it would follow that watching this community to learn the "meanings of the word 'God'" requires watching that larger community, too, setting the former within the latter. Differences between congregations and between the members of any one congregation — together with much of what they have in common — reflect attitudes and experiences that come from living with nonecclesial people and their products, within non-Christian groups and societies. These shape their understanding of doctrine, their reading of Scripture, and their practices.

Coherence and consistency among the members of any given con-

---

14. Frances Ward, "The Messiness of Studying Congregations Using Ethnographic Methods," in *Congregational Studies in the UK,* ed. M. Guest, K. Tusting, and L. Woodhead (Aldershot: Ashgate, 2004), p. 134.

15. Ethnographers seem to be increasingly concerned about this issue. See, e.g., J. D. Faubion and G. E. Marcus, *Fieldwork Is Not What It Used to Be: Learning Anthropology's Method in a Time of Transition* (Ithaca, N.Y., and London: Cornell University Press, 2009); Harry G. West, *Ethnographic Sorcery* (Chicago and London: University of Chicago Press, 2007).

16. E.g., Jenkins, *Religion in English Everyday Life.*

gregation are not, therefore, to be expected. Neither should we expect self-consistency on the part of each member since most of us disagree with ourselves, holding beliefs or engaging in practices that are in tension or conflict with others we also believe and practice.[17] Christians do not share a common understanding as to how significant such tensions and conflicts are, whether within ourselves or within the congregation or the church as a whole, for living the Christian life well. We do not even agree on the level of enthusiasm needed to be a good Christian. Not all of us think we need to be highly motivated, however much others insist that we should.[18]

Theological Method

I want to conclude from these points that ethnographic studies render the methodological turn to "this community" problematic, whether the church is taken to be a particular congregation or, *a fortiori*, the worldwide church. I argued earlier that theologians who watch the church have to make decisions as to what to watch and how to watch it, decisions that are contestable in various ways and for various reasons. The ethnographic view I have just described indicates a second possible difficulty with this kind of method, this time in regard not to the watcher so much as to what is watched. Congregational studies indicate how difficult it is to construct an account of a congregation's "common life and language," its distinctive culture or ethos, without ignoring — sometimes with adverse moral and theological consequences — what counters the construction. It is surely vastly more difficult to construct an account of the worldwide church's common life and language or its "specific shared way of interpreting human life as lived in relation to God," given the vastly diverse forms of life in, say, the congregations of China or Mexico or northern Canada, to say nothing of the diversity within them.

To be sure, there are vital aspects of the church's life and language that are probably shared everywhere. These are likely to be rather formal,

17. A point made convincingly, and with reference specifically to religious beliefs and practices, by Mark Chaves, "SSSR Presidential Address, Rain Dances in the Dry Season: Overcoming the Religious Congruence Fallacy," *Journal for the Scientific Study of Religion* 49, no. 1 (March 2010): 1-14. I owe the reference to Mary McClintock Fulkerson.

18. Charles Taylor offers a magisterial account of the historical background for the shift in what he calls our "social imaginary" that makes us this way in his *A Secular Age* (Cambridge: Belknap Press, Harvard University Press, 2007).

however: a focus on Holy Scripture (however it is read); an attempt (however diverse) to understand the meaning of our lives in relation to the God made known in Christ and the Spirit; and worship of that God (in whatever forms). Although these elements are present in virtually all congregations, the ethnographic view undermines the notion that they constitute the church as a "community" or a moral person in a sufficiently rich and consistent way to work as a principle for theological or ecclesiological method. There is simply too much, materially, that is not shared. Indeed, the worldwide church — the church that is often the subject of contemporary ecclesiology and the locus of modern theological method — when considered with a focus on detail, particularity, and the exceptional, is arguably little more than a congeries of diverse forms of life, languages, and meanings of the word "God." We cannot, then, start with the church as it exists; everything slips between the fingers unless we cement and shape according to our agenda, our construal of Christianity, and our formation within our particular world.

Considering the central role churchly virtues and practices play for Stanley Hauerwas and his followers reveals some of the issues here. It is much harder to describe what Christians do as "church practices" than they seem to assume, for concretely any given church-accepted practice is performed with intentions and contexts that can be diverse enough to alter the meaning of the practice. It is difficult to isolate a set of distinctly Christian virtues by watching the church, since the church consistently advocates very few particular practices, if any. Nor does it provide consistent guidelines for deciding which virtues should inform the others. Certainly one can make an argument that a certain set of practices should be found throughout the church, or that a certain Christian virtue should inform all other virtues and practices. But that would be to make an argument rather than discern it from watching the church as it is. And the argument is difficult to make. Hauerwas privileges practices of nonviolence, but very few church people practice or even preach nonviolence.

Though it would take far more space than I have to discuss it properly, it is worth remarking here that the ethnographic view may undermine confidence in both the cultural-linguistic approach of the so-called Yale School and the widely used critical correlation method. The difficulties of asserting a single grammar of Christianity are obvious from the ethnographic view and need no further comment. The problem with the correlation method lies in reasonably and fairly separating what is confusedly and quite thoroughly one into two distinct and correlatable things, such as the church and the world, or Christian belief and practice and worldly belief and practice. To construct the significant aspects and distinctive commonalities of each of the two things to be correlated is impossible without making a whole set of contestable selections and ignoring much that significantly, and often pressingly, undermines those selections. One's decisions in such matters may well reflect issues of power and authority, of inclusion and exclusion, and so on. But as we have seen with regard to the four theologians (Williams, Schleiermacher, Haight, and Hauerwas) I mentioned in the first section, they also reflect far more benign decisions and agendas, each of which is also contestable.

This is not at all to deny that there are very good reasons for reminding ourselves that theological inquiry is located within the church. Certainly it is important to remember that doctrines are not something handed down from heaven to us fully formed, that Christianity can be conceived and practiced only with due regard to historicity and lived experience, that we are formed by groups and individuals around us, and that we can be Christians only if we think and act in ways that draw upon at least some of the resources the church provides us. Certainly, too, we have no choice but to begin *within* the church in some way or other, but that is not the same as saying we begin by watching the church's common life and language. Nor is it necessary to assume that beliefs or practices shared, if not by all Christians at least by the best of them, or by most of them, are on that account to be accepted.

Why Community?

My second topic is ecclesiology and the church's self-understanding. Here I will cover some of the same ground, but in a rather different way. If the church is not empirically an individual life, not a "community" in any robust sense of the word, why do we so often say it is, and usually do so in reference to the empirical church? David Martin contends that "the forms of communitarian ideology propagated by mainstream religions are based on delusions. They do not 'correspond' to any reality."[19] He argues that "the emphasis on 'community' corresponds to a shrinkage in the constituency of persons influenced by the Church"[20] and "owe[s] a great deal to a middle-

---

19. David Martin, *Reflections on Sociology and Theology* (Oxford: Oxford University Press, 1997), p. 132.

20. Martin, *Reflections*, p. 131.

class nostalgia about lost community."[21] Martin's is perhaps a rather British-centered view, but I think one can see this in much writing about community in both Britain and the USA, Christian and non-Christian. In the USA, which has experienced relatively little fascism or collectivism, community is often uncritically presented as a good thing, virtually a term of perfection in the sense of the more community the better. None of this explains Schleiermacher's turn to *Gemeinschaft,* to be sure, but perhaps it, too, was an expression of a modern cultural phenomenon, the roots of which may lie in German thinkers like Herder. Another reason for using the word "community" is often to indicate solidarity among underprivileged groups. Thus one talks in the USA about the black community, the Latino community, the gay community. You can't refer to "the white community." It makes no sense, except perhaps in the case of white extremists. Likewise, and for much the same reason, in my view it makes no sense to talk of "the Christian community," except, possibly, if Christians are threatened in some way. And even then it is little more than a figure of speech.

A reply to this might be to say: Well, that may be so, but it remains a theological fact that community is constitutive of the church, so community should be fostered at all costs, and the church should counter as best it can the individualism and relativism rampant within modern societies. I would argue on ethnographic grounds that this cannot be the case if you mean the church-as-community must have a common life and language that are empirically describable. Since the church does not exist as that kind of community, it is hard to see how that kind of community could be an essential aspect of the church, on earth at least. The body of Christ need not be, and historically often has not been, considered a community in anything like the modern sense. Jesus did not say, "Where two or three are gathered together, there is community." An emphasis upon watching our communal selves may distract our attention from what is far more important, for theology, the church, and the world.

The Church's Distinctiveness

It is possible that modern theological talk about community is a particular version of a broader claim the church makes about itself, namely, that it is distinctive in some way, that it has some characteristics making it different

21. Martin, *Reflections,* p. 127.

and separate from all that is not the church. Wherein lies its distinctiveness, then? Not, I've argued, in its common life and language. Sometimes one or another of the churches has made strong empirical claims, such as the older Catholic notion of the *societas perfecta*. However, the church as such doesn't have a common institution or polity.

To be sure, it would be foolish to deny that people do know the church, or to be more precise, the churches, when they see it; churches have easily recognizable family resemblances. Discerning an individual Christian as a Christian just from watching him or her is generally much more difficult, often quite impossible — with the exception of the clergy, of course: those religious who wear habits, and theologians and teachers who talk and think about God for a living. Laypeople usually don't do anything distinctive except (some of them) on Sunday mornings, when non-Christians don't usually see them anyway. Some laypeople think it a good idea to make it known that they are Christians. They may wear substantial pectoral crosses (little crosses around the neck are too readily confused with a fashion accessory). They may affix signs to their cars — where I live the ichthys symbol has been replaced by "Keep Christ in Christmas." Or they may pray silently but noticeably before eating a meal in company, perhaps making others in their company feel rather uncomfortable. Many, probably the vast majority of Christians, don't do any of that. I cannot think of any good reason to conclude that it is better to signal in this way that one is a Christian rather than having it go largely unnoticed. An opportunity for genuine witness would be quite a different matter, but that is unlikely to be a daily occurrence.

Christian laypeople make up the vast majority of the church, yet perhaps because they are largely invisible, when people speak of the church, they often omit the laity by using synecdoche. Thus the media might say, for example, "the Catholic Church believes that life begins at conception" or "today the church asked forgiveness for its failure to act quickly enough on the child abuse scandal." We know what is meant: not the church but a particular denomination, and of that denomination only one part of it. In the first instance, only those who agree, while many do not; in the second, the bishops. Both are incorrect if understood as simple statements. But they are also an incorrect use of synecdoche.

The church's theological claims about its distinctiveness have often gone beyond difference toward separation and exclusion: the church is the ark of salvation, outside of which there is no salvation; without faith in Jesus Christ and baptism into his church, you cannot get to heaven. The church is the body of Christ, while the world is not; we are the people of God, everyone else is not. There is a tendency nowadays to move away from a strict connection between church membership and likelihood of salvation. Not incidentally, as Francis Sullivan, among others, has argued, "cultural factors have had a decisive influence" in this change.[22]

I think, though, one can reasonably generalize from a wide range of views to say that virtually all traditional ecclesiologies accepted by the churches, as well as those implicit in the churches' authorized ways of life, claim that being a member of the Christian church offers the possibility of getting closer to God than you could if you were not a member. To be sure, some Christians would deny that the church is distinct in this way at all. And, on the other side, some churches go considerably beyond this to say that you can and usually do get closer to God within the church than you could if you were a member of another religious or nonreligious body, or even than you could if you were a member of a different kind of Christian church. The basic claim I want to address here, though, is that the church's distinctiveness, assuming that it is distinctive in some such significant way, lies in its mediating function, its capacity to bring its members into a closer relationship with God, however that relation is understood.

The church's mediating function can be described in various ways. For the sake of the argument, I will give accounts of two fairly typical versions, then a third version more influenced by the ethnographic view. According to traditional Roman Catholic ecclesiology, the church's teaching authority — the magisterium — is in receipt of a body of revealed truths, the deposit of faith. This has been handed on by the magisterium from generation to generation, reaching all the way back to the disciples who received the gospel from Jesus. According to some accounts, it reaches even further "back" into the triune God. As the Word of God, Jesus Christ is the self-communication of the Father. The Holy Spirit is Christ's gift to the church's magisterium. The function of both the Spirit and the magisterium is, in their respective ways, to maintain the church's faith and life in the truth of the gospel. In this view, then, there is movement from God the Father, through the Son and the Spirit, to certain specially graced church leaders who teach the gospel with apostolic authority to the rest of us in the church. We are brought closer to God by means of our obedient acceptance of the magisterium interpretation of the gospel. This is what is dis-

22. Francis A. Sullivan, S.J., *Salvation Outside the Church? Tracing the History of the Catholic Response* (New York and Mahwah, N.J.: Paulist, 1992), p. 203.

tinctive about the church: by the special grace of the Holy Spirit, it possesses revealed truths that it mediates to the faithful through its authoritative teaching.

Rowan Williams has pointed out some of the problems with what he appropriately calls this "linear doctrine" of the Trinity, which he also finds in patristic and Protestant versions.[23] Two of the more significant problems are fairly obvious: the limitation of the role of the Spirit to an epistemological guarantor, and the failure to acknowledge our own responsive action within the dynamic of God's self-communication. Here I want to add the point that on this account, it is the teaching authority that determines the principles of selection by which to construct an ecclesiology. According to the authorities, they have been given the authority to determine who is closer to God; hence those who disagree with their teaching must be further away. Obviously this is a circular and arguably an institutionally self-serving argument. Yet it was also well meant, premised on a pastoral concern for the faithful, and as such was accepted for many years by many Catholics.

Williams and the other theologians I mentioned above share many elements of a rather different construal of the church's distinctive mediating role, one that finds expression in his methodological principle. If I may hazard a broad generalization, their common account might go roughly like this: The church and its members do not simply receive a body of revealed truths. They must discern and to some degree construct the meaning of the gospel. The success or failure of the church's *poesis* is contingent upon the active presence of the Holy Spirit (and, of course, what constitutes success or failure is also determined by the Spirit, and may often be hidden from us). Revelation is thus a complex dynamic process, emerging within the historical experience of the church's attempts to respond in faith to Jesus Christ. On this view, then, the distinctiveness of the church lies in its Spirit-guided participation in God's self-communication as this is mediated by Scripture, the church's history, and its traditions of practice and inquiry. The church and its members grow closer to God by their formation and participation within the distinctive Christian tradition.

Unlike the first way, here no one has absolute authority. Although the Holy Spirit ensures the overall indefectibility of the church, we can readily acknowledge the confusion and occasional misdirection of the teaching authorities. Furthermore, all Christians are to participate to some degree

23. Williams, *On Christian Theology*, pp. 113-15.

in the church's constructive response. All engage the tradition in light of their own background and concerns, informed by which they make judgments as to which aspects of the tradition are authoritative, which secondary. On this view, then, one should judge a theological proposal not by who makes it (though obviously some members of the church have far greater weight than others). Nor does its conformity to a set of authoritative statements or to a basic Christian logic make it necessarily acceptable. Its authority is dependent upon its reception, and thus upon whether or not it makes a convincing case to a sufficient number of Christians, especially to those well versed in the Christian tradition. As David Kelsey remarks, the "mode" of a theological proposal is "hypothetical." We say: "Here is an important theological question; try looking at it this way."[24]

The ethnographic view suggests the outlines of a third way of construing the church's mediating role that shares much with the second, but expands it in various ways. If the first account of the church's distinctiveness is congenial to some church authorities and the second to many theologians, the third way seems to have found its place among many ordinary Christians. However, church authorities and theologians are *also* ordinary Christians, so this way of thinking is arguably present throughout the churches, though often only implicitly or inconsistently.

I have remarked how most Christians, whether liberal or conservative, enthusiastic or largely uninterested, reject parts of the church's official teachings and some of the beliefs, practices, or attitudes found among the majority of their own congregation's membership. Their reasons for doing so may not be explicitly theological or even thought out to any extent. If pushed, they might appeal to all kinds of considerations, including a kind of intuition, deriving from their life experience, that a particular doctrine or moral rule just doesn't make any sense, to them at least. Critics characterize these people as picking and choosing among the offerings of the church, selecting what suits their needs and desires, rejecting whatever challenges them or makes them uncomfortable. If Roman Catholic, they may be called "cafeteria Catholics," accused of moral or religious failure, and derided as an ecclesial embodiment of the moral and religious relativism of modern decadent societies.

Such criticisms have been rejected in turn as inaccurate and misguided; indeed, they may say more about the psychology of the critics than

---

24. David H. Kelsey, *Eccentric Existence: A Theological Anthropology* (Louisville: Westminster John Knox, 2009), p. 9.

anything else. Charles Taylor's counterargument, made initially some time ago and expanded and further supported in his more recent historical work, is particularly appealing, in my view. He remarks that "one has to see what is great in the culture of modernity, as well as what is shallow or dangerous."[25] He argues that modern individualism, whether found in the church or anywhere else, need not be decadent, but instead may be a well-intentioned attempt to take full responsibility for what one believes and does. No doubt some of us are self-centered and self-indulgent, and all of us can be on occasion. In general, though, individual Christians — and non-Christians — do try, by and large, to live in ways that truthfully reflect their knowledge of the way things are as they understand it in light of their history and circumstances. They may talk of "self-fulfillment," and so appear narcissistic. But as Taylor contends, properly understood, "self-fulfilment, so far from excluding unconditional relationships and moral demands beyond the self, actually requires these in some form."[26] That is, the words and phrases of individualism like "being true to myself" and "self-fulfillment" do not in fact reflect the speaker's relativistic self-indulgence, but rather the speaker's quest to live authentically, in conformity to a larger whole.

Significantly, the kind of people accused of being cafeteria Catholics usually display a strong tendency to be nonjudgmental about the beliefs and practices of other Christians and non-Christians. They act much like Henry James's Owen Wingrave, of whom the author says: "He evidently didn't pretend that his wisdom was superior; he only presented it as his own." Again, this need not be relativism at all. Rather, it may well reflect the principle that we should live authentically, combined with genuine humility in the face of the massive difficulties of figuring out *how* to do so and then *actually* doing so. Of course, we may well make the wrong decision, living to regret our stupidity or just never knowing it. But on this view, our responsibility, *coram Deo,* is to respond as best we can, trusting in God's mercy and love. Thus it is arguable, I think, that it is through our engagement in the quest for an authentic response to God that we are drawn closer to God, irrespective of whether or not our quest issues in the correct decisions.

---

25. Charles Taylor, *The Ethics of Authenticity* (Cambridge: Harvard University Press, 1991), p. 120. Taylor develops his argument considerably further in his *A Secular Age,* especially pp. 473-535.

26. Taylor, *The Ethics of Authenticity,* pp. 72-73.

A similar kind of quest may lie behind the work of many modern theologians, I would think, as they search for the best way to think and live in relation to God. However, it may be more difficult for theologians to acknowledge their individualism — in this good sense — because theologians have been trained to assume that their moral and theological proposals have more authority. After all, their professional expertise is in "the Christian tradition"; they know more about the tradition than anyone, including most priests. The chief mistake here, of course, would be if we thought that working together in dialogue, giving papers and having conferences, thinking very hard and writing books, and doing all this securely within the Christian tradition — if we thought all this gets us *closer to God.* Besides the hubris, Pelagianism, and self-delusion, this would fail to acknowledge some of the problems inherent in all academic inquiry, one of which is that it can be hard sometimes not to think in schools of thought or view everything in terms of the latest fashionable question, or more generally, exhibit signs of *Fachidiotie.* Most Christians generally do not think like academic theologians. And that can be a very good thing, for it may spare them the egregious errors that can follow from subservience to some new academically authorized theory or to some mistaken doctrine or moral teaching supposedly authorized by the tradition.

Here, then, is another, rather broader picture of the church's relation to its members, to the world, and to God. The church's authorities are not the sole teachers of revealed truth. To be sure, the church needs suitable institutional forms through which it informs and guides its members in the ways of the gospel, and it will do this with authority, though of a more relative kind. But the church here is primarily a body of believing Christians who seek to live authentically by using the church's resources, thereby keeping those resources alive and available. As such, the life of the church constitutes a tradition, but one that is rather less coherent and distinctive than more theorized notions of a "tradition of inquiry." Based upon largely formal rather than material principles, the tradition in this third picture is not as separable from other traditions as some seem to suggest when they talk of and seek to work within "the Christian tradition." All Christians participate in this tradition, but do so as participants in the various traditions of their various cultures and societies.

In this third picture of the church, then, the tradition in question is the Christian expression and embodiment of the world, rather than an expression and embodiment of something based in itself. Distinctiveness here lies in its members' quest to live authentically as Christians within the world, and so in their using the resources of the church, as well as other resources. Accordingly, the church remains distinctive, but is less obviously so, its distinctiveness even hidden in important ways.

Implied in this third view is an ecclesiology, or possibly a range of ecclesiologies. A rough sketch of one ecclesiology might go something like this: Scripture tells us the triune God is active everywhere, not only in the church, and certainly not solely in its teaching authorities or in its own distinctive tradition. For the world is the object of God's love. It is to the world that the Father sent the Son, to reconcile it and bring it to eschatological consummation. It is in the world that the Spirit works in multitudinous ways to this same saving end, the outpouring of the Spirit at Pentecost not being limited to the empirical church. Theologically, as well as empirically, the church is in the world and of the world.

If the church's *empirical* distinctiveness is limited, its practices, beliefs, and attitudes largely determined by the resources of the world's cultures and societies, it is the church's *theological* distinctiveness that is of primary significance, what the church is *sub ratione Dei*. Scripture indicates its members are called to be the church, to respond to the gospel, the truth about the world. They do so haltingly and feebly for the most part, and that's all right, because God's salvation of the world is not contingent upon the church embodying or displaying the gospel successfully. Nor does the church possess the gospel. Rather, through the power of the Holy Spirit, the church is to point away from itself to the gospel of Jesus Christ. It is as a personal instrument of God, as it were, that it is theologically distinctive: here, if anywhere, we can talk about a moral person with a truly individual life. But this person and life is not empirically visible or even empirically actual; the church cannot display its special relation to God in, say, a shared set of distinctive practices or beliefs, or in some depth dimension of its essence. The church is theologically distinctive because of God's call, not because of its response to that call.

The church is thus not a sacrament if by that we mean a visible sign of an invisible reality that lies within itself. When people come to know the invisible reality of which the church is a sign, they know something other than the church, namely, God in the world, for our salvation. That said, the church *can* say it is an expression and embodiment of the world's response to the gospel of Jesus Christ, and thus is a kind of sacrament. But visibly it confuses as much as or more than it signifies. What we are as Christians and as the church is hidden by our own finitude, diversity, inconsistency, and the confusions of our places within the world. This is not to say that, hidden underneath all our worldliness, we are special. For who we are, as Christians and as the church, is what the world is, too. The church, then, is not an ark floating on the top of the waters. It lives and breathes within the waters. The world is the ark of salvation; the church is but the worldly expression of the Christian response to God's saving work in the world.

The church is called, then, to be the world's Christian expression. We are hidden, yet truly called by God, and we are the church irrespective of the quality of our response. As the church, then, our true center, our essential existence, lies outside ourselves, in God and in the world. As the Christian expression of the world, we remain a worldly product, for to be the church as it is called to be, we must be in and of the world; we are not called to leave the world, and anyway, how could we? But we are indeed called, so our lives as Christians are centered in God's call to us in the world. The world and God are the church; the church isn't the church apart from both the world and God working in it.

Obviously there is far more to be said to make sense of this kind of ecclesiology. But if the argument that supports it holds up to some degree, it may suggest two things. First, ethnographic and similar studies have a direct bearing upon systematic theology, both methodologically and materially, and especially with regard to the doctrine of the church. Second, a doctrine of God is of more significance as a guide and context for understanding the church than is admitted by those whose explicit methodical remarks (whether or not followed in practice) depend upon too strong a notion of "community" to bear the weight they load upon it.

CHAPTER 11

"In the Society of God":
Some Principles of Ecclesiology

John Webster

I

"So powerful is participation in the church," notes Calvin, "that it keeps us in the society of God."[1] *In dei societate* is fundamental to the being and the forms of the church; because of this, a doctrine of the church is a function of the doctrine of the Trinity. Intellectual apprehension of the being of the church requires us to explicate it as an element in the covenantal economy of God's goodness toward creatures; this, in turn, requires a theology of the divine missions, which is itself rooted in a theology of the inner divine processions. Like all Christian doctrines, the doctrine of the church is to be traced back to the immanent perfection of God's life and his free self-communication in the *opera dei exeuntia;* a theology of the church is not simply a phenomenology of ecclesial social history but an inquiry into that history's ontological ground in the being and works of the church's God.[2]

Put a little differently, ecclesiology proposes answers to the question:

---

1. J. Calvin, *Institutes of the Christian Religion* 4.1.3.

2. One of the most important recent treatments of ecclesiology that parallels some of the ideas pursued here is that of Hans-Peter Großhans in *Die Kirche — irdische Raum der Wahrheit des Evangeliums* (Leipzig: Evangelische Verlagsanstalt, 2003). Großhans's account is a well-judged and concentrated piece of biblical dogmatics, concerned above all to secure the right sort of relativity of ecclesiology to the doctrine of God. However, it does not make extensive use of Trinitarian doctrine, preferring to concentrate on an understanding of the church's relation to the truth of the gospel as the way in which its reference to that which lies outside its life is to be conceived.

What *kind* of society is the church? The answer ecclesiology returns is: the church is the human assembly that is the creaturely social coefficient of the outer work in which God restores creatures to fellowship with himself. The natural and historical properties of that society only become objects of intelligence (rather than simply of phenomenal regard) when they are understood as elements in the saving transit of creatures from their origin to their end in God's society. A corollary here is that ecclesiology has both a proximate and a principal *res*. Its proximate *res* is a form of human society, characterized by certain commonalities with, and by certain estrangements from, other such forms; its principal *res* is the temporal processions of God and the eternal processions from which they are suspended. In this double character, moreover, the *res* of ecclesiology is no more available, no less difficult of access, no less reserved from us than the Christian doctrine of God, for the simple reason that it is an extension of the Christian doctrine of God.

Such an orientation in dogmatic ecclesiology seems doomed to fall into idealism, since its core proposal is that the being of the church is not identical *simpliciter* with a human historical project, a social-material reality in time. Resistance to idealism commonly underlies appeals for the deployment of the social sciences in ecclesiology, or for a shift away from apparently abstract doctrines of the church, to accounts of "churchly practices" in which "theological reflection upon the church is in fact from the very outset a matter of practical rather than theoretical reasoning."[3] How might a dogmatic ecclesiology respond?

The threat of a failed connection between a dogmatic account of the church and the empirical realities of its history is always present. School dogmatics, especially in an exhausted tradition that has in some measure lost touch with the realities to which it is responsible, can rest content with abstractions of this kind, especially when organized as an exposition of ecclesiological "models." And this is not simply a problem within degenerate dogmatics: one of the temptations for a certain style of high ecumenical ecclesiology has been to think that a resonant theological description of the church — as *koinonia*, for example — holds the key to resolving the church's disunity and reestablishing its mission in the world. But the con-

---

3. N. M. Healy, *Church, World, and the Christian Life: Practical-Prophetic Ecclesiology* (Cambridge: Cambridge University Press, 2000), p. 46. For a significant correction, see N. Healy, "Practices and the New Ecclesiology: Misplaced Concreteness?" *International Journal of Systematic Theology* 5 (2003): 287-308.

cern to scour out idealism from doctrines of the church raises a deeper issue, one highlighted by Healy's identification of ecclesiology as a matter of
practical, not theoretical, reasoning. Behind the worries about idealism lies
a conviction, part metaphysical and part theological, and often only half-
articulated, that the real is the social-historical. This conviction commonly
promotes the metamorphosis of the proximate *res* of ecclesiology into its
principal *res*. "The principal object of ecclesiology consists in the empirical
organization or collectivity or communion called church":[4] so Roger
Haight in *Christian Community in History* (a book whose large ambitions
are thwarted by a mixture of dogmatic ineptitude and formulaic historical
exposition). Or again, note the principle enunciated at the opening of
Johannes van der Ven's *Ecclesiology in Context:* "God does not cancel out
the activities of people in the church, but inspires, intensifies, and orients
them. God gives to the people to form the church themselves, to do the
church themselves."[5] What presents itself as a principle of noncompetition
between divine and social agents turns out to require us to fold language
about divine action into language about the functions and codes of the
Christian society. Once more, in a much more penetrating essay by Joseph
Komonchak: "If the Church is the People of God, the Body of Christ, the
Temple of the Holy Spirit, it is all of these as a human reality, that is, because certain events occur within the mutually-related consciousness of a
group of human beings."[6] Notice the sequence: the church is the people of
God because certain events occur within a group of human beings — a
causal order at which even the most frankly intrinsicist theology of grace
might be dismayed.

Sometimes such proposals may express a sense of the irresistibility of
the modern turn to history; sometimes they may be warranted by appeal
to elements of the Christian faith, often rather randomly chosen, abstractly
conceived, and without much sense of their systematic linkages — appeal
to the doctrine of the incarnation, for example, or to the theology of grace
and created habit. The underlying assumption is, again, one concerning
the *res* of Christian theology: since the object of Christian theology is the
economy of God's works as creator and reconciler of humankind, then
theology should naturally direct its attention to the temporal and social as

4. R. Haight, *Christian Community in History,* vol. 1 (London: Continuum, 2004),
p. 5.

5. J. A. van der Ven, *Ecclesiology in Context* (Grand Rapids: Eerdmans, 1996), p. xiv.

6. J. Komonchak, "Ecclesiology and Social Theory: A Methodological Inquiry,"
Thomist 45 (1981): 269.

the sphere of God's presence and activity. And this conviction has proved companionable, not only to the deployment of modes of analysis of the phenomena of the church that derive from social and cultural science, but also to those kinds of ecclesiology that lay heavy emphasis upon the church as social body.

Sed contra: for Christian dogmatics, God is *ens realissimum,* God's acts are *acta realissima.*[7] The temporal economy, including the social reality of the church in time, has its being not *in se* but by virtue of God who alone is *in se.* Time and society are derivative realities, and that derivation is not simply a matter of their origination; it is a permanent mark of their historical condition. As Saint Thomas puts it, God's relation to creatures cannot be conceived as that of an agent who "is the cause of its effect in regard simply to the coming-to-be, and not directly in regard to the *esse* of the effect," for "the *esse* of all creaturely beings so depends upon God that they could not continue to exist even for a moment, but would fall away into nothingness unless they were sustained in existence by his power."[8] This, in the end, is why ecclesiology cannot be only a matter of historical sociology or practical reasoning: to make it such is to neglect the principle that all creaturely being is grounded in God, and by reason of that neglect to misapprehend the kind of historical society that the church is — in Thomas's terms, a society whose "essence is not its *esse.*"[9] Put simply: ecclesiology and ecclesial action are creaturely realities, to be set under the metaphysics of grace.[10]

---

7. See I. U. Dalferth, "Wirklichkeit Gottes und christlicher Glaube," in *Gedeutete Gegenwart* (Tübingen: Mohr Siebeck, 1997), pp. 99-132.

8. *Summa Theologiae* 1a.104.1 resp.

9. *Summa Theologiae* 1a.104.1 resp.

10. It is this emphasis that distinguishes my proposal from that of the late Dan Hardy in one of the most searching reflections on the dependence of the doctrine of the church upon the doctrine of God, "God and the Form of Society" (in *God's Ways with the World: Thinking and Practicing Christian Faith* [Edinburgh: T. & T. Clark, 1996], pp. 173-87). Hardy argues that the church's capacity to offer "a new orientation and impetus to the form of our society" (p. 174) by showing that social structures are relative to God is inhibited by the "marginalization of the Christian understanding of God" (p. 183) in Christian social theory, that is, by inattention to "the presence in human social structures of the social coherence which is embedded in God's very being and work." This marginalization he traces to monarchical conceptions of deity in Western theology according to which God is by nature "disinvolved from social structures and human relationships": by "allowing only extrinsic and occasional relations" between God and social forms, and by denying any "intrinsic relation between God and the natural or social orders" in the name of divine sovereignty, God is reduced to external agent, "occasionally related to the world when it pleases him" (p. 183). Hardy's counter to this is a doctrine of the Trinity that undergirds an intrinsic account of

Christian dogmatics does not concede the ontological primacy and self-evidence of the social-historical; and it considers that apprehension of the phenomenal visibility of social-historical realities is not possible in the absence of reference to their ordering to God, that is, in the absence of reference to their creatureliness. And so its account of the church is an extension of the doctrine of God, and therefore of teaching about God's immanent perfection and goodness. To speak of the church's being, dogmatics is required to speak of God who alone has being *in se;* to speak of the church's acts, dogmatics is required to speak of the *opera dei interna et externa.* In ecclesiology, much hangs on the doctrine of God — on the content of that doctrine and on the directness with which it is invoked. Whether such an approach is judged idealist will depend, in part, upon prior judgments about the nature of created community and its relation to the work of God. It is, doubtless, more exposed to the danger of extrinsicism that de Lubac exposed in *Catholicism* than, for example, those ecclesiologies that appeal to teaching about the *totus Christus,* or that deploy cultural ethnography, to prevent "a complete severance between the natural and the supernatural."[11] But apparent "extrinsicism" in talking of creatures may be no more than the at-

---

God's relation to created sociality. God, he writes, is "self-structured (in accordance with his own self-determined conditions) and self-identified in a complex and dynamic unity which rests on his energy to structure and restructure himself in self-sustaining cohesion . . . he is seen as an energetic unity (the Holy Spirit) which is true to its internal conditions (the Father) through ordering its interactions (the Son). But this is to be regarded not so much as a 'state of affairs' in God as an energetic faithfulness maintained in his dynamic relation to the world" (p. 186). There are intimations here of God's immanent life ("self-determined conditions" or "internal conditions"), but the main tendency is toward the economic. The "self-structuring of God," he continues, "is to be seen as a self-structuring which occurs in an ongoing 'relation' with human life in this world." "It is in the energising of his relationality that God reaches his fullness, and in this ordered relationality interacts energetically with human beings to enable them to structure their life together" (p. 186). If there is something problematic here, it is that what Hardy in a further essay calls the "social transcendental" ("Created and Redeemed Sociality," in *God's Ways with the World,* pp. 188-205) is too deeply embedded in human history, its immanent plenitude forming only a remote background to its economic presence, which is to be traced to "the *Logos* of God operative in creation" (p. 202). Hardy is entirely correct to root created social being in the doctrine of God; but his emphasis on the priority of creation over redemption, and his relatively thin description of the inner divine relations as the church's ultimate ontological ground, point in a significantly different direction from that followed here.

11. H. de Lubac, *Catholicism: A Study of Dogma in Relation to the Corporate Destiny of Mankind* (London: Burns, Oates and Washbourne, 1950), p. 166.

tempt to take with full seriousness and consistency the fact that God's relations to creatures are nonreciprocal, "mixed" relations, and to try to grasp how that condition shapes what it means for creaturely community to be and act *in dei societate*. Nor need this mean an abstract doctrine of divine transcendence, deployed, perhaps, to keep the church in its place or to underwrite sectarian disengagement. Properly undertaken, with the right kind of evangelical determinacy, it may be simply a way of identifying the kind of social history that the church is, namely, a social history that is one long reference to its origin in God's goodness. "To go back to origins is not to go back to annihilation, if we go back to the Origin of origins — to God. On the contrary, it is only in God that we can come to a positive position"[12] — so Barth in the Tambach lecture of 1919, the abstract term "Origin of origins" acting as a kind of placeholder for the doctrine of the Trinity, whose discovery still lay ahead of him. It is to that doctrine that Christian dogmatics turns in order to explicate the kind of positive social historical reality that the church is.

II

Dogmatics talks of the church by talking about God and God's works, and does so as its first and governing descriptive act. More closely, dogmatics arrives at the doctrine of the church by Trinitarian deduction, in this way conforming to the creedal sequence in which *credo in ecclesiam* succeeds *credo in Deum Patrem omnipotentem . . . et in Jesum Christum . . . credo in Spiritum Sanctum.*[13] Ecclesiology has its place in the flow of Christian doctrine from teaching about God to teaching about everything else in God. This means that ecclesiology is a derivative doctrine, concerned with the fulfillment of God's covenant with his rational creatures, and in its explication the doctrine of God is directly at work. And it means, further, that the life of the people of God is a necessary theme in Christian dogmatics, since dogmatics treats not only theology proper but also economy, and

12. K. Barth, "The Christian's Place in Society," in *The Word of God and the Word of Man* (London: Hodder and Stoughton, 1928), p. 294.

13. Bonhoeffer's grounding of the being of the church *extra se* (in *Sanctorum Communio: A Theological Study of the Sociology of the Church* [Minneapolis: Fortress, 1998]) is congenial to my argument here, though his appeal to revelation rather than Trinity ("Only the concept of revelation can lead to the concept of the church," p. 134) lends a rather abstract air to his presentation.

within the economy, the church. Because the one to whom dogmatics attends in theology proper is this one — the one who is moved by perfect goodness to bestow and maintain creaturely fellowship — there is a necessary ecclesial component to Christian teaching without which the doctrines of God and creation would be imperfectly apprehended.

Deduction of ecclesiological doctrine from Trinitarian doctrine is, of course, familiar in the kind of Trinitarianism in which the relations of the persons of the Godhead are "echoed" in the Christian community.[14] There are evident benefits here: in terms of the doctrine of God, getting beyond abstractly monist conceptions of God as an undifferentiated principle or cause of the church; in terms of the doctrine of the church, resistance to ecclesiological naturalism. But deploying "relation" (or, more abstractly, "relationality") as a bridge term between God and creatures can prove precarious, effecting the passage from God to church too comfortably, without securing an adequate sense of the unqualified gratuity of the church's created existence and of its difference from God who is the uncreated source of its life. The connection of theology proper and ecclesiology is best explicated not by setting out two terms of an analogy but by describing a sequence of divine acts both in terms of their ground in the immanent divine being and in terms of their creaturely fruits. The sequence has its rise in the eternal inner divine counsel, which then finds temporal execution in the missions of the Son and the Spirit, through which the Father's purpose is enacted.

God the Holy Trinity is alive with self-moved life. This movement of his is unlike creaturely movement because it is *self*-movement, *a se*, not moved from beyond itself, and so in its very mobility a kind of perfect repose, a movement without agitation or effort. As God moves himself, he does not come into being or stretch toward his fulfillment; his movement is not theogony but inexhaustible plenitude, the fullness of eternal life. The form of this life is the divine processions, in which God's perfection is enacted. We have only the faintest glimpse of these as we reflect on God's outer works, but we may identify them as the acts in which the Father generates the Son in the eternal relations of paternity and filiation, and Father

14. "Echoed" is Gunton's term in a representative essay, "The Church on Earth: The Roots of Community," in *On Being the Church: Essays on the Christian Community*, ed. C. Gunton and D. Hardy (Edinburgh: T. & T. Clark, 1989), pp. 48-80. For a more searching analysis, see C. Schwöbel's Heidelberg inaugural, "Gottes Ökumene. Über das Verhältnis von Kirchengemeinschaft und Gottesverständnis," in *Christlicher Glaube im Pluralismus. Studien zu einer Theologie der Kultur* (Tübingen: Mohr Siebeck, 2003), pp. 107-32.

and Son together breathe the Spirit in the eternal relation of spiration. These relations have no beginning or end, they suffer no diminution or increase; they are the eternal abundance and blessedness of God in himself. But that abundance — because it is *God's* abundance — is not self-enclosed or self-revolving, even in its repleteness, for God's perfection includes God's goodness, and God's goodness is manifest in his creative love. In his goodness, out of his own fullness and free determination, God bestows life upon a reality other than himself. In doing so, he does not replicate or communicate himself; creaturely being does not partake of the divine being but rather has its own identity and integrity at the hands of God, who gives life *(creatio)* and cares for what he creates by sustaining and governing it *(curatio, providentia)*. Amongst the beings so created and sustained are God's rational creatures, appointed to fellowship with the Creator. The history of this fellowship is the history of the covenant, that is, the history of Adam's race, which, after Adam's defection, is set again on the way to perfection through Israel and the church of Christ.

The Trinitarian deduction of the church may be described in a little more detail by tracing how particular external works of God with respect to the church may be appropriated to particular persons of the Godhead, always bearing in mind that all such external works are the work of the undivided Trinity, and that appropriation to one or another divine person may be eminent or distinct, but not absolute, appropriation.

The church has being because of the eternal will of the God and Father of our Lord Jesus Christ, who "destined us in love to be his children through Jesus Christ, according to the purpose of his will" (Eph. 1:5). The church exists as a form of human common life because and only because God the Father purposes that it should be. This intention of the Father emerges from the primal reality of the inner divine life. God the Father is the principle of the Holy Trinity, the infinite uncaused depth of God's triune being. The Father is properly and personally *autotheos,* not because he is superior or prior to the Son and the Spirit who share in divine aseity, but because he is the one who eternally generates the eternal Son and (with the Son) breathes the eternal Spirit. As this one the Father is also the divine person to whom the purposing of creaturely existence and the determination of its course and end are most properly to be attributed. This purposing is wholly antecedent; it is not a set of arrangements made in respect of an already existent reality upon which God comes to exercise his will; it is "before the foundation of the world" (Eph. 1:4). Further, this purposing is "in love"; not a dark imposition of order or an arbitrary restriction but a gift of history and form, "loving" because it wills the existence of another reality with its own identity. The divine counsel, and its application in predestination, is an act of divine benevolence. This purposing is effected with the Son. In classical Reformed dogmatics, this common engagement of the first two triune persons is brought to expression by the concept of the *pactum salutis* in which Father and Son agree together to effect the history of the covenant with creatures. The inner divine concord receives temporal administration in the Son's mission, the Son consenting that alongside his wholly unique relation to the Father there should also be other children of God, that he will be the "firstborn" (Rom. 8:29; cf. Heb. 2:10-13), graciously placing himself at the head of Adam's lost race to reestablish fellowship with the Father. All this is animated by the Father's goodness, his love for what is not God, his resolve that creatures should be and that their being should not be overcome by self-destruction.

So conceived, the life and activity of the triune God are the fundamental context in which the history of the common life of God's creatures is acted out. "See what love the Father has given us, that we should be called children of God. And so we are!" (1 John 3:1). For the apostle, the existence of the church is a matter for astonishment. The Father and the children are not simply elements within created sociality, but elements in the history in which created sociality is regenerated after sin has set human common life under the sign of death. The church's dynamic is thus that of adoption and the bestowing of status, a status that fulfills natural sociality but only by way of redemptive grace. The church is, therefore, society within the *foedus gratiae,* not the *foedus naturae.* "It was no common honour . . . that the heavenly Father bestowed on us, when he adopted us as his children," notes Calvin, for when the apostle says that "*love* has been *bestowed,*" he means that it is from mere bounty and benevolence that God makes us his children . . . for why are we sons? Even because God began to love us freely, when we deserved hatred rather than love."[15] A doctrine of the church is in this regard retrospective, drawing its substance from "that which was in the beginning" (1 John 1:1); that "beginning" includes the love of the eternal Father, the unoriginate origin of all things, who elects and adopts creatures into fellowship through the person and saving acts of the eternal Son.

The church has being because of the person and work of the eternal Son,

---

15. J. Calvin, *Commentary on the First Epistle of John,* in *Commentaries on the Catholic Epistles* (Edinburgh: Calvin Translation Society, 1855), pp. 202f.

the first and the last and the living one (Rev. 1:17f.). Relating ecclesiology to Christology depends in part upon ensuring that the full compass of Christology is brought to bear on the matter. When too narrow a selection of christological material is deemed pertinent, ecclesiology suffers disfigurement.[16] The person and work of the Son can be so identified with his incarnate presence that his eternal preexistent deity recedes from view; or the postexistence of the Son in his state of exaltation can be retracted. In both, Christology is constricted, as its central episode — the temporal career of the Son — is allowed to expand and fill the whole (and thereby the real force of that central episode itself is in some degree blunted). As a result, ecclesiology tends to be preoccupied with the question: What kind of continuity is there between the incarnate and the ecclesial body? The very form of the question narrows the range of ways in which the relations and differences between Christ and the church may be understood.

Retaining the scope of Christology in expounding ecclesiology involves giving due weight to three christological moments: the eternal deity of the Son, his temporal mission as reconciler, and his exaltation as the one under whose feet are all things (Eph. 1:22). Keeping each of these three moments in mind serves to ensure the relativity of ecclesiology to Christology and to prevent the ecclesiological functionalization of christological doctrine.

It is, first, ecclesiologically elemental that the Son shares in antecedent, wholly realized deity, that he is the eternal Son proceeding from the eternal Father, God of God, Light of Light, true God of true God, and replete in that procession. His identity as Son is, therefore, not wholly determined by the *status exinanitionis* of the incarnation. "Son" and "incarnate Son" are not wholly coincident realities, for the Son's becoming incarnate is not the divesting of deity or the mutation of deity into flesh; the Word becomes flesh without ceasing to be God. This does not mean that flesh is merely extrinsic to the Son's identity, but rather that his taking of flesh is a wholly spontaneous act of obedience to the will of the Father, and of love of creatures, an act that does not exhaust his deity. The Son is not made Son by the flesh; nor can he be deduced from it. There is that of the Son that is *extra* to the flesh he assumes. *Logos* and *sarx* are asymmetrical: to

---

16. Such problems emerge with some seriousness in J. Milbank, "The Name of Jesus," in *The Word Made Strange: Theology, Language, Culture* (Oxford: Blackwell, 1997), pp. 145-68; Milbank, "Ecclesiology: The Last of the Last," in *Being Reconciled: Ontology and Pardon* (London: Routledge, 2002), pp. 105-37.

grasp the identity of the *verbum incarnatum* we need also to look beyond its temporal occurrence to the Son's antecedent divine capacity, a capacity not expended in the act of incarnation but remaining full and free. Why is this ecclesiologically elemental? Because it identifies the right sort of externality in Christ's relation to the church: not an externality that presupposes a gulf between God and creatures, crossed by occasional divine forays into created time, but rather the irreversible relation-in-distinction between the uncreated and created that is the energy of God's covenantal fellowship with his rational creatures. It is this distinction that may be breached in, for example, ecclesiologies organized around the concept of *totus Christus,* at least in versions of that concept in which the full identity of the Son is achieved only as he takes the church into union with himself: Calvin's strictures against a *crassa mixtura* of God and creatures[17] ought not to be passed over too quickly in reaching a judgment about contemporary ecclesiologies of *koinonia.* The distinction between uncreated and created, expressed in the Son's transcendence of the flesh even in its assumption, is elemental to a theologically intelligent grasp of the historical forms and acts of the church.

Second, it is ecclesiologically elemental that the incarnate Son of God is the reconciler of lost creatures. The Son's deity issues in an outward movement, that is, in the temporal mission of reconciliation. Out of the groundless depth of his divinity he comes to creatures by taking creaturely form, and with it creaturely distress and culpability; in so doing, he effects the destruction and reconstitution of Adam's race. The first Adam was lawless, withholding assent to the nature and end bestowed on him by divine goodness and drawing down upon himself and his heirs deathly alienation from God and the dismembering of created society. The second Adam fulfills the law by obeying the Father's will, taking upon himself the curse of Adam's race, and so restoring creaturely fellowship with God and bringing into existence a community that is, indeed, *in dei societate.* As lordly reconciler, the Son "creates in himself one new man" (Eph. 2:15). His history — the fact that there and then, this one, the incarnate Son, spoke and acted and suffered thus — is the ontological condition of the church: not simply a symbol to provoke creatures to common life but a *making,* a bringing to effect or setting forth of the mystery of the Father's will that creatures should attain their end by being united in him (Eph. 1:10).

Third, it is ecclesiologically elemental that the Son of God is in

17. Calvin, *Institutes* 3.11.10.

heaven. "He who descended is he who ascended far above all the heavens" (Eph. 4:10). The Son's exaltation entails his removal from direct historical presence among creatures. This in turn reinforces the ecclesiological importance of affirming that the Son's relation to the church is external, but not in such a way as to contradict the union with Christ that is proper to the church as one of the fruits of redemption. The church is indeed "made alive together with Christ"; it is "raised up with him," it "sits" with him in the heavenly places (Eph. 2:5f.). This "with Christ" has ontological weight: the church has its being with him. But what is the force of this "with"? It indicates an intimacy of relation between Christ the Lord and those whom he exalts to share his location, but one in which he retains his free, sovereign incommunicable identity. His co-location with the church is not such that his identity as the exalted Son becomes porous, or that he is no longer gracious toward the community. The church adds nothing to the identity of the exalted Son. "By grace" (Eph. 2:5, 8) is not merely the means of the church's entry into union with Christ but the permanent characteristic of that union, and therefore a signifier that the church's relation to its Lord is characterized by ever greater dissimilarity.

This element of distinction between the church and its Lord is routinely muted in ecclesiologies ordered around a particular construal of the "body of Christ" metaphor. Jenson's account of the matter is a striking (because drastic) example. Embodiment is a person's "availability to other persons and thereupon to her or himself"[18] (note that the account begins from observations about embodiment rather than from the identity of the agent of whom the metaphor is predicated). The ecclesiological extension of the principle of embodied availability runs thus: "That the church is the body of Christ . . . means that she is the object in the world as which the risen Christ is an object for the world, an available something as which Christ is there to be addressed and grasped. Where am I to aim my intention, to intend the risen Christ? The first answer must be: to the assembled church, and if I am in the assembly, to the gathering that surrounds me."[19] And so "[t]he church with her sacraments is truly Christ's availability to us just because Christ takes her as his availability to himself. Where does the risen Christ turn to find himself? To the sacramental gathering of believers."[20] It

---

18. R. Jenson, *Systematic Theology,* vol. 2 (Oxford: Oxford University Press, 1999), p. 213.

19. Jenson, *Systematic Theology,* 2:213.

20. Jenson, *Systematic Theology,* 2:214.

is surely odd to ask where the risen turns to find himself; one could hardly ask that question of God unless the attribute of perfection had ceased to bear any real weight, and to ask it of the risen Christ assumes that his identity is in the process of construction rather than eternally replete. This requires Jenson to develop a — strained — account of the otherness of Christ to the church, focused on the eucharistic elements: "the object that is the church assembly is the body of Christ, that is, Christ available to the world and to her members, just in that the church gathers around objects distinct from herself, the bread and the cup, which are the availability *to her* of the same Christ. Within the gathering we can intend Christ as the community we are, without self-deification, because we jointly intend the identical Christ in the sacramental elements in our midst, which are other than us."[21] But this is surely an emergency measure, which can scarcely compensate for the absence of a sense of Christ's singular, self-constituting, and church-creating subjectivity as the enthroned Son.

To say that the church is the body of Christ is to say that its being is a predicate of his lordly and complete identity and activity.[22] "He is the head of the body, the church; he is the beginning, the first-born from the dead, that in everything he might be pre-eminent" (Col. 1:18). The metaphors here — headship, origination, primogeniture, preeminence — are all, of course, terms of relation. The exalted one is not separate from the church; *fellowship* flows from his work, for he is the reconciler. But the fellowship he brings about is not such that the identity of the exalted one is extended, completed, or enacted in the community over which he presides. The eternal Son *creates* the church by exalting it to his side, but he does not thereby create or intend himself, for his identity is antecedently replete; as himself *autotheos,* his identity as Son is given him by the Father in full measure. As this perfect one, he is "far above all the heavens."

This train of thought simply observes some basic dogmatic rules: that "we with God" derives from "God with us," and that "God with us" does not mean the diffusion of God's life but its generativity. Because this is so, there really is fellowship with God, there really are brothers and sisters of Jesus Christ. The risen Christ does not cast about him for some other reality through which to find his identity or intend himself; he *declares* himself: "Here am I, and the children God has given me" (Heb. 2:13).

The third element in the Trinitarian deduction of the church is

---

21. Jenson, *Systematic Theology,* 2:213.
22. See here Großhans, *Die Kirche,* pp. 31-54.

pneumatology. *The church is and acts by virtue of the Holy Spirit, the Lord and giver of life.* The sequence of this confession about the Spirit is significant: the Spirit gives life because he is Lord. Whatever is said about the economic activity of the Spirit is therefore predicated upon his consubstantiality with Father and Son. His quickening is "the work of the Eternal Majesty";[23] its effectiveness rests upon the fact that the Spirit is no immanent created power, that he is "not amongst but above all things."[24] Ambrose's point is that the Spirit is not to be numbered among creatures; but it is precisely as this one, sharing in the eternal lordship of God, that the Spirit is active in the created realm, distributing the gift of life from the store of the divine generosity. The Holy Spirit is the divine agent of creaturely perfection, that is, the one in whom the works of God toward creatures are completed so that creatures attain their end. Creatures do not have life in themselves, and so cannot maintain their own life; they are maintained by the Spirit, through whose presence and activity creatures do indeed *live* — act in spontaneity, move through time, deliberate and relate. Above all, the Spirit gives new life, since he is the divine agent who consummates Christ's objective work of reconciliation and realizes in a final way God's purpose for creaturely being in fellowship with himself. In fulfillment of the Father's decree, and in consequence of the Son's perfect work of reconciliation, the Spirit animates and preserves a human social world in which the old order of sin and death has been set aside and the life of the children of God is unleashed. Through the Spirit it comes about that there exists a temporal, cultural, bodily reality in fulfillment of the divine appointment: "You shall be my people." All this takes place as the accomplishment of the Spirit's mission, that is, his being sent by the Father and the Son, in order to effect in time the full realization of the economy of redemption. There is a stream of life that flows from heaven toward creatures, whose source is God the Father and whose power is God the Son; this is the Holy Spirit, by whom God's covenant with his rational creatures takes social-historical shape.

With this we turn to consider the church as social-historical phenomenon.

---

23. Ambrose, *On the Holy Spirit* 2.29.
24. Ambrose, *On the Holy Spirit* 1.19.

III

We are to be led by the questions: What kind of social-historical phenomena characterize the society that exists in God's society? By what modes of action and suffering may the life of this society be picked out? And what kinds of acts of observation do these acts and sufferings require if they are to be known? Three initial points by way of orientation.

First, the acts of the church are characterized by the fact that their motive power is not inherent within themselves. They are modes of action whose movement is itself moved. It is not easy for us to access the concept of moved movement, still less to incorporate it into ethnographical description. This, because at least since the seventeenth century, natural motion has been immanentized and eventually secularized, so that, for example, the entelechy of society finds sufficient explanation in description of its natural agents and course.[25] At best, divine causality in respect of the world is restricted to the efficient causality that establishes the conditions for the world by setting it in motion; but appeal to divine causality is not required for observation of the way things now are, beyond simply invoking the fact that what now is has come into being. The most obvious casualty of the immanentization of divine motion is, of course, the Christian doctrine of providence, but its wider effect is erosion of the category of *creatureliness* from our explanation of ourselves and its replacement by the categories of pure nature, history, and society.

The muting and eventual exclusion of reference to divine motion were closely tied to the emancipatory potential of the study of human society in and of itself. To liberate society from divine motion is to open a space for free human action and social spontaneity. The deep assumption here is that natural motion is *purely* natural or nothing at all; put differently, that to talk of human acts as creaturely is simply to indicate their ultimate origin, not the ontological condition for their present performance. Yet it is elemental to a scriptural metaphysics that the motion of God and the motion of creatures are not inversely but directly proportional: the more God moves the creature, the more the creature moves itself. In the case of the church, then, the acts by which this society realizes itself are acts whose description requires constant deployment of language about God.

---

25. On this, see M. J. Buckley, *Motion and Motion's God: Thematic Variations in Aristotle, Cicero, Newton, and Hegel* (Princeton: Princeton University Press, 1971); S. Oliver, *Philosophy, God, and Motion* (London: Routledge, 2005).

The phenomena of church action have to be traced back — reduced — to God as their exemplary, efficient, and final cause. The divine wisdom by which God ordains the church's life and activity and the divine providence by which God enacts what he purposes have to be primary elements in the description of what the church does in time. The phenomena of the church are not only phenomena within a stream of empirical history; they are also — primarily — phenomena in the history by which God conducts creatures away from the ruins of the earthly city toward the heavenly.

Second, because the acts of the church are not acts of pure natural spontaneity, but movements moved by God, they bear within themselves a certain excess. That is, they are signs, ostensive acts that refer beyond themselves to the triune being and work by which the church is brought into and maintained in being. "Do you not know that you are God's temple and that God's Spirit dwells in you?" Paul asks the Corinthians, not without a measure of exasperation (1 Cor. 3:16). Our temptation in handling such imagery is to think that "temple" is the *signum*, and the goings-on at Corinth the *res*. The opposite is the case: God's temple is what the Corinthians *are*, not what they might be said to be by metaphor. It is not their active self-realization that determines their being, but rather the fact that they are the temple of God. They are this temple, further, by virtue of being indwelt by the Spirit and set apart or made holy. The dynamic of the life of the church is not self-derived, and its acts are indicative.

Third, there is by the nature of the case a certain obscurity to the historical-practical reality of the church.[26] Its temporal forms are not unconditionally transparent; they do not show the church's source of life without ambiguity. The church is *spiritually* visible. To speak of the church as spiritually visible is to make a twofold claim, about the church's being and about the way in which that being may be apprehended. The church's spiritual visibility means, first, that its being is not exhausted in its phenomenal surface, because the church is constituted by the presence and action of God "who is invisible" (Heb. 11:27). By the church's invisibility is meant this reference to God that is ontologically primal to the church as *creatura verbi divini* — as an evangelical, rather than simply a social-historical, reality. Second, spiritual visibility is visibility to prayerful reason illuminated by the Holy Spirit to see and trust the work of God in creaturely occurrence. This is why ecclesiology is first an exercise in con-

---

26. For what follows, see E. Jüngel, "Credere in ecclesiam. Eine ökumenische Besinnung," *Zeitschrift für Theologie und Kirche* 99 (2002): 177-95.

templative science, and only derivatively of practical social science: knowledge of the church is ordered to knowledge of "things not seen" (Heb. 11:1). Spiritual visibility, however, is not the antithesis of practical-historical form but a characterization of it. De Lubac dismissed such talk as baleful Protestant "monophysitism," dissociating the divine and the human. "Having stripped [the church] of all its mystical attributes, [Protestantism] acknowledged in the visible church a mere secular institution."[27] That is a bad misjudgment. The church that is spiritually visible has historical shape and endurance, but only because it is granted to exist in that way by the secret energy of the Spirit.

At this point, a comprehensive ecclesiology would move to treat the fundamental forms of the church; here only the barest outline can be offered. The fundamental forms of the church are the primary structures of its creaturely, social-historical existence. By speaking of the church's fundamental forms, dogmatics picks out attributes and activities by which the church can be identified. Though they are encountered in particular concretizations of practice in the history of the church, fundamental forms are not wholly identical with those practices. Talk of the church's fundamental forms thus has a critical or relativizing function with respect to the empirical life of the church. In this respect, talk of the church's fundamental forms functions similarly to talk of the church's marks: both are concerned not simply to make empirical observations but to grasp how even in defect or misperformance the church remains under the determination of the divine appointment and its attendant promises. Statements about the church's fundamental forms describe the divine gifts promised to the church as the *coetus electorum*, the imperatives those gifts bear within themselves, and the certainty that the church's temporal declension cannot annul its being.

Three examples from a larger set may be given: assembly, hearing the divine Word, and order.

First, the church is a human assembly or form of association. But its human act of assembly follows, signifies, and mediates a divine act of gathering; it is a moved movement of congregation. To describe the human assembly as what it is, therefore, reference must be made to certain antecedent divine works: choosing before the foundation of the world, predestination to be the sons and daughters of God, appointment to live for the praise of God's glory (Eph. 1:4-12). These divine works are the ex-

27. De Lubac, *Catholicism*, p. 29.

emplary cause of the church's temporal assembly. Further, reference must be made to certain divine works in the present, such as the work of the glorified Christ in whom the assembly is joined together and grows into a holy temple (Eph. 2:21). The church assembly is a social-historical reality "in the Lord" (Eph. 2:21) — "in the Lord" being no mere rhetorical flourish through which the ethnographer penetrates to some more primary natural level but rather metaphysically irreducible.

The historical actuality of the church is determined by its being as the *coetus electorum et vocatorum,* that is, as that society by the election and summons of the triune God. Election and calling are not simply features of the distant origin of the church; they determine not only its inception but also its continuance, permanently marking its life. These divine acts of determination, election, and vocation precede, accompany, and direct the action of the community that is chosen and summoned. The communion of the saints exists on the basis of and in virtue of the divine work. Indeed, the primal sin in the history of the covenant is neglect of the fact that the covenant people has its life *ab extra,* that it is "a chosen race, a royal priesthood, a holy nation, God's own people" (1 Pet. 2:9), and instead thinking of its life as self-assembled and self-governed. Because the church is a creature, self-realization is not fundamental to its being, and its (necessary) acts bear the traces of this creaturely status.[28] The practical-historical acts of the church are not self-making, but a following of its given nature. This does not make the church *less* than a historical project; what it does suggest, however, is that the project that the church is, is more than a rather indeterminate set of cultural negotiations in which the church figures out some kind of identity for itself. The church is not finished; it learns itself over time; it does not possess itself wholly, because its source of life is the infinity of God.[29] But God's infinity not only opens up a historical horizon that the church fills with social forms; it is the *law* of churchly action, giving direction and shape. The church is not an indefinite or arbitrary social-cultural assembly, but is shaped by the divine plan, and its history unfolds as that plan moves toward fulfillment.

---

28. M. Beintker, *"The Church of Jesus Christ:* An Introduction," *Ecclesiology* 1 (2005): 45-58; Dalferth, *Gedeutete Gegenwart,* pp. 57-59; see Schwöbel, "The Creature of the Word: Recovering the Ecclesiology of the Reformers," in *On Being the Church,* pp. 110-55.

29. A point consistently emphasized by Rowan Williams in, for example, "Word and Spirit," in *On Christian Theology* (Oxford: Blackwell, 2000), pp. 107-27, or "A History of Faith in Jesus," in *The Cambridge Companion to Jesus,* ed. M. Bockmuehl (Cambridge: Cambridge University Press, 2001), pp. 220-36.

Second, the church is a society built upon the foundation of the prophets and apostles whose testimony to the gospel is set before the church in Holy Scripture.[30] Its common life and culture flourish as it submits to that witness. The church is a mode of common life established and edified by God's communicative presence mediated through the biblical writings; in this sense it is the creature of the divine Word. Its acts of intelligence and speech are, therefore, receptive and attentive acts, referred to God's self-communication in Holy Scripture. Any adequate ethnography of the church's communicative economy will need to follow the ways in which that economy makes reference to Holy Scripture.

Holy Scripture is the unified canon of texts appointed by God as the herald of his self-publication. The canon is holy, that is, it is a set of creaturely textual acts sanctified to serve God's revelatory presence. By the divine act of sanctification these creaturely acts are made fitting attestations of the divine Word. As a field of the Spirit's operation in its production, Holy Scripture is inspired, that is, God undertakes that Scripture's prophetic and apostolic authors give creaturely voice to what the Spirit says to the churches. As a field of the Spirit's operation in its reception, Holy Scripture possesses clarity, because the Spirit who inspires Scripture also illuminates its readers, making the prophetic and apostolic word intelligible and effectual. As an attestation of the rule of Christ and his gospel, Holy Scripture is authoritative; in reading Holy Scripture the church receives an embassy from the church's Lord, so that its speaking can legitimately require the attention that is properly given to the *viva vox Christi*. As that to which Christ entrusts the task of instructing the church, Holy Scripture is sufficient; it is not one of a number of potential creaturely mediations of revelation, but is fully adequate to guide the church into the comprehensive truth of the gospel. None of these affirmations entails thinking of Scripture as other than a creaturely product, but simply specifies the way in which God acts mediately through its testimony (a robust theology of mediated divine action provides release from a modern quandary according to which Scripture is either a purely natural religious product that represents the circumstances of its production, or a supernatural reality only incidentally related to creaturely processes). The scriptural embassy presents an overarching account of the *magnalia dei* as the fundamental line of God's history with creatures. This account orders the

---

30. O. O'Donovan, "What Kind of Community Is the Church?" *Ecclesiology* 3 (2007): 171-93.

church's identity, both in relation to its divine ground and in relation to its temporal passage, and it also presents the imperative force of the divine work, as not just a condition in which the church rests but as a legitimate directive of the church's action.

The church exists in the wake of divine revelation; it is a "convocation," gathered by and around Jesus Christ's presence as himself prophet and apostle who exercises his office through creaturely auxiliaries. What may reliably be predicated of the practical-historical life of the church is that his reality — Christ's inexhaustible eloquence, his voice resounding in Holy Scripture — is a promise beneath which the church is set. The reality and trustworthiness of that promise are the basis of some primary activities of the church: expectant reading of Scripture as Christ's address of his community through the Spirit; discursive repetition and intensification of the prophetic and apostolic message in proclamation; governance of the church's public life and assemblies by the scriptural norm, and deference to that norm in the church's decisions. There is a proper churchly self-negation, an ascesis of the church's mind, which is part of the process whereby the church comes to act out its relation to the truth. Its history is, we might say, one of learning the truth, a learning that is, however, not un-directed curiosity but a matter of being "sanctified in the truth" (John 17:17) by the Father through the Spirit in response to the Son's petition. The church reads Scripture and tries to speak what it hears and order its life accordingly; and this happens because at the Son's behest "the Spirit of truth" is active in the church's life to "guide it into all truth" (John 16:13).

Third, the church exists and enacts its life in a distinctive and limiting *order*.[31] It is a ruled society, common life under "law." It has a determinate shape, received from its origin in the purpose and acts of God, and by that directed to its end in fellowship with him. Order promotes identity, integrity, and duration over time. It does so, positively, by safeguarding the church's access to its fundamental resource, and, negatively, by indicating that which the church is not authorized to be or do. The basic signs of the church — Scripture and sacraments — are its primary instruments of order, but they are administered by derivative instruments: creeds and confessions, canon law, a publicly authorized ministry. Order *sanctifies* human common life, and so is a provision of divine goodness.

---

31. On this see E. Radner, "To Desire Rightly: The Force of the Creed in Its Canonical Context," in *Nicene Christianity: The Future of a New Ecumenism,* ed. C. Seitz (Grand Rapids: Brazos, 2001), pp. 213-28.

The relation of order to divine goodness is easy to overlook; feeling its full weight requires some spiritual discrimination, a grace acutely hard to exercise in the agonistic cultures of crisis that afflict some mainstream denominations. The order of the church, its existence in limitation, is a grace because it is essential to the healing of created society from the disarray by which it is overcome. Sin is a repudiation of creaturely vocation, and thereby a transgression of the limits that form the good order in which creaturely life is blessed. In the realm of sin, desire is detached from intelligent perception of human nature and ends, and becomes chaotic, untethered to the human good. This chaos also engulfs the common human realm and corrodes its good. Healing comes by the restoration of creatureliness, that is, through the saving gift of determinate form: hence the covenant enunciations "You are a people holy to the LORD your God" (Deut. 14:2), "You are . . . a holy nation" (1 Pet. 2:9). Reception of this gift involves passion, frustrating culpable desire, wrenching affections away from what is worthless — only thus can creatures be set again on the path to perfection. The church is the theater of this mortification, not merely as a kind of association of those undergoing spiritual transformation, but as a society whose public forms of life instantiate and promote the discipline in which creatures may come alive.

IV

What kind of society is the church? To ask that question is already to suggest that the term "society" is used equivocally of the church. Because the church is the society that keeps us in God's society, because it is the convocation of the elect and the community of the Word, the church does not possess its social properties after the manner of other societies, for it is, as Donald MacKinnon put it in a remarkable early tract, "a society which, though visible and distinguishable among many others, is not as those others are."[32] The church is not simply social nature but created and fallen social nature re-created by the saving missions of the Son of God and the Holy Spirit and so reconciled to God and on the way to its perfection. This already means that the ethnography of such a society will be irregular, even aberrant, utterly enigmatic if we restrict the matter of ethnography to purely natural motion. The church is a society that moves itself as it is

32. D. M. MacKinnon, *The Church of God* (London: Dacre, 1940), p. 21.

moved by God. Without talk of this divine movement, of the electing, call-ing, gathering, and sanctifying works of God, an ethnography of the church does not attain its object, misperceiving the motion to which its at-tention is to be directed, and so inhibited in understanding the creaturely movements of the communion of saints.

Ecclesiological investigations are of two sorts. One pursues the ques-tion of the origin of the church — "origin," not in the sense of inner-historical genetics but in the sense of the theological-metaphysical depth from which the church arises as an apostolic society. Investigation of the origin of the church is the task of dogmatics, as it offers a Trinitarian re-duction of the Christian society. A second investigation concerns itself with the phenomena of the church. These phenomena are characterized by a certain elusiveness. They are signs whose matter does not inhere in them-selves; they have a special visibility; they do not exhaust themselves in their natural manifestation. There is a proper hierarchical arrangement of the two sets of ecclesiological investigations: at least in the order of being, in-vestigation of origins precedes and governs investigation of phenomena (in the order of knowing, which comes first is probably a matter of indif-ference). Respecting the hierarchy is important because pursuit of the sec-ond set of inquiries can find it difficult to resist becoming naturalized, re-garding the phenomena of the church while suspending their reference to the depth from which they come into being. In a naturalized ecclesiology, the first set of inquiries into the church's depth is interrupted or overtaken by the second set of inquiries; or answers to the second set of inquiries are taken to be answers to the first set of inquiries. In both cases, the proper object of ecclesiology finds itself relegated to the shadows. Dogmatic ecclesiology resists this by keeping alive the distinction between and due order of uncreated and created being; by indicating that the phenomena of the church are not irreducible but significative; and by introducing into each ecclesiological description and passage of ecclesiological argument direct language about God, Christ, and the Spirit. The condition for these acts of dogmatic reason is, however, the conversion of intelligence from love of temporality, which is why prayer is indispensable in ecclesiological understanding.

What are the conditions, then, for profitable deployment of ethnog-raphy in ecclesiology? Here are four closing suggestions: (1) Questions about the suitability of modes of inquiry or disciplines are properly de-cided in relation to objects and ends of inquiry. An ethnography that serves in the project of constructing the church as natural social body is quite different from one that tries to observe the church as an element in the divine mystery set forth in Christ. (2) The use of ethnography in ecclesiology requires metaphysical clarification, including clarification of the distinction and relation between uncreated and created being, and between divine and social action; this, because "[t]he concept of church is conceivable only in the sphere of reality established by God."[33] (3) Ethnography may find itself frustrated by the concealed, secret character of the church as social body or lifeworld; the church remains in some measure indiscernible, because its motion is not purely spontaneous or original to itself but "in the Lord." (4) Theology is not one science among others; it is inquiry into God and all other things ordered in some way to God; and so it is inquiry into the conditions for all science, including social science.

33. Bonhoeffer, *Sanctorum Communio,* p. 127.

CHAPTER 12

The Church "Taking Form" in Mission: Reimagining Family Ministries within the *Missio Dei*

Richard R. Osmer

Joydeep Prasadam emigrated from India with his wife fifteen years ago and became an American citizen shortly thereafter. He runs his own small company that provides financial services to individuals and small businesses. While his company has struggled during the recent downturn of the global economy, Joydeep believes that his business is well positioned to do well when the economy recovers. During this period, his wife, Sandhi, became a saleswoman at Macy's, working in the men's department. Joydeep laughed as he commented: "She has no experience in sales, and yet she's now top in sales in her department. And selling *men's clothes* too! She's always been pretty good at helping me figure out what to wear." Since Sandhi has started working full-time, Joydeep has taken over more of the responsibilities of taking care of their two children after school and on weekends. "I never thought I'd have to juggle being a father and starting my own company when I came to the U.S.," he reflected, "so, I guess I'm really an American now," laughing once again.

Joydeep is a member of a small Presbyterian church located in a part of New Jersey with one of the largest concentrations of emigrants from India in the United States. Historically, the congregation was located in the town center of a rural area with many large farms. Most of these farms were sold after the 1950s, and the area subsequently experienced enormous population growth and residential development. In spite of these trends, the congregation was teetering on the brink of extinction as recently as a decade ago, as its aging, white members gradually began to become shut-ins and die. In the face of this crisis, the congregation made an intentional

decision to reach out to and welcome the changing population of the surrounding area. Today, it has families who emigrated from India, China,
Korea, Colombia, and Uganda, as well as African Americans and Anglos.
For a congregation of 150 members, it also has a disproportionately large
number of interracial couples.

The church is to be commended for its strong sense of mission, especially its welcome of families from around the world. Yet, at present, it has
no family ministries, which might provide Joydeep and Sandhi with models and skills needed by families with children in which both parents work.
Nor does it provide them with the opportunity to think about the meaning
of Christian marriage and the sorts of moral decisions involved in balancing work and family. While they are loved and supported in a general way
by the congregation, it does not offer them crucial support and guidance
that might help their relationship grow and even thrive during this time of
transition.

This chapter argues that family ministries are underdeveloped and
undervalued in many American mainline congregations. Addressing this
shortcoming necessarily requires practical theology to carry out four interrelated tasks:

> Descriptive-empirical: What is going on? Gathering information to
> better understand particular episodes, situations, or contexts.
>
> Interpretive: Why is this going on? Entering into a dialogue with the
> social sciences to interpret and explain why certain actions and
> patterns are taking place.
>
> Normative: What ought to be going on? Raising normative questions
> from the perspectives of theology, ethics, and other fields.
>
> Pragmatic: How might we respond? Forming an action plan and un-
> dertaking specific responses that seek to shape the episode, situa-
> tion, or context in desirable directions.

In my book *Practical Theology: An Introduction,* I describe each of
these tasks more fully, arguing that they are interrelated along the lines of a
hermeneutical circle or spiral.[1] I make no claim to originality in this description of practical theology. Indeed, I believe that something like these
four tasks has been common for many years in the writings of various

---

1. Richard Osmer, *Practical Theology: An Introduction* (Grand Rapids: Eerdmans,
2008).

practical theologians, as well as clinical pastoral education and doctor of ministry programs and field education seminars.[2]

In this chapter, I give special attention to the descriptive-empirical task of practical theology, without neglecting the other tasks altogether. I illustrate the important role of empirical research in practical theology by addressing the current state of family ministries in American mainline congregations. How would practical theology gain an accurate understanding of the family ministries of such congregations without empirical research? How might it offer a picture of good practice without such research? Moreover, how would practical theology draw on the interpretive frameworks of the social sciences in a responsible fashion if it did not assess the empirical research on which such frameworks are based? In these and many other ways, it is clear that practical theology cannot address important concerns like the state of the American family unless it carries out, draws on, and interprets the empirical research of a number of fields.

For the purposes of this chapter, it is especially important to draw on empirical research. To claim that family ministries are underdeveloped and underappreciated, as I did above, is counterintuitive. Are not American mainline congregations all about families, confining their mission safely to the private sphere of modern life? The short and simple answer is no, an assessment that will be defended more fully on empirical grounds over the course of this chapter. Even congregations with a renewed sense of mission, like the one described at the beginning of this chapter, often view

---

2. For a small sampling of U.S. and U.K. practical theology covering tasks or dimensions analogous to those identified in my book, see Seward Hiltner and Lowell Colston, *The Context of Pastoral Counseling* (New York: Abingdon, 1961); Allen Moore, "The Place of Scientific Models and Theological Reflection in the Practice of Ministry," *Pastoral Psychology* 22, no. 210 (January 1971): 25-34, and "A Recovery of Theological Nerve," *Religious Education* 79, no. 1 (Winter 1984): 24-28; James Whitehead and Evelyn Whitehead, *Method in Ministry: Theological Reflection and Christian Ministry* (New York: Seabury Press, 1980); Don Browning, ed., *Practical Theology: The Emerging Field in Theology, Church, and World* (San Francisco: Harper and Row, 1983); James Poling and Donald Miller, *Foundations for a Practical Theology of Ministry* (Nashville: Abingdon, 1985); Charles Gerkin, *Widening the Horizons: Pastoral Responses to a Fragmented Society* (Philadelphia: Westminster, 1986); James Poling and Lewis Mudge, eds., *Formation and Reflection: The Promise of Practical Theology* (Philadelphia: Fortress, 1987); Duncan Forrester, ed., *Theology and Practice* (London: Epworth, 1990); Paul Ballard and John Pritchard, *Practical Theology in Action: Christian Thinking in the Service of Church and Society* (London: SPCK, 1996); John Swinton and Harriet Mowat, *Practical Theology and Qualitative Research* (London: SCM, 2006).

the family as a kind of obstacle to the church's public witness. They are wary of expending too much energy on their own members.

Don Browning offers an important historical perspective on the origin of this way of thinking in mainline congregations in the United States. Using Gibson Winter's influential book *The Suburban Captivity of the Churches* as an example of a trend emerging in the 1960s, he points to the long-term implications for family ministries in the American mainline:

> From then on, I believe, an implicit split between public and private began to affect the mission strategies of the mainline churches. Family life, sexuality, and intimate relations were seen as part of the private world, and issues of work, legislative matters, education, the economy, and foreign policy were perceived as matters of the public. It was thought that a church with a heroic mission . . . should address the latter and let the former be more or less a matter of individual Christian preference and lifestyle. For over two decades there has been the implicit assumption in the mainline churches that mission to the public world was somehow antithetical to mission focused on the family.[3]

Elsewhere, Browning makes this point in broader terms, describing American churches, particularly the mainline, as being slow to help families make the transition from the period of the Industrial Revolution to a new postindustrial, postmodern society.[4]

Building on these insights, this chapter will move in three steps. First, it will outline a theology of congregational mission that might be used to frame a renewed emphasis on family ministries as part of a broader shift in the identity and mission of mainline Protestant churches. Second, it will point to social scientific research that underscores the importance of families in the well-being of individuals, civil society, and public life, as well as the role religious communities can play in nurturing strong families. Third, the chapter will explore two congregations with well-developed family ministries that also have strong programs for children and adults of divorced families.

---

3. Don Browning, "Religion and Family Ethics: A New Strategy for the Church," in *Work, Family, and Religion in Contemporary Society,* ed. Nancy Tatom Ammerman and Wade Clark Roof (New York: Routledge, 1995), p. 159.

4. Don Browning et al., *From Culture Wars to Common Ground: Religion and the American Family Debate* (Louisville: Westminster John Knox, 1997), p. 1.

The Missional Church

It is, in fact, the case that a renewed emphasis on family ministries might end up being one more initiative designed to attract new members to American mainline congregations. Mainline denominations have been in decline for quite some time, and a recent comment to me by a Presbyterian elder captures the sense of desperation that many are feeling at the congregational level: "Tell us what to do. We're pretty much open to anything that will help us attract new members. Before long, we're not going to be able to pay the bills and, in the not so distant future, we're going to have to close the doors." Heartfelt as this cry for help might be, it is misguided. As long as mainline congregations merely look for new programs designed to bring in new members to help pay the bills, they are avoiding the deeper issues of identity and mission that need to be at the top of their agenda. A renewed emphasis on family ministries, thus, must be part of a broader shift in the theological identity and mission of mainline churches. One strand of contemporary Protestant theology giving explicit attention to these issues is sometimes identified as the "missional church" discussion.

The longer history of this discussion stretches back to the emergence of the theological concept of the *missio Dei* in the middle of the twentieth century. This initially took place in the Willingen conference of the International Missionary Council in 1952 and, then, in the World Council of Churches. The *missio Dei*, described more fully below, subsequently was developed in the writings of a wide range of theologians.[5] In North America it is closely identified with the Gospel and Our Culture Network, which emerged in the late 1980s as an extension of the Gospel and Culture discussion initiated in Great Britain by Lesslie Newbigin.[6]

Newbigin served as a missionary and bishop of the Church of South India for over three decades, and upon returning to England was shocked

---

5. For an overview, see David Bosch, *Transforming Mission: Paradigm Shifts in Theology of Mission* (Maryknoll, N.Y.: Orbis, 1991). For a historical study of the emergence of this discussion, see H. H. Rosin, *"Missio Dei": An Examination of the Origin, Contents, and Function of the Term in Protestant Missiological Discussion* (Leiden: Inter-university Institute for Missiological and Ecumenical Research, 1972).

6. This discussion was initially sparked by Newbigin's *The Other Side of 1984: Questions for the Churches,* published originally by the British Council of Churches for a year-long discussion and subsequently reissued by the World Council of Churches. For an overview of Newbigin's writings, see *Lesslie Newbigin: Missional Theologian* (Grand Rapids: Eerdmans, 2006). A link to the Gospel and Our Culture Network is http://www.gocn.org/.

by the advanced state of secularization in his home country. What once had been a Christian society was now clearly post-Christian. In his writings and speaking, Newbigin evoked a theological discussion of the implications of this shift for the church. In North America, this discussion has attracted a highly ecumenical group of scholars and pastoral leaders, including Lutherans, Presbyterians, Mennonites, Canadian Baptists, and the leaders of nondenominational and emergent church communities. While individual scholars drawing on this perspective have developed very different theologies, it may be helpful to outline some of the key concepts of this discussion, which are particularly relevant to practical theology.

The central, orienting concept of this theological framework is the *missio Dei,* the mission of God. It marks a shift in thinking about mission, from an ecclesio-centric to a theo-centric perspective. Instead of thinking of mission as activities the church does (i.e., outreach programs, evangelism, sending missionaries overseas), it views mission, first and foremost, as something God does in sending the Son and Spirit into the world. David Bosch puts it like this:

> We have to distinguish between *mission* (singular) and *missions* (plural). The first refers primarily to the *missio Dei* (God's mission), that is, God's self-revelation as the One who loves the world, God's involvement in and with the world, the nature and activity of God, which embraces both the church and the world, and in which the church is privileged to participate. . . . *Missions* . . . refer to particular forms, related to specific times, places, or needs, of participation in the *missio Dei.*[7]

Discussion of this concept unfolded during a period in which many theologians were beginning to recover the importance of the Trinity in the doctrine of God, the mystery of the oneness and threeness of the Godhead.[8] Some theologians, like Karl Barth and Lesslie Newbigin, emphasized the oneness of God; other theologians emphasized the threeness, like Jürgen Moltmann, Katherine Mowry LaCugna, and Stanley Grenz.[9] This

---

7. Bosch, *Transforming Mission,* p. 10.

8. Rosin, "*Missio Dei,*" pp. 5-6.

9. Karl Barth, *Church Dogmatics* I/1, *The Doctrine of the Word of God* (Edinburgh: T. & T. Clark, 1975), chapter 2; Lesslie Newbigin, *Trinitarian Doctrine for Today's Mission* (Eugene, Oreg.: Wipf and Stock, 1988); Jürgen Moltmann, *The Church in the Power of the Spirit: A Contribution to Messianic Ecclesiology* (San Francisco: Harper and Row, 1977); Catherine Mowry LaCugna, *God for Us: The Trinity and Christian Life* (San Francisco: Harper-

accounts for some of the diversity within the missional church discussion. Yet within this diversity, there is a consensus that mission refers primarily to God's activity in creation, redemption, and glorification, and only secondarily to the church's mission. This means that practical theology cannot focus exclusively on clergy functions or church ministries, commonly known as the clerical and ecclesial paradigms of practical theology, respectively. It must take its bearings from God's mission, which is larger than the church. Indeed, the church finds its mission through *participation* in God's mission. While the upbuilding of the church is part of the subject matter of practical theology, so too is its understanding of the social context in which it is located and what God is calling the church to do and be within this context.

A second concept that is important in the missional church discussion is *election*. In the Christian tradition, this concept has commonly been used to describe God's creation of a special covenant people, Israel and the church, who embody God's purposes in a fallen world. Across the tradition, however, election has often been associated with the special privileges, blessings, and status of the church.[10] The church is the "dispenser of salvation," giving it control over those who desire eternal life. Or it is the "community of perfect righteousness," which alone understands and obeys God's will. Or it is a community of individuals predestined for salvation before the foundation of the world and may look to their experience for evidences of God's favor. Or it is the evangel of "saving truth," elected to save individuals from eternal damnation.

In contrast to these understandings of election, many theologians in the missional church discussion describe election in relation to the *missio Dei*. God elects a particular people to give witness to his saving purposes toward the whole of creation. Election is calling to service and witness, not primarily the reception of special blessings, benefits, or privileges. Perhaps the text most often used to warrant this view of election is Genesis 12:2-3, which describes God's call of Abraham: "I will make of you a great nation, and I will bless you, and make your name great, so that you will be a blessing . . . and in you all the families of the earth shall be blessed." Darrell Guder comments on this passage:

Collins, 1973); Stanley Grenz, *The Social God and the Relational Self: A Trinitarian Theology of the Imago Dei* (Louisville: Westminster John Knox, 2001).

10. For an excellent discussion of this issue, see Darrell Guder, *Be My Witnesses: The Church's Mission, Message, and Messengers* (Grand Rapids: Eerdmans, 1985).

When God calls Abraham to make of him and his descendants a blessing, the universal scope of God's action is emphasized: "By you all the families of the earth will bless themselves." . . . Those whom God calls experience the benefits of that call, that is, the goodness and spiritual excitement of knowing God and sharing in his grace and love (which is really what blessing means). But these benefits are integrally connected to the mission for which they are given. "Mission" has to do with "the purpose for being sent out." Ultimately, God called Abraham so that a people could be set apart and then sent out to be God's agents to accomplish his saving purposes.[11]

This understanding of election has important implications for practical theology. It leads to a fundamental rethinking of the nature and purpose of the church. The church does not merely have a mission; its very being is missional. Bosch, once again, is helpful in drawing out what this means for practical theology. He portrays the church as an ellipse with two foci: "In and around the first it acknowledges and enjoys the source of its life; this is where worship and prayer are emphasized. From and through the second focus, the church engages and challenges the world. This is a forth-going and self-spending focus, where service, mission and evangelism are stressed. Neither focus should ever be at the expense of the other; rather, they stand in each other's service. The church's *identity* sustains its *relevance* and *involvement*."[12]

Bosch's portrait of the church as bi-focal points to the reciprocal relationship between the church's inner life and its involvement in the world. This has implications for our understanding of ministries like spiritual formation, which commonly focuses solely on the inner life of the congregation. Bosch invites us to view spiritual formation differently. The church "takes form" in the Spirit, not only as it teaches its own members certain practices of the spiritual life, like prayer and small group Bible study, but also as it involves them in ministries of service and self-giving. Spiritual formation is inclusive of both poles.

This opens out to a third concept: *missional vocation*. Vocation

---

11. Guder, *Be My Witnesses,* pp. 9-10.

12. Bosch, *Transforming Mission,* p. 385. Bosch is drawing here on the thinking of the German theologian Jürgen Moltmann, who portrayed the church both as a contrast society, which must embody in its own way of life God's purposes for creation, and as a catalyst of social transformation, a community actively involved in other spheres of life to contribute to the common good.

comes from the Latin, *vocare,* to call. In classical Protestantism, it was used to depict the calling of every Christian to service and witness in his or her everyday life. In many ways, it was an outgrowth of Martin Luther's understanding of the priesthood of all believers, which portrayed every member of the church as being called to ministry, not the ordained alone. Within the missional church discussion, this concept continues to include the vocation of individual Christians but gives primary attention to the *congregation's* missional vocation. As George Hunsberger puts it: *"Personal* vocation is shaped and molded in the context of a community that has clarity about *its* vocation. A Christian's personal sense of vocation is a derivative from that 'one hope of our calling' (Eph. 4:4) shared with the whole church, those 'called out' *(ekklesia)* into the mission of God!"[13] From the perspective of practical theology, this underscores the importance of leaders and processes that invite congregations to discern their own particular missional vocations, giving attention to questions like these:

- *where* they are, in a geographic, social, cultural context
- *when* they are, in the flow of history and change
- *who* they are, in continuity with a tradition, re-forming it in the present
- *why* they are, welcoming God's call, entering God's coming reign[14]

Obviously, these concepts and others stand in need of greater development in a full-fledged practical theology of the missional church. But enough has been said to indicate some of the ways this discussion challenges congregations rooted in American mainline denominational traditions to rethink their identity and mission, moving beyond the sort of thinking and practices to which they became accustomed while the "religious establishment" of American society. The crisis of membership and resources that many of these congregations are currently experiencing is an opportunity for their leaders to reframe their missions within God's mission and to reform their way of life accordingly.

---

13. George Hunsberger, "Discerning Missional Vocation," in *Treasure in Clay Jars: Patterns in Missional Faithfulness,* ed. Lois Barrett (Grand Rapids: Eerdmans, 2004), p. 38.
14. Hunsberger, "Discerning Missional Vocation," p. 39.

Ministries to Families in Missional Perspective

One of the areas in which American mainline congregations need to re-think their identity and mission is family ministries. As noted above, Don Browning argues that after the 1960s mainline churches tended to dichotomize family ministries and mission. The former were part of the private sphere and a matter of personal preference among diverse life-styles. The latter primarily focused on the public sphere, where social jus-tice was enacted through advocacy or charitable programs. In terms of the theological framework developed above, this understanding of mission is reductionistic. It reduces mission to activities the church does "out there" and ignores the ways a congregation's very being is missional, serving as a sign and witness to God's purposes for creation. This includes the care and guidance congregations offer their families, which impact the way couples relate to one another, raise their children, and communicate God's love in the home. Beyond this sort of theological reductionism, moreover, there are good empirical reasons on social scientific grounds to question the di-chotomy of public mission and private preference framing family minis-tries in the mainline. Here, three such reasons are explored.

1. *While the family and religion are located primarily in the private sphere in North America, they continue to have an important impact on public institutions and civil society.* Implicit in the dichotomy of public mission and private preference is a particular understanding of modernity, given theoretical expression in a wide variety of theories of modernization and secularization.[15] These theories predicted that as societies modernized and structural differentiation promoted greater secularization, institutions lo-cated in the private sphere would gradually grow weaker as many of their functions were taken over by public institutions of the state and economy. This was especially thought to be the case with regard to religion and the family. Yet, the story has proved more complex, and a number of telling criticisms of this perspective have been raised in recent decades.

One criticism is the very obvious empirical fact that religion has not withered away and continues to play an important role in *both* public and

15. The early work of Peter Berger in the sociology of religion represents an extremely influential example of this perspective. See *The Sacred Canopy: Elements of a Sociological Theory of Religion* (Garden City, N.Y.: Anchor Books, 1969), and *The Heretical Imperative: Contemporary Possibilities of Religious Affirmation* (Garden City, N.Y.: Anchor Books, 1970). For an overview of secularization theory, see Steve Bruce, *God Is Dead: Secularization in the West* (Oxford: Blackwell, 2002).

private life in the United States and around the world.[16] It is impossible to imagine the civil rights movement in the United States or the Solidarity movement in Poland without the participation of religious communities. Nor is it really possible to understand the political and cultural polarization in the United States and around the world without taking account of the "faith factor."[17] Religion remains an important force in modern life.

The same is true of families. As Pankhurst and Houseknecht point out, "Little that happens in the public realm is without its private side. Attitudes toward work and spending and leisure and politics are all shaped and nurtured in the family and among friends and acquaintances."[18] Drawing on social capital theory, Blankenhorn and McLanahan and Sandefur have presented convincing empirical evidence that families play a crucial role in mediating social relationships, psychological support, educational and economic opportunities, and other assets that enable children to become contributing members of the workforce, civil society, and politics.[19] The relative health or decline of families has an enormous impact on public life.

Perhaps, most important of all, developments in the sociology of culture and religion have raised questions about the adequacy of focusing solely on large-scale institutions and cultural trends in depicting modernization, ignoring the way they are mediated by different cultural and religious communities.[20] Drawing on these theoretical developments, Wilcox has carried out empirical research in which he identifies the very different religious subcultures of conservative and mainline Protestantism, which

16. José Casanova, *Public Religions in the Modern World* (Chicago: University of Chicago Press, 1994).

17. For the impact of religion on voting behavior, for example, see John Greene, *The Faith Factor: How Religion Influences American Elections* (Westport, Conn.: Praeger, 2007).

18. Sharon K. Houseknecht and Jerry G. Pankhurst, eds., *Family, Religion, and Social Change in Diverse Societies* (Oxford: Oxford University Press, 2000), p. 3.

19. David Blankenhorn, *Fatherless America: Confronting Our Most Urgent Social Problem* (New York: HarperCollins, 1995). Sara McLanahan and Gary Sandefur, *Growing Up with a Single Parent: What Hurts, What Helps* (Cambridge: Harvard University Press, 1994).

20. For an overview, see Diana Crane, ed., *The Sociology of Culture: Emerging Perspectives* (Cambridge: Blackwell, 1994). See particularly, Robert Wuthnow, *Communities of Discourse: Ideology and Structure in the Reformation, the Enlightenment, and European Socialism* (Cambridge: Harvard University Press, 1989) and *Meaning and Moral Order: Explorations in Cultural Analysis* (Berkeley: University of California Press, 1987). Christian Smith develops subcultural identity theory in *American Evangelicalism: Embattled and Thriving* (Chicago: University of Chicago Press, 1998).

shape the attitudes and behaviors of fathers along different lines.[21] Modernization is *not* unilinear. It is accommodated, resisted, and adapted in ways that are shaped by religious communities and their families.

Taken together, these criticisms of older theories of modernization call into question clear distinctions between the public and private spheres, as well as the thesis that secularization will necessarily lead to diminished roles for religion and the family in modern life. Not only do religion and families continue to make important contributions to primary relations in the private sphere, but they also impact public institutions and civil society both directly and indirectly.

2. *Greater participation by women in higher education and the workforce poses important challenges to families in which both husband and wife work outside the home.* Of all degrees conferred in American higher education in 2009, nearly 60 percent were awarded to women.[22] According to the U.S. Bureau of Labor Statistics, in 2008 59.5 percent of all women were in the labor force, and between 1975 and 2000, the percentage of working mothers with children under age eighteen rose from 47 percent to 73 percent.[23] Clearly, many married couples today face the challenge of balancing work and parenting, like Joydeep and Sandhi Prasadam, described at the outset of this chapter.

Empirical research indicates, however, that men continue to do less than an equal share of the parental, domestic, and emotional work associated with family life, though they are doing more of this work than men did in earlier generations.[24] This unequal division of labor not only impacts the long-term psychological well-being of women and their marital satisfaction, but also may contribute to gender inequality in wages and promotion in the workplace.[25] Working wives continue to bear more of

---

21. W. Bradford Wilcox, *Soft Patriarchs, New Men: How Christianity Shapes Fathers and Husbands* (Chicago: University of Chicago Press, 2004).

22. See *Digest of Statistics*, U.S. Department of Education, which offers the following summary: *associate's degrees:* 167 for women for every 100 for men; *bachelor's degrees:* 142 for women for every 100 for men; *master's degrees:* 159 for women for every 100 for men; *professional degrees:* 104 for women for every 100 for men; *doctoral degrees:* 107 for women for every 100 for men. http://nces.ed.gov/programs/digest/d07/tables/dt07_258.asp; accessed February 2010.

23. See http://www.bls.gov/cps/wlf-intro-2009.htm; accessed April 2010.

24. See Wilcox, *Soft Patriarchs*, pp. 5-6, for an excellent overview.

25. For research on the division of labor in the family, see Frances K. Goldscheider and Linda J. Waite, *New Families, No Families? The Transformation of the American Home* (Berkeley: University of California Press, 1991), chapter 6. For discussion of the impact of

the burden of the "second shift," experiencing more intensely than their husbands the tensions between working, parenting, and caring for aging parents.

Historically, strong interinstitutional relationships have existed between religion and the family, and there are many reasons to believe that this continues to be the case.[26] Churches and other religious communities, thus, may be in a unique position to help dual-career families respond to the particular challenges they face, offering moral and theological frameworks, mentoring groups, and family programs, as well as advocating for public policies promoting the well-being of families.[27]

3. *The high rate of divorce among Americans places families under stress, with many long-term, negative consequences for their members.* The rate of divorce among Americans began to rise following World War 2, rose significantly during the 1960s and 1970s, leveled off in the 1980s, and has declined slightly in recent decades. When this trend is coupled with the rise of out-of-wedlock births, the number of children living in single-parent homes is quite large. For children born between 1970 and 1984, it was estimated that 44 percent would live with a single parent before the age of sixteen.[28]

One of the more pernicious consequences of the American mainline's tendency to view the family as a matter of personal preference among diverse lifestyles was to misjudge the negative impact of divorce on children, mothers, and fathers. In one denominational statement after another in the 1970s and 1980s, this was ignored in an attempt to affirm an inclusive attitude toward different family forms and "committed relationships."[29] While the mainline's willingness to grapple with gay and lesbian families

---

the "second shift" on gender inequity in the workplace, see Paula England, "Marriage, the Costs of Children, and Gender Inequality," in *The Ties That Bind: Perspectives on Marriage and Cohabitation,* ed. Linda Waite (Hawthorne, N.Y.: Aldine de Gruyter, 1986), and Arlie Hochschild, with Ann Machung, *The Second Shift: Working Parents and the Revolution at Home* (New York: Viking Press, 1989).

26. Houseknecht and Pankhurst, *Family, Religion, and Social Change in Diverse Societies.* This book is particularly interesting, for it compares the interinstitutional relationships of the family, religion, and other institutions across cultural lines.

27. See the recommendations of Browning, *From Culture Wars,* chapter 11, and Bonnie Miller-McLemore, *Also a Mother: Work and Family as Theological Dilemma* (Nashville: Abingdon, 1994).

28. Browning, *From Culture Wars,* p. 53.

29. For a brief overview of some of these statements, see Browning, *From Culture Wars,* pp. 43-48.

and to welcome single-parent families and single elders is commendable, it can no longer afford to ignore the substantial body of social scientific research documenting the long-term, negative impact of divorce on all family members. What are these findings?

Let us begin with children. Drawing on longitudinal data, McLanahan and Sandefur document the negative impact of divorce on children's educational achievement, on entry into the workforce, and on the ability to establish a stable family during young adulthood.[30] Others have noted the connection between divorce and adolescent at-risk behaviors, like substance abuse, sexual activity, delinquency, and dropping out of high school.[31] Yet the long-term impact of divorce is not just seen in these kinds of at-risk behaviors. It has a subtle but very real effect on children who go on to live productive lives without outward signs of serious social or emotional problems. This is the clear finding of the Project on the Moral and Spiritual Lives of Children of Divorce, codirected by Norval Glenn and Elizabeth Marquardt.[32] This project focused exclusively on the American context.

Marquardt describes the impact of divorce on the inner lives of children in the following way: "For those of us from divorced families, a deep and enduring moral drama was ignited the moment our parents parted. After their parting we spent our childhoods crossing a widening chasm as their divided worlds grew more different every year. Our constant journeys between their worlds had lasting consequences."[33] Facing the task of negotiating the increasingly different worlds of their parents, children of divorced families often experience feelings of loneliness they cannot share with others. Many also feel like little adults, who must take on more responsibilities in the home, cope with being alone, and offer emotional support to their primary parent. They sometimes feel caught between the different values, household rules, and lifestyles of their parents, left to sort out on their own where they belong and what they believe.

The impact of these kinds of ongoing, everyday experiences does not disappear as the children of divorce grow older. In what is sometimes described as the "sleeper effect," it often reemerges when these children be-

30. McLanahan and Sandefur, *Growing Up with a Single Parent.*

31. Joy Dryfoos, *Adolescents at Risk: Prevalence and Prevention* (Oxford: Oxford University Press, 1990).

32. Elizabeth Marquardt, *Between Two Worlds: The Inner Lives of Children of Divorce* (New York: Crown Publishers, 2005).

33. Marquardt, *Between Two Worlds,* p. 17.

come young adults and face the task of forming long-term commitments and relationships. It also influences their participation in religion. Young adults from families of divorce are less likely than their peers to become involved in organized religion, even though they view themselves as being just as spiritual as their peers.[34] Perhaps the most damning finding of this study for organized religion is the fact that two-thirds of those people who were involved in a church or synagogue at the time of their parents' divorce report that *no one* from their religious community reached out to them — not a clergyperson or congregation member.[35] This finding alone should be enough to shock American mainline leaders into thinking more deeply about their stance toward marriage and divorce!

Divorce has a negative impact on adult women and men as well. Of all single-parent families, 86 percent are headed by mothers.[36] The income of divorced mothers and their children is less than half the average income of two-parent families. Single mothers commonly face the daunting challenge of providing both emotional support and discipline to their children, handling the household tasks and working, and trying to find the time to maintain friendships and develop new relationships. It is little wonder that following divorce, women have higher rates of depression and alcohol abuse than their peers.[37] Men, too, fare worse following divorce. They commonly revert to the sorts of at-risk behaviors characterizing single, young males. They drink more, have poorer diets, engage in more fighting, and neglect regular medical checkups and following through on their doctor's orders.[38]

---

34. Marquardt, *Between Two Worlds,* p. 139.

35. Marquardt, *Between Two Worlds,* p. 155.

36. Browning, *From Culture Wars,* p. 54. This includes families in which the mother has never married.

37. Elizabeth Menaghan and Morton Lieberman, "Changes in Depression Following Divorce: A Panel Study," *Journal of Marriage and the Family* 48 (May 1986): 319-28. Whether alcohol abuse precedes or follows divorce is more complicated. Empirical studies have found that women and men with drinking problems have higher rates of divorce. But some studies have found increased rates of heavy alcohol consumption following divorce. For an overview, see M. Fe Caces et al., "Alcohol Consumption and Divorce Rates in the United States," *Journal of Studies on Alcohol* 60 (1999).

38. Linda Waite and Maggie Gallagher, *The Case for Marriage: Why Married People Are Happier, Healthier, and Better Off Financially* (New York: Broadway Books, 2000), pp. 53-58.

Family Ministries and the Mission of the Church

On both theological and empirical, social scientific grounds, thus, there are compelling reasons for American mainline churches to view family ministries as a central part of their mission. In this final section we will examine two congregations in the United States that view family ministries in precisely this way, drawing on a small research project in which I currently am engaged.[39] These congregations are Peachtree Presbyterian Church in Atlanta, Georgia (Peachtree), and First Presbyterian Church, Berkeley, California (Berkeley). Both churches are atypical of congregations in the Presbyterian Church (U.S.A.), which average 200 members. In 2008, Peachtree had almost 9,000 members and a budget of around $11 million. Its membership has grown steadily since 2004, following a period in which it cleaned up the rolls. In 2008, Berkeley had slightly over 1,900 members, reflecting a steady rise in membership since 1998. Its budget was just under $4 million.

Unlike most Presbyterian congregations, thus, Peachtree and Berkeley have large, growing memberships, as well as physical, financial, and human resources. They also are atypical in their theology. They represent what might be called a Reformed evangelical strand of Presbyterianism, which along with other mainline evangelical congregations may represent a unique niche in American Protestantism. Peachtree and Berkeley do *not* identify with the Religious Right or Left and, when possible, avoid the polarizing social issues creating so much conflict in their denomination. Yet they are deeply invested in social justice, community service, and global outreach, which is reflected in their organizational structure and budget. At the same time, they place a great deal of emphasis on nurturing the personal spirituality of their members, through small groups, Sunday morning programs, the home, and many other venues. Both congregations have leaders who are participants in the missional church discussion and have been interviewed as part of a small research project in which I currently am engaged.[40]

39. This project is the Missional Leadership Project, which is examining the understanding of spiritual formation and leadership informing the work of "missional leaders." My coresearcher in this project is Drew Dyson, a doctoral student at Princeton Theological Seminary, who was recently appointed professor of evangelism at Wesley Theological Seminary.

40. The Missional Leader Project, which I am codirecting with Drew Dyson, Wesley Theological Seminary, is currently beginning its third phase. To this point it has interviewed pastoral and lay leaders in thirty congregations identified by knowledgeable insiders as

These congregations, I believe, are good examples of some of the ways congregations might face up to the challenge articulated by Browning and his colleagues: "The fundamental family issue of our time may be how to retain and honor the intact family without turning it into an object of idolatry and without retaining the inequalities of power, status, and privilege ensconced in its earlier forms."[41] They do so by simultaneously making two ministries central to their missional identities: family ministries, designed to support strong intact families over the course of the marriage life cycle, and caring ministries, designed to support children, youth, and adults of divorced families. As one of Peachtree's pastors put it:

> We want to build strong families in this church. This is central to our mission. We baptized 183 babies last year. (laughs) We want our members to honor the covenant of marriage, not as a kind of law, but as a way of living as full, thriving, and complete human beings who are created by God for relationships. Our programs and LifeGate (their counseling center) support this. We don't want it to be easy for people to bail out of their marriages. When people come to us, and one of them has had an affair, and their marriage is on the rocks, we begin by saying, "We're going to support you no matter what, but you need to know from the beginning that we want you to work through this and stay together if at all possible." That's our starting point, and in the end, it's really only the Holy Spirit that can make that happen. At the same time, we want to be a grace-filled church. We recognize our common sin, whether we're married or divorced, and the free gift of God's grace in Jesus Christ. So we accept and love divorced people, and we do everything in our power to walk with children when their parents are going through a divorce.

This sort of theology of the church's mission to both intact and divorced families is communicated through sermons, pastoral relationships, programs, and friendships. It is part of the ethos of these congregations. While the remainder of this chapter focuses primarily on the programmatic dimensions of family and caring ministries, it is important to keep this congregational ethos in mind. Developing strong family and caring

---

"missional churches." In the second phase, it compared these congregations with a smaller sample of congregations that are known to have strong spiritual formation programs but are not a part of the missional church network.

41. Browning, *From Culture Wars*, p. 71.

ministries is not just about programs. It also is about the formal and informal ways congregations communicate the centrality of families of all sorts to their mission. We will examine three ways this is embodied in these congregations: (1) programs specifically targeting the special needs of families over the course of the marriage life cycle, (2) counseling centers and caring ministries, and (3) communicating a theology of families through multiple channels.

1. *Programs specifically targeting the special needs of families over the course of the life cycle.* Peachtree and Berkeley both offer a variety of programs on Sunday morning and at other times that are oriented to couples who are newly married, have children of different ages (preschool, elementary, or adolescence), and are dealing with "empty nest" issues. These are in addition to classes for young singles and the elderly, and classes not oriented to a specific age or stage of life. In both churches, these classes do more than provide information. They teach marriage and parenting skills and help couples understand the unique issues they face at their particular stage of the marriage life cycle. They also use these classes to build a sense of community among people who face similar life issues.

Berkeley, for example, offers "marriage small groups" for couples at the same stage of the marriage life cycle. The groups use the Prepare/Enrich inventory and are led by trained mentor couples. The church also offers ongoing classes that are structured in a curriculum-like way around the stages of the marriage life cycle, like Marriage 101: Starting a Healthy Marriage, Marriage 102: The Cooperation Years, and Marriage 103: The Second Half of Marriage. It offers a similar "curriculum" on parenting skills for couples with children at different ages.

Peachtree also is sensitive to the specific needs of couples at different stages of the marriage life cycle but handles it differently. It has dropped the language of "church school" or "Sunday school," replacing it with "Sunday classes and communities." This signals the church's desire that participants will join one of these groups on a long-term basis and that these groups will combine study, service, spiritual friendship, and social activities. In a congregation of 9,000 members, they are seen as a primary way of building both a sense of community and a sense of mission. Many of these communities are composed of couples who are in the same stage of the marriage life cycle and, periodically, make use of materials that focus on their special needs.

2. *Counseling centers and caring ministries.* Both Berkeley and Peachtree support counseling services as part of their broader caring min-

istries, available to church members and nonmembers alike. These centers balance therapeutic and enrichment approaches. They offer support to people in crisis or with special problems, but they also offer services designed to help individuals, couples, and families to thrive. They also employ counselors with clinical training and a Christian background, viewing Christian spirituality as part of a holistic approach to psychological and familial well-being.

Peachtree sponsors LifeGate @ Peachtree, which has several campuses around Atlanta. While some of LifeGate's services are directed to children, youth, adults, and couples with special problems, they are also oriented toward building strong relationships in the family across the life cycle. The centers offer "marital checkup" therapy for couples who want to improve their communication skills and intimacy. They also sponsor "enrichment" workshops, with such titles as "Bringing Baby Home," "Managing Stress and Conflict," and "Making the Magic Last." Berkeley's counseling service follows similar lines. It offers counseling for those experiencing problems, as well as classes and groups for people with specific needs, like the experience of significant loss, male sexuality, and spirituality for older women.

Independent of these counseling centers, Peachtree and Berkeley also sponsor divorce recovery groups as part of their broader caring ministries. These attract a significant number of participants beyond their own members. While their formats differ slightly, they are high-commitment groups that maintain confidentiality. Trained facilitators use a book to explore common issues and emotions surrounding divorce, combining study and personal sharing. Both churches also sponsor programs developed by national organizations for children. Peachtree sponsors Kids' Turn, specifically designed for children whose parents have divorced.[42] Berkeley sponsors Rainbow, for children in families experiencing significant losses, like the death of a family member and divorce.[43] According to knowledgeable "insiders," the pastoral leaders of Berkeley's very large university ministry are sensitive to the lingering effects of divorce on college students. As one leader put it, "We've got our antennae up for these kinds of issues. Hey, my parents divorced when I was 12, but I didn't really start acting out until I was a sophomore in college. I listen carefully to what people share in small group Bible studies and in personal conversations. I try to build a deeper relationship if I get the feeling that something is going on."

42. http://www.kidsturn.org/pages/page.php?pageid=75; accessed April 2010.
43. http://www.rainbows.org/; accessed April 2010.

3. *Communicating a theology of families through multiple channels.* One of the ways Peachtree and Berkeley support intact and divorced families is by consistently talking about their issues in biblical and theological ways. The pastors preach sermon series on these issues and offer sermon illustrations from family life. Their Web sites communicate the importance of family and divorce ministries in ways that are framed "theologically." In my research team's conversations with divorced members, moreover, the theme of pastoral support and acceptance repeatedly came to the fore. As one woman put it, "You know, it really meant a lot when one of our pastors was there to welcome us at our first divorce recovery group meeting. There's still a lot of shame about being divorced, and most of us are pretty cautious in what we share at church. But Debbie (the pastor) was there to greet us in a non-judgmental way. That said a lot about our acceptance in the church."

It is rare among American mainline Protestant churches today to find congregations that affirm simultaneously family ministries committed to building strong, intact families that can continue to grow over the course of the marriage life cycle and caring ministries offering healing and support to the members of divorced families. But it can be done, as the two examples just explored make clear. Though the size and resources of Peachtree and Berkeley are atypical for their denomination and the mainline in general, there is no reason that churches of other sizes cannot develop family and caring ministries appropriate to their own circumstances. This, after all, is what discernment of missional vocation is all about. We can only hope that serious engagement of these ministries will be part of a broader transformation of mainline churches' identity and mission.

Conclusion

This chapter began by outlining a model of practical theology in which empirical research figures prominently. It has illustrated the importance of such research by exploring in depth the state of families in the United States, arguing that mainline congregations must rethink the relationship between family ministries and mission. No claim has been made that the theology and contextual analysis of this chapter are sacrosanct. But it should be clear at this point that they can only be challenged by perspectives that take empirical research as seriously as has this chapter. Simple appeals to Scripture, church tradition, and Christian doctrine will not be enough, for they inevitably will work intuitively or make naive appeals to common sense in their interpretation of the present context. This alone should make it clear why the other theological disciplines need practical theology, for it alone carries out the descriptive-empirical task of theology most fully.

Index

Action Research — Church and Society (ARCS), 167-81, 167n. *See also* Practical ecclesiology and ecclesial practices

Adams, Nicholas, 99, 148-50

African Methodist Episcopal churches and congregations: love feast (communal worship centered on eucharistic ritual), 61-65, 69, 70; typical characteristics of, 61-65

Alinsky, Saul, 152

Ambrose of Milan, 213

Ammerman, Nancy, *Congregation and Community*, 38, 41-42

Anglican parish of St. Mary's, Battersea, 173-74

Anthropology: confrontations with postcolonial realities and founding assumptions, 101; uses of the term "ethnography," 6-7, 13-17, 102. *See also* Ethnographic research methods; Ethnography

"Application" model. *See* Deduction/deductive methods

Apprenticeship: and broad-based community organizing (BBCO), 150-56; and craft knowledge, 153-56; and em-

bodied knowledge, 54-55, 68-69, 70; Hauerwas's reflections on, 153

L'Arche communities, 73n

Arendt, Hannah, 138, 157, 158

Aristotle, 157

Atkinson, Paul, 6, 37-38

Attention and attentiveness. *See* Theological attentiveness

Augé, Marc, 118

Augustine, Saint, 25-26, 165

Baggett, Jerome, 185-86

Balmer, Randall, *Mine Eyes Have Seen the Glory: A Journey into the Evangelical Subculture in America,* 97

Balthasar, Hans Urs von, 27

Barbour, Ian, 21-22, 24-25; *Religion in an Age of Science* (Gifford Lectures), 21-22

Barth, Karl, 26, 149, 205, 228

Baxter, Michael, 88-89

Becker, Penny Edgell, 130-31

Bellah, Robert, 158n

Berry, Thomas, 57

Bhatti, Deborah, 167-81

Big Bethel African Methodist Episcopal (AME), 61-65, 69, 70

"Biography as theology," 97-98, 149